Courthouse Research
for Family Historians

COURTHOUSE RESEARCH FOR FAMILY HISTORIANS

YOUR GUIDE TO GENEALOGICAL TREASURES

BY

CHRISTINE ROSE

SAN JOSE, CALIFORNIA

2004

ISBN 0-919626-16-8

FIRST PRINTING 2004

10 9 8 7 6 5 4 3 2 1

PUBLISHED BY  CR Publications
1474 Montelegre Dr., San Jose, CA 95120-4831

PRINTED BY THOMSON SHORE, INC., DEXTER, MI

AUTHOR: <CHRISTINE4ROSE@CS.COM>

COVER DESIGN: ANN SILBERLICHT

COVER CREDIT: COURTHOUSE IMAGES FROM ECONOMIC RESEARCH SERVICE, U.S. DEPT. OF AGRICULTURE, HTTP://WWW.ERS.USDA.GOV

ACKNOWLEDGEMENTS

First, my deepest thanks to Kay Germain Ingalls, a skilled professional genealogist, who spent many hours reading this manuscript and offering sage advice and grammatical tips. And always with good humor. Thanks also to Diane Gravel, a New England research professional and a former law-student recruiting manager, for reading, correcting, and offering suggestions from her own research. And thanks to James Hansen, Genealogy Reference Librarian of the Wisconsin State Historical Society, an expert genealogist, and to Donn Devine, another talented genealogist and an attorney. Jim offered immensely useful suggestions, and Donn made sure my legal observations were on target. To my long-time friend Kathy Nichols, who is working on her own family's history for publication, a huge thanks for reading the draft from the vantage point of one who has not yet visited a courthouse. And thanks most of all, to my husband Seymour, who has accompanied me into most of those 500 plus courthouses. He read and reread, and offered many suggestions. His enthusiasiam and encouragement for this project never wavered, as it never does. And, I can't overlook the many courthouse clerks and archivists who willingly answered my questions and helped provide illustrations. In particular, thanks to the Chester County, Pennsylvania, county archivists who spent a morning pulling records and making suggestions for the book, and to the archivists and volunteers at Prince William and Fairfax Counties, Virginia for their assistance. I envy them, working daily with such precious records!

To all of you, the depth of my gratitude is endless.

ABOUT THE AUTHOR

Christine Rose, CG, CGL, FASG, is a Certified Genealogist, a Certified Genealogical Lecturer, and a full-time professional genealogist. She was elected Fellow, American Society of Genealogists, an honor bestowed by peers based on quantity and quality of publications, and limited to only 50 at any time. She is a resident of San Jose, California, and has been active in genealogy for many years. She was the recipient of the prestigious Donald Lines Jacobus award in 1987 for two genealogy books. Compiler of numerous genealogies and articles; an Associate of the Board for Certification of Genealogists; former Vice President of Association of Professional Genealogists; Past Director, Federation of Genealogical Societies, and columnist for the latter's *Forum* for over fifteen years. Christine, widely known as a national lecturer, has lectured in many cities across the country, at national conferences, at the National Institute of Historical Research in Washington, D.C., and has been on the faculty of the Samford University Institute of Genealogy and Historical Research for a number of years. She is a member of numerous genealogical societies, and founder and editor of the *Rose Family Association*. Her popular *Nicknames: Past & Present*, is now in its 4th edition., and her *Family Association, Organization and Management, A Handbook* is in its 3rd edition. She has also published *Military Pension Acts 1776-1858, Genealogical Proof Standard*, and others. She is co-author of the best-selling *The Complete Idiot's Guide to Genealogy*, published by Alpha Books, a division of Macmillan Reference USA. Christine's specialities include onsite research in courthouses and repositories across America; also military research, and federal land records.

To Kay Germain Ingalls, CG
who enjoys courthouses as much as I do.
Thank you, dear friend!

Book Notes

Explanations of types of documents, and definitions, appear throughout the chapters. All the terms and definitions have also been consolidated in the Glossary. See pages 205-212.

The book references mentioned throughout the chapters have also been consolidated. They appear (with some additional suggestions) on pages 201-204.

Each chapter ends with "Chapter Points to Ponder," reflecting a few important points.

Enjoy!

TABLE OF CONTENTS

Chapter 1: Preparation is the Key   1

START IN A COUNTY COURTHOUSE ... or? 1
COUNTIES CAN HAVE PARENTS TOO 2
   Counties Formed From The Initial County Of Research 2
DOES THE COUNTY STILL EXIST? 2
INDEPENDENT CITIES 3
OTHER CONSIDERATIONS 3
   Will They Be Open? 3
   Can You Handle the Record Books? 4
   Packing With a Purpose 4
   What's In Your Briefcase 5
   Taking Files 5
MAPS 6
SKILLS TO PRACTICE BEFORE LEAVING 7
   Reading the Handwriting 7
   Transcribing Faithfully 8
   Books and Tapes will Assist 9
   Abstracting 10
OTHER PRACTICAL CONSIDERATIONS 10
   Should You Take Your Computer into the Courthouse? 10
   Photocopying 10
CHAPTER POINTS TO PONDER 11

Chapter 2: You're There—Now What?   13

ARRIVING AT THE COURTHOUSE 13
   Starting the Search 14
EXPECTATIONS 14
HINTS FOR SUCCESS 15
DIFFERENCES IN INDEXES 16
   Numbering of Record Books 16
   A Variety of Indexing Systems 17
   Russell Index System 17
   Additional Hints With the Russell System 19
   The Campbell System and other "first name" indexes 19
   Cott Indexes 20
   Graves Tabular Initial Indexes 21
   Additional Indexes 21
CAN'T FIND A NAME IN THE INDEX? 21
   Did the Index Err? 21
   Did You Miss Some Entries? 22
   What's Missing in the Index? 22
   Using the Index for Maximum Results 22
   After the Index is Examined 23
BROUGHT YOUR COMPUTER? 23
LEGAL AGE 24
THERE WAS A FIRE! 24
THOSE OTHER RECORDS ON THE SHELVES 25
CHAPTER POINTS TO PONDER 25

Chapter 3: Property Matters   27

IMPORTANCE OF LAND OWNERSHIP 27
STATE-LAND STATES vs. FEDERAL-LAND STATES 28
   Surveying Differences 29

CHAPTER 3, con't..

    LAND SURVEYS 30

INDEXES FOR LAND RECORDS 30

    ENTRY BOOK INDEXES 33

    PECULIARITIES OF DEED INDEXES IN LAND RECORDS 33

    WHAT DO DEED INDEXES INCLUDE? 34

    INDEXES PREPARED BY OTHERS 35

    TYPES OF DOCUMENTS 35

TERMINOLOGY 40

CHAPTER POINTS TO PONDER 45

Chapter 4: Searching for Property Records   47

THE OFFICE FOR LAND RECORDS 47

TYPES OF RECORD BOOKS 47

    DEED BOOKS 47

    SURVEY BOOKS AND WARRANTS 47

    PLAT BOOKS AND PLAT MAPS 49

    POWERS OF ATTORNEY BOOKS 49

    MORTGAGE BOOKS 49

WHAT A DEED TELLS US 50

THE RECORDING PROCESS 51

CLUES IN THE DEEDS 53

OTHER CONSIDERATIONS 55

    PHOTOCOPYING 55

    SR. AND JR., ELDER AND YOUNGER, 1ST AND 2ND 56

    ABSENCE OF RECORDS 56

STRATEGIES FOR SEARCHING LOCAL LAND RECORDS 57

    CONNECTING FAMILIES THROUGH THEIR DEEDS 58

RECORDS NOT A PART OF THE LOCAL LAND RECORDS 58

LAND RECORDS ARE CRUCIAL TO RESEARCH 59

CHAPTER POINTS TO PONDER 60

DEED TRANSCRIBED AND ANNOTATED 61

Chapter 5: Estates Galore   65

WHICH OFFICE HANDLED ESTATES? 65

WAS THE ESTATE PROBATED? 66

WOMEN AND WILLS 67

KINDS OF ESTATES 67

THE PROBATE INDEXES 68

TERMINOLOGY 72

UNDERSTANDING THE LAW 74

    NAMING CHILDREN IN THE WILL 75

    PRIMOGENITURE OR DOUBLE PORTION 75

    DAUGHTERS 76

    INTESTATE DIVISION PER STIRPES OR PER CAPITA 77

    HEIRS AT LAW, SONS-IN-LAW, AND OTHERS 77

PROBATE COURT MINUTES and COURT ORDERS 78

THE ESTATE PACKETS 79

    BUT KEEP IN MIND 80

CHAPTER POINTS TO PONDER 81

Chapter 6: Estate Documents   83

WILLS (Testate Proceedings) 84

    CODICILS TO WILLS 85

MORE THAN ONE KIND OF WILL 85

THE PROBATE PROCESS 86

OTHER DOCUMENTS ASSOCIATED WITH ESTATES 88

CHAPTER 6, con't.
PETITION 88
BOND 89
"LETTERS" ISSUED 90
INVENTORY 90
ACCOUNT 91
ACCOUNTS OF SALE AND SALE BILL 92
PETITION FOR SALE OF REAL ESTATE 92
FINAL SETTLEMENT OR FINAL DISTRIBUTION 93
RENUNCIATIONS 94
ADMINISTRATIONS 95
RELINQUISHMENT IN AN ADMINISTRATION 95
PUBLIC ADMINISTRATOR OR OTHER PUBLIC OFFICIAL 96
GUARDIANSHIPS 96
GUARDIANSHIP OF MINORS 96
BONDS FOR GUARDIANS 96
ENTAILED PROPERTY IN THE HANDS OF MINORS 97
CHOOSING A GUARDIAN FOR A MINOR 97
NEXT FRIEND 97
GUARDIANSHIPS FOR INCOMPETENTS 97
COMMITTEE (IN CASES OF INCOMPETENCY) 98
GUARDIAN'S ACCOUNTS 98
CHAPTER POINTS TO PONDER 98

Chapter 7: Milking Every Clue from Estates   99

LET'S CONSIDER 99
ENTAILS 99
WERE THERE TWO WILLS? 100
WILLS OF UNMARRIED ADULTS 100
MAKING IT FAIR 101
GLEANING CLUES FROM WILLS 101
MORE ON PACKETS 103
VARIED DOCUMENTS IN THE ESTATE PACKET (ANNOTATED) 104
TRANSCRIBING A WILL 105
ABSTRACTING A WILL 106
WILLS ARE MARVELOUS IN MORE WAYS THAN ONE 108
IS A SEARCH AMONG ESTATES WORTH THE EFFORT? 109
DON'T BE CONTENT WITH ONE RECORD 110
CHAPTER POINTS TO PONDER 110

Chapter 8: Understanding the Court System   111

THE COURT SYSTEM 111
TYPES OF COURTS 111
OUR LEGAL SYSTEM 113
RECORD BOOKS 114
TYPE OF DOCUMENTS 118
CIVIL COURT INDEXES 120
THE FILE PACKETS: Civil and Criminal 121
TERMINOLOGY 122
CHAPTER POINTS TO PONDER 126

Chapter 9: Civil and Criminal Court   127

CIVIL RECORDS 127
FINDING CIVIL COURT RECORDS IN THE COURTHOUSE 128
INDEBTNESS 128
JUDGMENTS 129
YOUR STRATEGY IN BECOMING ACQUAINTED WITH CIVIL COURT RECORDS 130
THE CIVIL COURT PROCESS 130
OTHER RECORDS WHICH MIGHT BE FOUND 131

CHAPTER 9, con't.
    CHANGES OF NAME 131
TAX RECORDS 131
    HOW TAX RECORDS HELP YOU 132
    WHAT WAS TAXED 133
    LAND BOOKS 133
    TAX ASSESSOR 134
    TAX FORECLOSURES 135
ROAD RECORDS 135
    ROAD COMMISSIONERS 135
CORONER'S RECORDS 136
REGISTRAR OF VOTERS 136
NATURALIZATIONS 137
    LOCATING THE NATURALIZATION PAPERS 138
    NATURALIZATION OF WOMEN 139
    FORMATION OF BUREAU OF IMMIGRATION AND NATURALIZATION 139
DIVORCES 140
    CAN'T FIND THE DIVORCE PROCEEDING? 141
CRIMINAL MATTERS 141
    THE "GAOLS" 142
    BAIL BOND 142
    DUTIES OF A CRIMINAL COURT CLERK 142
JURIES 143
CHAPTER POINTS TO PONDER 143

Chapter 10: Birth, Marriage, and Death   145

REGISTRATIONS OF VITAL RECORDS 145
WHICH COURTHOUSE OFFICE? 146
    CITIES MAY KEEP THEIR OWN RECORDS 146
    ARE THE RECORDS OPEN TO THE PUBLIC? 146
    REGISTER BOOK INDEXES AND THEIR ORGANIZATION 147
    TRANSCRIBING AND ABSTRACTING VITAL RECORDS 148
BIRTH RECORDS 148
    DELAYED OR CORRECTED BIRTH RECORDS 149
    OTHER COURTHOUSE DOCUMENTS CAN SUBSTITUTES FOR BIRTH RECORDS 149
    LOCAL CUSTOMS HELP 151
MARRIAGES 152
    THE PROCESS BY LICENSE OR BY BANNS 152
    MARRIAGE APPLICATION AND THE LICENSE 153
    MARRIAGE BONDS 154
    MARRIAGE CERTIFICATES 154
    MARRIAGE REGISTERS 154
    MARRIAGE CONTRACT 155
    WHERE DID THEY MARRY? 155
    SUBSTITUTE MARRIAGE RECORDS 156
    BREACH OF PROMISE 156
    COMMON-LAW MARRIAGES 157
    SPECIAL NOTES ON MARRIAGES 157
DEATHS 157
    WHERE IS THE DEATH REGISTER AND WHAT'S IN IT? 158
    WHEN YOU CANNOT FIND THE DEATH RECORD 159
    SUBSTITUTE RECORDS CAN PROVE A DEATH 159
    VITAL RECORD ASSISTANCE 160
ONE ACTION CAN PROVE BIRTH, MARRIAGE, AND DEATH 161
CHAPTER POINTS TO PONDER 162

Chapter 11: The Internet, Microfilm, and Libraries   163

THE INTERNET AND COURTHOUSES 163
    CYNDI'S LIST IS ALWAYS A PLACE TO START 163

CHAPTER 11, con't.
    OTHER CYNDI'S LIST RESOURCE ITEMS 164
    USGENWEB 164
    COUNTY FORUMS 165
    COUNTY SITES OTHER THAN USGENWEB 165
    STATE ARCHIVES ON THE INTERNET 166
    FEDERAL LAND RECORDS ONLINE 166
    LOCAL LAND RECORDS ONLINE 167
    PROBATE RECORDS ONLINE 167
    VITAL RECORDS ONLINE 168
    CIVIL RECORDS ONLINE 169
    ON-LINE SUBSCRIPTION SERVICES 169
MICROFILM FOR COURTHOUSE RECORDS 169
    FAMILY HISTORY LIBRARY (FHL) AND THEIR MICROFILM 169
    FINDING FAMILY HISTORY CENTERS 170
    FHL CATALOG 170
    ORDERING FHL MICROFILM 171
    MICROFILM OTHER THAN FHL 173
    MICROFILM PROBLEMS 173
LIBRARY GENEALOGICAL COLLECTIONS 173
    FAMILY HISTORY LIBRARY BOOKS 173
    OTHER MAJOR LIBRARY COLLECTIONS 173
ADVANTAGES OF LIBRARY PREPARATION 175
    USE WORLDCAT OCLC 177
    LAW LIBRARIES FOR STATUTES 177
    UNITED STATES STATUTES 177
NEWSPAPERS 178
OTHER FINDING AIDS 178
    USING NUCMC 178
    PERSI INDEX TO PUBLISHED ARTICLES 179
    COUNTY INVENTORIES AND COUNTY GUIDES 180
    WORK PROJECT ADMINISTRATION (WPA) 180
ORIGINAL COURTHOUSE RECORDS FOUND ELSEWHERE 181
UNUSUAL SITES 182
CHAPTER POINTS TO PONDER 182

Chapter 12: Strategies that Work   **183**
    EXAMPLE 1: ALLOW ONE RECORD TO LEAD TO ANOTHER 183
    EXAMPLE 2. LOCATING THE CHILDREN 185
    EXAMPLE 3: LOCATING PARENTS 187
    EXAMPLE 4: FOLLOWING THE SEPARATIONS AND DIVORCES 188
    EXAMPLE 5: THE WILL IS MISSING 189
    EXAMPLE 6: WIDENING THE SEARCH 190
STRATEGIES FOR LETTER WRITING 193
    GENERAL RULES WHEN WRITING 193
    STATING THE REQUEST CLEARLY 194
STRATEGIES FOR FINDING AFRICAN-AMERICAN RECORDS 195
STRATEGIES FOR "KNOWING" OUR ANCESTORS 197
KEEPING US GOING 198
    THE SAGA OF A REVOLUTIONARY SOLDIER 199

Resource References   **201**
Glossary   **205**
Index   **213**

LIST OF FIGURES

Figure

1-1	Illustration to determine county of search	2
1-2	List of independent cities in Virginia	3
1-3	Bookshelves and file boxes in a typical courthouse	4
1-4	Example of a one-page summary	6
1-5	7.5 Minute topographical map	6
1-6	County highway map	7
1-7	Example of "thorn"	8
1-8	Example of "ff"	8
1-9	Examples of tailed "s"	9
2-1	Russell index	17
2-2	Russell index enhanced	18
2-3	Russell index surname pages	19
2-4	Cott index	20
2-5	Variation of a Cott index	20
2-6	Graves index	21
3-1	Rectangular survey township after 1796	30
3-2	Rectangular survey township before 1796	30
3-3	General deed index	34
3-4	Illustration of "ss"	44
4-1	A plat map	48
4-2	Illustration of chains	49
4-3	A township grid for research purposes	58
4-4a, 4b, 4c	Three pages of a transcribed deed, annotationed	61-63
5-1	General Index to estates	68
5-2	Estates index, and Proceedings dockets	68
5-3	Block in a proceedings docket	69
5-4	Example of a published index	71
5-5	Court Order Book entry	78
6-1	Example of initials for a signature mark	84
6-2	Summary of probate process	87
6-3	Petition for probate of will	88
6-4	Bond for an administratrix	89
6-5	Inventory of an estate	91
6-6	Final distribution in an estate	93
6-7	Court orders for an administration	95
6-8	Appointment of a guardian	96
7-1	Example of seals on three signatures	106
8-1	Example of a bond	114
8-2	A court docket	116
8-3	A docket entry	119
8-4	A writ	119
9-1	Example from a court order book	129
9-2	Civil Court process	130
9-3	A tax list	132
9-4	Occupations from a tax list	133
9-5, 9-6	A voting register	136
10-1	Marriage certificate and return	154
10-2, 10-3	Death register	158
11-1	Family History Library search criteria	170
11-2	Example of a Family History Library catalog search	172

INTRODUCTION

The thrill never diminishes. Over 500 courthouses later, I still feel excited when approaching the courthouse. The scenes are similar—the town square, the "locals" sitting on the benches for their daily confab, the marble soldier in front commemorating the county's war casualties. As I walk up the courthouse steps, worn over time, I wonder who passed there before me. Within its walls, perhaps high on a dusty shelf, will I find the answer to that genealogical puzzle—that court case, that marriage record, that guardianship proceeding, which will finally provide the missing piece? Who has last seen it? When I hold it in my hand, will I feel connected to the ancestors who held it so many years ago while signing or making their marks on its pages?

Though many counties do not have the time or resources for preservation, many are striving to do so. In one, a young teenager had been hired during the summer to apply a light oil preservative to the leather bound books and polish them until they gleamed. In another, my husband and I were astonished when entering the record office to see a room that looked like an old English library. The cabinets , pullout drawers, and desktops were a delight to behold.

We've been in courthouses of every description. Some very large —so large that in one I was totally lost after going to the ladies room at closing time to wash off the dust of the books. Then I couldn't find my way back to the proper entrance until a janitor came to my rescue! Other courthouses were so small that upon entering the vault to do research, three people were too many. We've been up marvelous marble stairs, adorned with columns. And up the splintering stairs in poor, rural counties. In one we were offered doughnuts; in others a cheery smile. In some, we were as unnoticed as if we were invisible.

We've arrived during the strawberry festival, with the courthouse lot full of delicious offerings at homemade booths. We've arrived during the area's craft shows, Octoberfests, and other local activities, all giving a flavor of the community.

While working we've heard the town gossip and tidbits of legal entanglements as the attorneys and title company searchers endeavored to solve a knotty land problem.

"Over 500 courthouses later, I still feel excited ..."

We've used the wonderful law libraries in many of the court-houses, in peace with easy access to the statutes of the state.

We've had numerous courtesies extended—allowing us to remain in the record room searching while the office was closed for lunch, and taking the time to escort us to little-used storage areas.

We've passed through countless security systems, and been in courthouses where notorious trials were being held. In one, the guard amiably chatted while he looked in my brief case and my purse, asking from where we hailed, and generally appearing to take little notice of what he was examining. We told him we were headed for the register of deeds office. "It's on the second floor," he helpfully supplied, "and you can pick this up on your way out." In his hands was my *very* small pocket knife—hardly an inch and a half—his sharp eyes missed nothing!

In some, I've been required to sign a register before entering the record room. In most, I simply walked into the vault and worked as I pleased.

We've also at times been subjected to the rejection which some clerks accord genealogists. In one courthouse, the clerk was insistent that I could not access the probate records unless I found the family name in a slim printed book which was only a listing of wills. My question, "What if he died without a will? I need to see other indexes, too" brought no response. Finally, I simply pointed to one of the wills in the printed list, indicating I was there to see that document. Only then was I allowed to enter the record room. And there, among the shelves, were all the important additional probate records that the clerk would not admit to having.

In another courthouse, I was making wonderful discoveries in the probate indexes. The files were stored offsite, but they had been microfilmed and the rolls were available. Rather than wait a day until the clerk could retrieve the original files I opted to use the film. Imagine my surprise when I discovered that some of the sheets in the loose probate packets had been filmed upside down and sideways. This would not in itself have deterred me—but, the microfilm reader was old and would not allow rotation of the pages. Upon inquiry, the only solution offered was to call for the original packets and wait a day. I was back to square one!

I could imagine the clerks amusement watching me, wondering how long it would take me to discover I had to read upside down!

I've worked at my own pace, poking and hunting and amassing records, thinking all the while no one paid attention. And most times that was true. But the clerks are sometimes surprising. In one, while I pursued clues for 4-5 hours, the lone clerk of the small county was obviously busy and, I supposed, paying no heed. I reached up to get a Death Register, unaware that in that state it was closed to the public. The clerk, whom I thought was paying little attention, immediately boomed, "Don't touch that!" Obviously, he had been aware of my activities all along!

In one courthouse, when I could not locate the court books I needed, I was told they might be in the basement. But, still not finding them there, I stumbled into one of the best sources of such knowledge—the janitor. With his assistance we were led to a locked second floor room (which did not contain the particular ones I desired) and finally, up a separate staircase to the attic. There, little used and mostly unknown were all the record books I needed to solve the problem.

Do I have to go personally to the courthouse? Yes and no. Certainly, we are fortunate that many records have been microfilmed. The Family History Library in Salt Lake City and their centers throughout the United States are evidence of the magnificent effort to preserve on film early deeds, probates and other selected records. But selected they remain—within the walls of courthouses are countless other records, waiting to be discovered. In particular, the "loose" papers remain largely unfilmed—those files and packets that have been stored, usually in tin boxes, and relegated to obscure nooks and crannies of the courthouse as space became scarce.

I've been asked what percentage of courthouse records have been microfilmed. Though difficult to estimate, the figure is nonetheless low enough to know that many are still only available in their original form.

The research can start directly in the courthouse, bypassing alternative strategies. Or, it can commence with what is available at the Family History Library on microfilm. Records abstracted or transcribed in book form are also useful, though subject to the compiler's errors of interpretation or errors in copying and publishing. However, using these publications as a foundation, the search can proceed to on-site inspection of the documents in the courthouse to verify the published abstracts, and to ferret out originals only available on-site.

This book will help you get started—tell you what to expect, and how to get the most from the few hours you may be there. You will feel intimidated at first. But each visit will instill more confidence. The day will come when you will give the clerk a smile, pass into the vault housing the records, and feel as comfortable as those who work there daily. I believe that you will feel the same as I do, the thrill of sharing the lives of our ancestors through the records they left. Their joys and their hardships are often revealed through the court records. We can wonder at events that forced children into apprenticeships, or what circumstances precipitated the family feuds captured in the court minutes. And we can be thrilled over their first purchase of land, or the birth of a child.

Do I have to go personally to the courthouse? Yes and no.

Should you go? Yes! Go. Go as often as you can. Practice with your local courthouse—go there to the different offices, take a simulated research problem with you if you don't have a real one. You're just there for the experience. Look around. Observe. Examine the books, the indexes. Get a feel for what is there. Several practice sessions will infuse you with confidence for the trip you make into the county of your ancestors. Read the guidebooks. Note what they say about the records of that state. Check the websites for the county you are to visit. And, don't worry if you feel intimated at first—we all do. That will pass.

USING THIS GUIDEBOOK

Many examples in this guide are of the Rose surname—most not our own family, but from other Rose records across the country which I've collected over the years. They should apply to your MacDonald, Sneider, or other ancestors, too. I've done extensive courthouse (and town hall) research in New England, Pennsylvania, New York, Ohio, Indiana, Illinois, and various other eastern, southern and midwestern states. The examples used are those I had with me while writing this guidebook, but be assured that research is the same across the country. You look for indexes, read the documents, and evaluate what you find, no matter where you are.

I had to make some editorial decisions. First, I quicky found that when I tried to include both sexes in examples, I was constantly referring to "he or she." It was so cumbersome that I relented and used "he" throughout, though the examples should be inferred to relate (when appropriate) to women, too.

Secondly, I planned to use the "proper" suffixes to executor and executrix, administrator and administratrix, etc., to distinguish between male and female. This too became a problem and I decided on a generic suffix of "or" except in quoted passages. Thus, "executor" and other similar titles may be male or female. For similar reasons I discarded such terms "grantor(s)" and "buyer(s)" to show that more than one person could be involved. But keep in mind that "the grantor" could be "the grantors," "the buyer" could be "the buyers," etc.

The most difficult decision was tense—whether to use present or past. I opted for past tense since researchers will encounter many early records as they progress. In most cases the same tips and observations should be applied to the present, too.

In the end, my goal was to give you a guide that would read easily, and excite you so you'll visit the courthouses, either by a personal visit, or a forage into microfilm and books.

But do go personally if you can. I think you will become as addicted to courthouse research as I am!

C.R.

"East or west, north or south, the search strategies are similar.

1 PREPARATION IS THE KEY

START IN A COUNTY COURTHOUSE ... or?

Deciding where the onsite research will be conducted requires some study. Will it be in a *county* courthouse? For most of the United States, the answer is yes, but important exceptions exist. Some states are not on a county system. Their records are housed in Town Halls, Probate Districts, and other non-county divisions. Deed records for Connecticut, for instance, are housed in the Town Halls. But probate records of that state are in probate districts, which usually encompass several towns. In some states, deeds, probates and civil records are at the county level, while vital records—births, marriages and deaths–are in the town records. Also, a few counties have two courthouses. You may be looking in the wrong one.[1] To determine whether these exceptions affect your search, consult a guidebook[2] or access the county's website.

An especially good source for Internet help with the counties is the U.S. GenWeb project at <http://www.usgenweb.com>. This volunteer program maintains websites for almost all of the counties of the United States. At their website click on either the table or map of states, and from that link access the counties within the state. These county websites vary in their quality and quantity, but contain valuable information. Maps, titles of published books of the county, queries, some court records, and even offers of local help may appear. (See also Chapter 11.)

Photocopy the pages from your guidebook (for your personal use only) listing the parent counties for the state you will visit. You will need this as your search proceeds onsite, or even if you do long-distance search through microfilm, Internet, or books.

The guidebooks include the telephone numbers of the courthouses, as do the county websites.

---

[1] As an example, Santa Clara County, California, has its original courthouse in San Jose, California (1850), while another, established in the late 1900s, is located in Palo Alto. Each courthouse must be searched; their records do not duplicate. A number of other U.S. counties also have multiple facilities.

[2] Some of the guidebooks useful for courthouse research include: Alice Eichholz, ed., *Redbook* (Salt Lake City: Ancestry, 1992) which includes a description of the record-keeping system in each state. Also helpful is the *Handy Book for Genealogists,* Tenth Edition (Logan, Utah: Everton Publishers, Inc., 2002). For those researching in New England see also Marcia D. Melnyk, *Genealogist's Handbook for New England Research,* Fourth Edition (Boston: New England Historic Genealogical Society, 1999).

COUNTIES CAN HAVE PARENTS TOO

Before you visit the courthouse, determine in which county to conduct the research. When did your family live in the area? Examine the records you have accumulated—births, gravestone records, Bibles, and others. Estimate dates. Then use one of the guidebooks to determine *when* the county was formed. Example: You are tracing a family that lived in Jefferson County, Ohio. The family Bible states your ancestor was born there in 1804. Family recollections are that the family lived in that area for a number of years previous to your ancestor's birth. Noting that Jefferson County was formed in 1797 from Washington County, you should add the latter county to your research list.

Sometimes the need to know about the parent county won't become apparent until you are onsite. Perhaps your records place the family in the area in the 1850-60 period. Once you discover the surname in an index earlier than those dates, you'll need to know the date the county was formed, and the parent county(ies) from which it was taken. Only then can you judge whether your search must extend to those earlier localities. By ascertaining the parent county and date before you arrived onsite, you are well prepared.

COUNTIES FORMED FROM THE INITIAL COUNTY OF RESEARCH

You may have the opposite problem than above. Your ancestor may have stated that he was born in Columbiana County, Ohio, on 3 August 1801. This is also recorded in his Bible and on his gravestone. Now you learn that Columbiana County didn't even exist when he was born. What happened? Check the formation of the county. At the time of his birth it was Jefferson County; Columbiana County was not created from it until 1803. Now Jefferson County is added to your locality research list.

The formation of new counties can also uncover records of "lost" families. Perhaps your ancestor vanished from the records of Albany County, New York. Where did he go? Try the counties formed from that county. Noting that Montgomery County was formed from Albany you have a new clue—he may be in records there.

DOES THE COUNTY STILL EXIST?

Some counties no longer exist: Tennessee County, for one, surrendered its name when Tennessee became a state in 1796. Consult printed sources or state and regional repositories to deter-

---

TO ILLUSTRATE SPECIFIC RESEARCH

PARENT COUNTY
Washington County, Ohio, original county formed in 1788.

NEW COUNTY
Jefferson County, Ohio, formed from Washington County in 1797.

The search should not stop with Jefferson County. Note from the guidebooks that several other counties were formed from parts of Washington County, not just Jefferson County. It may be necessary to search them, too.

Note also that the counties formed from parts of "original" counties (that is, the first counties) often later spawned other counties. For example, Columbiana County was formed in 1803 from parts of both Jefferson and Washington Counties.

Figure 1-1. The above demonstrates the necessity of knowing the parent counties.

Besides the guidebooks mentioned in this chapter, the state repositories usually have an excellent listing of the formation of the counties in the state. The listing may also be posted at the state archives' website. One fast way to search the Internet for the state's archives is to enter into your search engine the name of the state, followed by the word "Archives."

mine the location of extant records for extinct counties. Examine the guides[3] for listings or contact the state's archives to ascertain where the records are preserved.

INDEPENDENT CITIES

Other exceptions to county divisions are independent cities, especially prevalent in the state of Virginia. This state now has 95 counties, but additionally, there are 41 independent cities. The latter usually have their own courthouses and court systems. Several early independent cities of Virginia were abolished, or merged into other counties or cities. A few of the independent cities have their records maintained by the adjoining county. See Figure 1-2. If the city you need is listed, call them to ascertain where their records are held.[4]

A few other states have independent cities,[5] but none to the extent of Virginia.

OTHER CONSIDERATIONS

Take some time to consider what your visit will entail. A few preparations can smooth the way.

WILL THEY BE OPEN?

It is discouraging to arrive at the courthouse, with only a few hours available for research, and find locked doors. States honor different holidays. One celebrates statehood in February, another in November. One courthouse may close on Good Friday, while another remains open. Ascertain the hours and holidays. Different jurisdictions within a state may have differing regulations. The opening of deer hunting season may cause a closing of at least some of the departments, as might remodeling, storm damage, or other misfortune. Years ago my husband and I left one Tennessee county at noon on a Wednesday (eating granola bars and bananas in the car on the way to conserve time!) and drove 50 miles to get to another courthouse. Much to my dismay, we found the courthouse was closed Wednesday afternoons, but open Saturday mornings. If only I had checked, I could have reversed my schedule and visited that courthouse in the morning.

INDEPENDENT CITIES
in Virginia (present-day)
Alexandria
Bedford
Bristol
Buena Vista
Charlottesville
Chesapeake
Clifton Forge
Colonial Heights
Covington
Danville
Emporia
Fairfax
Falls Church
Franklin
Fredericksburg
Galax
Hampton
Harrisonburg
Hopewell
Lexington
Lynchburg
Manassas
Manassas Park
Martinsville
Newport News
Norfolk
Norton
Petersburg
Poquoson
Portsmouth
Radford
Richmond
Roanoke
Salem
South Boston
Staunton
Virginia Beach
Waynesboro
Williamsburg
Winchester

Figure 1-2. Above are the present-day independent cities of Virginia. If you are working in records of another state, check the guides of that state to determine if they too have independent cities. You can then decide whether they should be added to your research plan.

---

[3] See footnote 2 on page 1.

[4] Also consider the division of Virginia in 1863 when West Virginia was created. After the division, the records of the Virginia counties which formed West Virginia remained in their respective courthouses in the new state of West Virginia, even though those records were created before the 1863 division. Thus, these pre1863 Virginia records are now found in West Virginia.

[5] As an example Baltimore, Maryland, and St. Louis, Missouri are independent cities.

CAN YOU HANDLE THE RECORD BOOKS?

The books in the courthouse are very big and very heavy. Earlier ones are often kept at the top of high shelves, requiring the use of a ladder. Getting those books down can be treacherous if you are not used to ladders or cannot lift the weight. If that is the case, bring someone with you who can. Busy clerks are generally not available when you need them—considerable time can be lost waiting for some help.[6]

Figure 1-3. A typical courthouse, with heavy record books filling the shelves. At the top are tin file boxes in which original court packets are stored.

PACKING WITH A PURPOSE

Now that you've decided to go, what should you take? First, consider clothing. Because of often unkempt conditions, the courthouse is not the place for pastels for women, or light colored pants for men. Nor for shorts or other "tourist" clothing. Your reception in the courthouse will improve if you arrive in clothing that reflects you are a serious researcher. Not "dressy," but simple and practical. Darker clothing or mixed backgrounds (checks, flowers, plaids, etc.) make it more likely you'll leave looking as respectable as when you arrived. The dusty shelves and even dirtier attics will otherwise leave their mark. Clerks are sensitive about the conditions of their basements and attics. They will hesitate to tell you about their storage rooms knowing that your light colors will be soiled when you finish. Assure them that you understand there may be lots of dust.

Women, wear flat shoes. The spiral staircases, worn ladder rungs, and stepping stools are not for heels. And standing for several hours at the high counters will be more comfortable in low shoes.

Put some coins in your brief case too—sometimes you need them for the photocopy machine, and the clerk may not be able to supply them. (You can use them for parking, too!)

---

[6] Sometimes local restrictions will prevent you from retrieving the record books if a ladder is required. The clerk in those instances must do it for you.

WHAT'S IN YOUR BRIEFCASE

Bring a lined notepad and pens and pencils. (Some courthouses do not allow the use of pens.) Pack a magnifying glass to read difficult handwriting. Courthouses that don't allow photo-copying will probably allow the use of a camera, so take one with you.[7] Maps and your notes on courthouse location and hours need to go, too.

Other tools can help. One colleague reports that after encountering a clerk's reluctance to allow the use of some fragile original records, she pulled out a pair of archival gloves and promised to wear them. With a big grin, the clerk took her to the books!

Add a small flashlight and extra batteries. Some areas lose power frequently. The prudent researcher will be prepared to work under adverse conditions.

Check your briefcase for items that won't get past security guards. Knifes, nail files, scissors, etc. are best left in your car or hotel room. If you take them, you can leave them with the guard if they are prohibited, but remember to retrieve them when you leave the courthouse.

TAKING FILES

Your thick files should not go into the courthouse with you. They will slow you down if you try to read a large record book with your numerous papers spread on the courthouse counter. When preparing for the trip, sort through your collected data on the family to be researched. Focus on what you want to locate in the county's records. *What is your goal?* Are you trying to find the name of the parents? The maiden name of the wife? A list of children? List your goals by priority. Once focused on the purpose of the visit, prepare a one-page summary[8] of what is known of the family in that time period. Set that summary on the courthouse counter as you work. It will keep you centered. A thick file would only scatter your attention and become a burden. You could bring the pertinent family sheets and some family notes, but keep them in a file in your briefcase or car, not on the courthouse counter.

On the following page, Figure 1-4, you will see an example of a research plan. That plan stays with you during your courthouse visit. It will help, immensely.

---

[7] Even if allowing a camera, they may restrict flash.

[8] Before you tackle the courthouse do some census research, if the time period falls after the first federal census of 1790. Census records of the surname can help tremendously, often providing clues to proximity to others of the surname in the county, name similarities, and age brackets of at least the head of the home. Armed with that information, you'll be better equipped to pick up on clues as you tackle the courthouse records.

TAKE WITH YOU TO THE COURT-HOUSE
- lined paper pad
- pen/pencils
- summary of family listings of the courthouses and their "parents"
- addresses of courthouses, and other local repositories or cemeteries you want to visit
- magnifying glass
- coins for the photocopier and parking
- camera (optional—handy if you are not allowed to photocopy)
- flashlight and batteries (lights go out, and attics are dim)
- membership cards in genealogical societies—some states will require this membership in one of their state-based societies
- If you are doing client work, take an authorization from the client granting you permission to obtain records on the client's behalf. (In some areas, such permission is required.)

After you leave the courthouse and are 100 miles away, you will be distressed if you have forgotten to retrieve your "confiscated" articles. Remember to pick them up as you leave the courthouse.

HYPOTHETICAL EXAMPLE

Your family was in Belmont County, Ohio, from 1825. Your ancestor died in 1875. Your priority is to determine the date of the marriage of your ancestor and the names of his children.

SUGGESTED SUMMARY

GOAL: 1) Establish marriage, and 2) names of children of George and Sarah Wooten.

SUMMARY: George Wooten is listed as aged 25, living with his father John Wooten aged 56 in 1850 Belmont County, Ohio. In the 1860 census of the county George Wooten is HOH [Head of Household] aged 36, Sarah 30, Joseph 4 and Martha 2, all born Ohio. Not located the 1870 census of that county. George died 1875 (gravestone in Good Hope Cemetery, ABC township, same county).

RESEARCH POSSIBILITIES. [Here you will list some records with which to begin.]

➢ Marriage record
➢ Birth records of children
➢ Probate records of George and his wife Sarah. (If he predeceased her, check for a possible remarriage— her estate may be under a different surname if she remarried.)
➢ Deed records among parents and children

[As you do the search in the courthouse other ideas will come to you. Perhaps the estate of the grandfather John Wooten would name some grandchildren.]

Figure 1-4. The above first states the goal, and then a summary of the known information. Following that data is a prioritized listing of possibilities for research. It is a reminder to yourself of your goals and where to start.

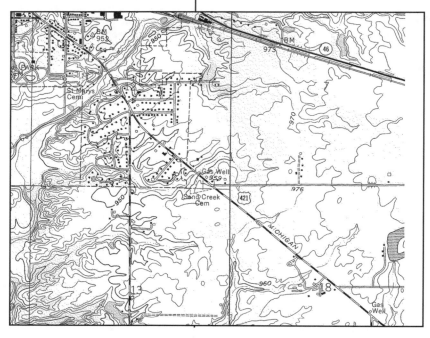

Figure 1-5 above is part of the 7.5 Minute map for the Greensburg Quadrangle, Decatur County, Indiana.

MAPS

Make time to do more than courthouse research while in the area. Plan to visit the cemetery, walk the land, or photograph the church. Three types of maps may be especially useful:

1) topographical 7.5 minute maps

2) county highway maps

3) state/county outline maps.

Topographical Maps. The topographical "7 ½ minute" maps of the U.S. Geological Survey (USGS) can be ordered from their website.[9] Check their online indexes to determine which maps you need. Sometimes these maps are also available in book stores in the local area. They are detailed and often show cemeteries.[10]

County Highway Maps. These can be purchased from the state transportation department in the state's capital and often locally, at the courthouse or a county transportation department. Nominally priced, they are especially useful in showing the main and secondary roads, and often cemeteries. Township divisions are included.

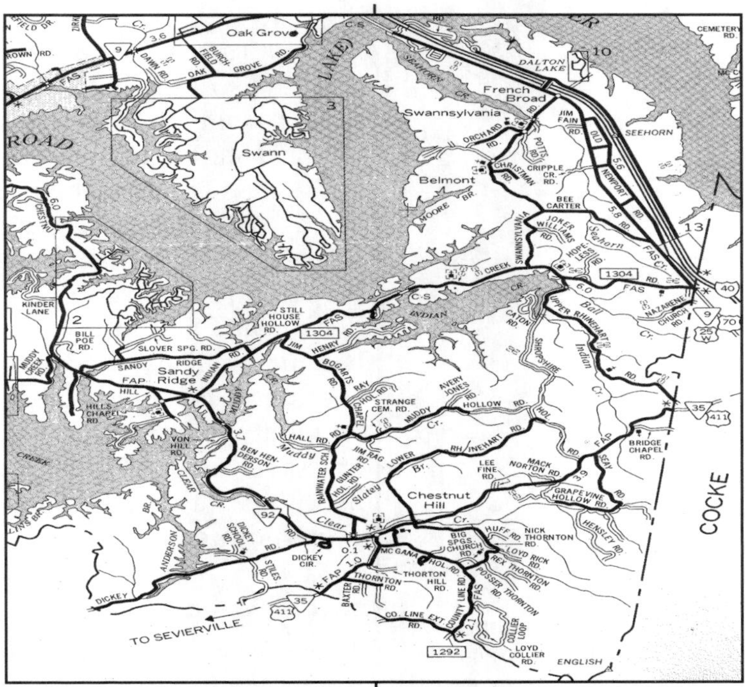

Figure 1-6. County maps prepared by the state's transportation services are useful and often include cemeteries. The above shows a small part of Jefferson County, Tennessee.

Township divisions can also be viewed in a county atlas, county history or county gazetteer. Visit the public library and photocopy the page (for study purposes only)[11] which includes the map.

State Outline Maps. Also useful is an outline map of the state's counties. You'll want this for the whole state so you can immediately spot adjoining counties. The closer your family lived to the edge of the county, the more probable it is that records you need might be found also in the adjoining county. Some guidebooks have these outline maps; also try the Internet.

SKILLS TO PRACTICE BEFORE LEAVING

You may be on vacation or on a pleasure trip, and have allotted only a few hours to search. To make the best use of the time, acquire some skills before the trip. Particularly important is the ability to read the old handwriting accurately and quickly.

READING THE HANDWRITING
The ability to read the documents is the key to maximizing a few hours. To develop this skill, use any of the documents you

---

[9] United States Geological Survey at <http://www.usgs.gov>.

[10] There are subscription-based websites such as <http://www.topozone.com> which allow you to download USGS topo maps for a fee.

[11] Older atlases and county histories, depending upon year published, are likely out of copyright. But, even if they are still in copyright you can photocopy the page strictly for your own study purpose, but be sure not to publish those that are still copyrighted, nor send them to others.

have already collected during your past research. *Transcribe them word for word.* This is the best training possible. Some documents will be discouraging. When I first encountered a 1650 court document from Virginia, I despaired. I could barely read a few words. I started by transcribing the identifiable. Using a magnifying glass to study the formation of the letters, I added a few words with each rereading. Eventually I succeeded. This was followed by fully transcribing a variety of documents—every revolutionary pension file, every deed, every will, every court document I had in my files, learning with each. As a "plus" I became familiar with the "boilerplate"—those repetitive clauses inserted for legal understanding, legal protection, or just custom, but don't contribute genealogical clues. It is a tremendous timesaver to be able to examine a document and quickly extract its important details. That is only possible if the handwriting poses no problem.

TRANSCRIBING FAITHFULLY

A transcription should not alter anything in the original. All capital letters, all punctuation, all misspellings should be copied as they appear in the original. Some transcribers even prefer to keep the transcription line by line as it is in the original, though that is a personal preference and not required. *But in no event should changes be made in the original.* If you feel it is essential that a correct name or other remark be included, add it within square brackets [ ] so that it is clearly understood that you added this comment. There are some exceptions. The Board for Certification of Genealogists and scholarly journals now recommend that the following be transcribed for the letters they are intended to represent. At the library, study the issues of those journals and note the transcriptions of the old documents contained in their articles.

The Thorn. The thorn, which is intended for "th," looks very much like a "y." The words "the" and "that" look like "ye" and "y^t." To conform to modern-day practices, the part which looks like "y"should be transcribed as "th" for which it is intended. The thorn is commonly found in the words "the," "that," "them," as well as in others.

The "ff." During certain periods "ff" was commonly used to designate the capital letter F. We encounter names written as "ffrancis" and "ffrederick," for "Francis" and "Frederick." When the letters are transcribed as "ff" indexing becomes a problem. When the index is automatically generated, entries for ffrancis would not appear with Francis. The current practice is to transcribe the "ff," when clearly meant as a capital at the beginning of a word, as "F" for which it was intended.

The tailed "s." We often see the long-tailed "s" in documents. It was common and was often represented in printed works as

RULES FOR TRANSCRIBING.
- Follow punctuation exactly.
- Follow spelling exactly, even capitalization.
- If you supply missing letters, guess at a word, or insert a comment, use square brackets to surround your addition.
- Add the source citation to the transcription.

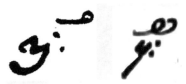

Figure 1-7. Two examples of the thorn. They both represent the word "the." The example on the top left used the peculiar e on its side, seen especially in 1600 and early 1700 writings.

Figure 1-8. Example of the "ff" used as the initial letter of a name. In this case, it is best to transcribe ffoster as Foster.

8

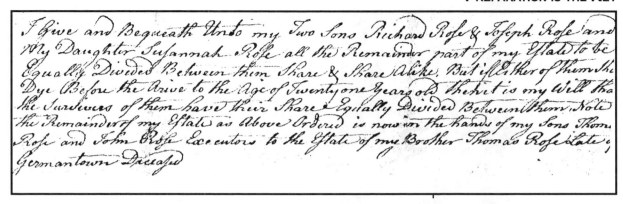

Figure 1-9. The above shows a number of instances of the tailed "s," including the words Susannah Rose, the word Estate, and others. There are twelve—can you find them all?

an "f." However, if a tailed "s" is transcribed as an "f" it can cause serious problems. Consider the word "wise." If a tailed "s" in the original is transcribed as "f," it erroneously becomes "wife." Other words could also cause similar problems. Prevent misinterpretation by using "s" in your transcriptions.

BOOKS AND TAPES WILL ASSIST

The subject of old handwriting is treated in a number of books.[12] Study their examples as you practice transcribing. It will be time well spent.

Lectures on the subject which were taped at national conferences can help.[13] Get two or three and listen to the tips. Try to get a copy of the syllabus material which accompanied the lecturer's presentation of the topic. The syllabus from that conference may be in a library near you. Or contact the Allen County Public Library in Fort Wayne Indiana.[14] For a small fee, they copy syllabus material if the lecturer has given them permission to do

Study the examples in the guide books, and practice with documents. Rapid reading is essential in courthouse research, especially when you have only a few hours onsite.

---

[12] Some of the titles include:

E. Kay Kirkham, *Handwriting of American Records for a Period of 300 Years* (Logan, Utah: Everton Publ. Co., 1973).

Elizabeth Shown Mills, ed. *Professional Genealogy: A Manual for Researchers, Writers, Editors, Lecturers, and Librarians* (Baltimore: Genealogical Publishing Co., 2001). See particularly Chapter 16, Mary McCampbell Bell, "Transcripts and Abstracts."

Kip Sperry, *Reading Early American Handwriting* (Baltimore, Md.: Genealogical Publishing Co., 1998). Includes an excellent twenty-seven page bibliography.

Ernest Thode, *German-English Genealogical Dictionary* (Baltimore, Md.: Genealogical Publishing Co., 1992). Includes illustrations of German script.

[13] Go to Repeat Performance's website at: <http://www.audiotapes.com>. In the search engine enter "handwriting" for a listing.

[14] Allen County Public Library, 200 East Berry Street, Fort Wayne, IN 45802, <http://www.acpl.lib.in.us>.

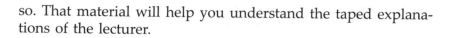

so. That material will help you understand the taped explanations of the lecturer.

ABSTRACTING

If the document is one you want to preserve in its entirety, make a photocopy. But also abstract it on-the-spot. Otherwise the clues that document can yield and the opportunity to follow those leads while still onsite will be lost. An abstract includes all the important points in the original: names, dates, residences, signatures, witnesses, date that the document was proved or acknowledged, and any special clauses within the document. (See other chapters in this guide for information on specific documents described in those chapters.)

OTHER PRACTICAL CONSIDERATIONS

SHOULD YOU TAKE YOUR COMPUTER INTO THE COURTHOUSE?

My personal opinion? No. The courthouse is an awkward place in which to use a computer. Usually the counters on which you will work are tall and slanted. They may or may not have a "lip." Without that lip, your computer could slide onto the floor. Trying to type an abstract of a record from one of the very large and heavy record books, with the computer sitting to the side, not only takes a lot of counter space, but is almost impossible if the record book won't stay open. (Sometimes the courthouse has a table on which researchers can work, and if so, it might be possible. But that is uncommon.) Additionally, if you type your abstract into the computer, it will take longer for you must check it for typing errors. Abstracting by hand is faster and allows for easy simultaneous use of a magnifying glass.

If you have notes on your computer you need to consult (for instance, if you have been to the courthouse previously and don't want to duplicate the research), print your computer notes to take with you.

As an alternative, consider loading your family compilation and notes into a Palm reader.[15] But don't eliminate the one-page summary mentioned previously in this chapter for it will keep you focused.

PHOTOCOPYING

In most courthouses, a photocopier is available. However, the clerk may restrict photocopying of selected older records and, particularly, loose originals. Many researchers are taking digital cameras into the courthouse in case such restrictions exist. There may be no problem in using a camera if you don't use flash, but

---

[15] Small hand-held computer.

ask first. Some courthouses are imposing a "no camera in the courthouse" policy. If so, you'll need to return the camera to your car, or leave it with the guard.

CHAPTER POINTS TO PONDER

✓ Determine the right facility in which to conduct the search.

✓ Be prepared with information on the date of formation of the county and parent counties.

✓ Prepare a one-page sheet of goal and summary.

✓ Be prepared with addresses and maps, and the hours the facilities are open.

In the next chapter we will enter the courthouse and learn what to do upon arrival.

2 You're There— Now What!?

ARRIVING AT THE COURTHOUSE

You did all the preparation, climbed those stairs, and at last, you are inside the courthouse. Where to go? Find the directory– usually posted in the hallway near the entrance. The department where the deeds are recorded may be listed as Recorder of Deeds, Land Records, or various close alternatives. The Probate division may be listed as Wills (or in some states, the Surrogate's office). Also listed, depending upon the court structure of the state, may be County Clerk, or Circuit Court Clerk, or Chancery Court, or others. If in doubt, look around for an information desk, and if not found, go into one of the offices and ask "In which office will I find land records?" or whatever others you have decided to search first. Your initial efforts most likely will be in one of the following:

Deeds. The recorded deeds, mortgages (land and chattel), survey books, plat books, and other records associated with land will be here.[1]

Estates. These records will be found in an office variously designated Probate, Wills, or Surrogate. It houses wills (testate proceedings), administrations (intestate proceedings), bond books, inventories, accounts, guardianships, and a host of related estate records.

Vital Records. Here you should find the births, deaths, and perhaps, marriages. In modern times these are often housed in offices other than the courthouse, for example, a Department of Health.

Civil Court Records. This office will contain the records involving plaintiffs and defendants (including divorces, name changes, adoptions, and others.

Courthouse offices are known by different names from area to area.

---

[1] Sometimes there were wills or other records intermingled in the land recordings, depending upon the area and the time period.

These are broad definitions. Actually, the offices in various states, and indeed, even within the same state, vary widely. The Recorder of Deeds' office may house the early court minutes; the marriage records may be in there too, while the births and deaths may be in the civil records office or a separate Health Department. The best you can do is to start in one office, examine what is there, and then proceed to another office.

STARTING THE SEARCH

Know what it is you are specifically seeking—land records, marriages, or others. Have in mind the time frame you are searching, and the date the county was formed. Before you can access any records, you need to access *the indexes* to the records. When you are in the specific office in which you've decided to start (land, or marriages, etc.) greet the clerk but don't say, "I'm a genealogist," and start reciting details of your search. When the clerk inquires as to what you need, merely say, "I am looking for the indexes from — to —," giving a range of dates. Or perhaps say, "from the formation of the county to 1850—," or whatever dates are pertinent to your search. The clerk may just wave you through the door to the record room, or may go with you and show you where the indexes to those records are located. The only other necessary questions at this time: "Is the photocopy machine self-serve?" and "How much are copies?"

If the clerk did not accompany you, when you enter the record room look around to get oriented. The indexes will likely be grouped together in one area, with the rest of the room devoted to the actual books to which the indexes refer. If after searching you do not find the indexes, or can't locate those for the time period you need, ask the clerk. The older indexes, and perhaps even the records themselves, may be available only on microfilm, or may have been removed to another room—the attic, the basement, or even to an off-site facility.

EXPECTATIONS

Commonly, clerks are too busy to assist other than answering questions about their recording system or the location of the records. They usually do not have the time (or the genealogical inclination) to digest details of your problem. There are exceptions. Sometimes the clerk is also an enthusiastic genealogist who will offer hints. There may even be a volunteer or a part-time clerk specifically assigned to genealogy. But that is rare. More likely, you'll arrive in the midst of a busy morning when current court matters absorb their attention.

You cannot expect the clerks to go up and down the ladders to bring down the books you need, or at least, not when you need

> "Where would I find the indexes?"

them. As mentioned in the previous chapter, if you are unable to do that yourself, bring someone with you who can.

For your part, certain things are expected of you, as a matter of courtesy and to preserve the records.

Find a good spot to store your personal items. If you go into another office, take purses and briefcases with you.

- When you first arrive, look around. Is there a place you can deposit your jacket, your briefcase, purse, umbrella, or other personal belongings? (I like to pick the top of a bookshelf which is high and easy to watch as I am working.) Usually counter space is limited. Keep only what you need on the counter. If you go into another room to continue the search, take personal items such as a briefcase or purse with you. Theft is as possible in courthouses as in other work areas.

- If you have someone with you, keep conversation to a minimum and speak quietly.

- Keep your note paper off of the book page while writing. It can leave impressions on those valuable original record books. Keep your notepad to the side.

- Don't make any correction in a book. (If it is something obvious and important, and you feel it must be noted, advise the clerk. Or later, write them a letter with details.)

- In some courthouses, posted notices prohibit the use of pens. Be prepared with a pencil, though they may be provided. (If pens *are* permitted, make sure yours doesn't leak!)

- Return record books to their proper place on the shelves.

- If you are using original loose records, *keep them in the same arrangement you found them.*

- Do not eat, drink or smoke around the records.

- No talking or singing to yourself! While working in solitude we can develop habits which are distracting to others.

HINTS FOR SUCCESS

In each department you visit, keep a log of which record books you have examined, even if the search was negative. Otherwise, six months from now you'll find yourself duplicating your efforts in the same sources. Your listing might resemble the following:

Deed Index 1 1798-1830 – see listings copied
Deed Index 2 1831-1850 – no Adams listings
Survey Book 1 (1798-1810) – no Adams listings
Survey Book 2 (1811-1820) – no index; conducted page by page search
Marriage Book 1 – groom index only; did not search page by page for brides in the index or the register
Marriage Book 2 – bride/groom index; part of "A" surnames faded and unreadable

If the book you examined does not have the title on the spine (or the spine has deteriorated or is missing), look inside to determine the contents. Examine the first and the last pages to get an idea of dates. Your log might then show:

[Survey Book – spine missing, dates about 1821-1835]

By enclosing in square brackets the title and description you supplied, it will be clear later that you added this information.

DIFFERENCES IN INDEXES

In my first few visits to courthouses, I didn't fully understand the various indexing systems. "How difficult could an index be?" thought I! It didn't take long to realize there are numerous and assorted styles of indexes. Some can trap the unwary user. Some basics follow. (See also Chapters 3, 5, 7 and 9 for indexes specific to those chapter contents.)

How Difficult Can it Be?!

Original Index. Often the earlier record books have their own indexes. Thus, Deed Book A and Will Book A may each have an index, Deed Book B and Will Book B, etc. As the years passed, users found that using individual indexes for a long span of time was time consuming. A consolidated index (see below) encompassing several years may have then been created. But if it wasn't, the only recourse is to examine each record book individually.

In another variation, the "original" index may have covered a long period but only one type of document. A deed index might cover 20 years but list only deeds and not powers of attorney. A will index might cover only wills and not inventories or bonds. In this case, each *type* of record book index would need to be examined.

Consolidated Index. This index can assist immeasurably. Usually compiled years after the "original" indexes, the consolidated index combines several types of records into one easy-to-use listing. Sometimes called a "general" index, its broader inclusions facilitate a quicker search. For example, a consolidated index in the probate department may include the early index to wills, administrations, inventories, accounts, and guardianships (or other combinations of records). There is a downside. Since that index was prepared years after the events, the consolidation is subject to errors by the creators who may not have been familiar with the old family names, or with the old script. Human error can also cause the omission of an entry or insertion of an erroneous date, number or name.

NUMBERING OF RECORD BOOKS

Record books may start out with letter descriptions, A, B, C, etc. After Z it may then continue with Book AA, BB, CC. Or, after

---

The original index may have covered a span of years, or may have been created for each individual book. Original indexes may have included a variety of documents. Or, there may be several indexes, each covering a specific type of document—wills, bonds, inventories, and others.

A consolidated index is usually prepared years after the original entries. It combines a variety of documents into one index. Though a huge help, errors can creep in depending upon the clerk's skill in interpreting early handwriting, and human error when recopying.

Book Z the numbering may switch to Book 1, 2, 3. Another variation: earlier books were designated A, B, C, and after Z the next series started with A1, B1, C1. After rotating to Z1 it restarted with A2, B2, C2, and so forth.[2]

In a few states, such as Maryland, it was popular to use the initials of the head clerk. If the man was named John Walford, then the books under his term would be JW1, JW2, JW3 etc. This style of numbering doesn't furnish a clue as to which are earlier books unless you know when that clerk was in office, or a span of dates was added to the spines by subsequent clerks.

A Variety of Indexing Systems

Different states (and even counties within states) use diverse indexing modes. Some are simple, some are complicated.

Instructions on how to use the index, and visual examples of those indexes, are usually either on the inside cover of the index or on its first few pages. If you are availing yourself of microfilm instead of the original books, it is easy to overlook these explanations unless you specifically roll the film to the beginning of the microfilmed record book to locate them.

Russell Index System

This was a common indexing system (and still is in some areas). It is based on the key letters of l, m, n, r, and t. Those surnames not containing a key letter are listed under "Misc." With this system, you need to first find the index book with the initial letter of the surname you seek. If you are looking for "Kelly," go to the index book with "K" on the spine.

Once you have found the correct index book, ignore the initial letter, in this case K. Now determine if there is a key letter in the remaining letters, and use the *first* key letter you find. If the surname has more than one key letter, you are looking for the *first* key letter following the initial letter of the surname. In the example above, i.e., Kelly, you find that "e" is not a key letter. The first "key letter" in that name is l. You need to search no further. Having found the key letter "l" along the top row, you will use the page numbers listed under "l" as shown in the illustration, i.e., 11, 21, 31, 41, 51, and 61. Now that you have settled the question of the surname, your next step is to determine which column you will use for the first name. Check

ORIGINAL INDEXES
May start Deed A, B, to Z, then restart with A1, B1, to Z1, and restart with A2, B2, to Z2, etc. Or, Books may start with A, B, to Z, and then restart with AA, BB, to ZZ, and restart with A3, B3, to Z3, etc.

There are a multitude of indexing styles. Check the inside cover of the record book, or the first few pages. The record book should include an illustration and description. Study it, but ask the clerk for assistance if needed.

TO LOCATE NAMES IN INDEX

Determine first key-letter following initial letter in Family Name. Find section number in the column headed by said key-letter, opposite given name initial desired. Names not containing a key-letter will be located under "Misc." Corporations, etc., will be located under the first key-letter following the initial letter in the first word of the name, or if no key-letter, under "Misc." Always omit the article "The."

Given Name Initials	Key Letters and Section Numbers					
	l	m	n	r	t	Misc.
ABCD	11	12	13	14	15	16
EFGHI	21	22	23	24	25	26
JKL	31	32	33	34	35	36
MNOPQR	41	42	43	44	45	46
STUVWXYZ	51	52	53	54	55	56
Corps., etc.	61	62	63	64	65	66

Patented and Patents Pending   RUSSELL INDEX COMPANY, PITTSBURGH, PA.

Figure 2-1. Russell index, based on key letters of l, m, n, r, and t.

---

[2] There are always exceptions. A clerk may have inserted a Book BB between A and C, etc.

the column along the left, which represents the initial letter of the first name. Looking for John Kelly? Go to page 31. Looking for William Kelly? He will be on page 51 of the record book.

On the example of Penton, (still in Figure 2-1), look for the letter "P" on the spine. Once in that index book, check for the first key letter. The letter e (in Penton) is not a key letter, but the letter n is. Following the the method given, for Arthur Penton go to page 13. For George Penton, go to page 23.

What about a name with no key letters? If you are looking for the surname Robb, note that after the initial R of the surname, there are no key letters. Those surnames with none will use the "Misc." column. If the name is Alan Robb, look along the left for given names starting with A, B, C, and D, since Alan falls there, then look across to the Misc. column. Any listing for an Alan Robb will be page 16 (still in Figure 2-1). In some heavily populated areas, the Russell index may be further defined (Figure 2-2) by including two key letters. Instead of l, m, n, r, and t, they are broken further as the illustration below depicts.

RUSSELL INDEX VARIATION for more heavily populated areas. Key letters of l, m, n, r, and t are combined with the second key letter. If the surname has two key letters, you need to use that combination to find the specific column. The key letters are:

L, LM, LN, LR, LT
M, ML, MN, MR, MT
N, NL, NM, NR, NT
R, RL, RM, RN, RT
T, TL, TM, TN, TR

Remember to disregard the initial letter of the surname—you will pick the index book marked with that initial letter. Do not count that initial letter as a key letter.

Figure 2-2. Variation of the Russell index to accommodate heavily populated communities. Assume that you are in the "R" surname index. If looking for Alexander Romine, disregard the initial letter of the surname since you are already in the R index. Find the first key letter of l, m, n, r, or t. In this case for Romine it is m. Then look for the next key letter, if any. In this case, for the name Romine, the second key letter is n. Therefore, you will use the column along the left and look for "MN." To find Alexander Romine, look to the top row letters which are shown as "Given Name Initials and Section Number." Use the column under A for the given name of Alexander. Any entries for him will therefore be on page 120. Bernard Romine would be on page 220.

TO LOCATE NAMES IN THE INDEX

Determine the first and second Key-letters after the initial letter in the Surname. In the column headed by the Given Name initial of the name for which you are searching, and opposite the Key-letters contained in the Surname, the number of the section is designated where the name will be found. Duplications of the same Key-letter are disregarded. Surnames, not containing a Key-letter, are found in the sections designated by the numbers opposite "Misc." All names other than those of individuals are found in the sections designated by the numbers in the column headed "Corps., Etc.", and opposite the Key-letters contained in the first word of the name, disregarding the article "The."

LETTERS KEY.	A	B	C	D	E	F	G	HI	J	KL	M	NO	PQ	R	S	TUV	W	X Y Z	Corps Etc.	LETTERS KEY.
L	110	210	310	410	510	610	710	810	910	1010	1110	1210	1310	1410	1510	1610	1710		1810	L
LM	110	210	310	410	510	610	710	810	910	1010	1110	1210	1310	1410	1510	1610	1710		1810	LM
LN	110	210	310	410	510	610	710	810	910	1010	1110	1210	1310	1410	1510	1610	1710		1810	LN
LR	110	210	310	410	510	610	710	810	910	1010	1110	1210	1310	1410	1510	1610	1710		1810	LR
LT	110	210	310	410	510	610	710	810	910	1010	1110	1210	1310	1410	1510	1610	1710		1810	LT
M	120	220	320	420	520	620	720	820	920	1020	1120	1220	1320	1420	1520	1620	1720		1820	M
ML	120	220	320	420	520	620	720	820	920	1020	1120	1220	1320	1420	1520	1620	1720		1820	ML
MN	120	220	320	420	520	620	720	820	920	1020	1120	1220	1320	1420	1520	1620	1720		1820	MN
MR	120	220	320	420	520	620	720	820	920	1020	1120	1220	1320	1420	1520	1620	1720		1820	MR
MT	120	220	320	420	520	620	720	820	920	1020	1120	1220	1320	1420	1520	1620	1720		1820	MT
N	130	230	330	430	530	630	730	830	930	1030	1130	1230	1330	1430	1530	1630	1730		1830	N
NL	130	230	330	430	530	630	730	830	930	1030	1130	1230	1330	1430	1530	1630	1730		1830	NL
NM	130	230	330	430	530	630	730	830	930	1030	1130	1230	1330	1430	1530	1630	1730		1830	NM
NR	130	230	330	430	530	630	730	830	930	1030	1130	1230	1330	1430	1530	1630	1730		1830	NR
NT	130	230	330	430	530	630	730	830	930	1030	1130	1230	1330	1430	1530	1630	1730		1830	NT
R	140	240	340	440	540	640	740	840	940	1040	1140	1240	1340	1440	1540	1640	1740		1840	R
RL	140	240	340	440	540	640	740	840	940	1040	1140	1240	1340	1440	1540	1640	1740		1840	RL
RM	140	240	340	440	540	640	740	840	940	1040	1140	1240	1340	1440	1540	1640	1740		1840	RM
RN	140	240	340	440	540	640	740	840	940	1040	1140	1240	1340	1440	1540	1640	1740		1840	RN
RT	140	240	340	440	540	640	740	840	940	1040	1140	1240	1340	1440	1640	1640	1740		1840	RT
T	150	250	350	450	550	650	750	850	950	1050	1150	1250	1350	1450	1550	1650	1750		1850	T
TL	150	250	350	450	550	650	750	850	950	1050	1150	1250	1350	1450	1550	1650	1750		1850	TL
TM	150	250	350	450	550	650	750	850	950	1050	1150	1250	1350	1450	1550	1650	1750		1850	TM
TN	150	250	350	450	550	650	750	850	950	1050	1150	1250	1350	1450	1550	1650	1750		1850	TN
TR	150	250	350	450	550	650	750	850	950	1050	1150	1250	1350	1450	1550	1650	1750		1850	TR
Misc.	160	260	360	460	560	660	760	860	960	1060	1160	1260	1360	1460	1560	1660	1760		1860	Misc.
	A	B	C	D	E	F	G	HI	J	KL	M	NO	PQ	R	S	TUV	W	X Y Z	Corps Etc.	

Each of these divisions is assigned a page number (see this illustrated in Figure 2-2) In this type of amplified Russell system, you need to determine the first *and second* key letters in the surname. If you were searching the name of Romine, you would go to the R surname index book (or perhaps a combination such as P, Q, R). Once there, look down the left column for MN, the first and second key letters in the Romine name.

ADDITIONAL HINTS WITH THE RUSSELL SYSTEM

With the standard Russell system a surname such as Robb has no key letters. It therefore falls under "Misc." and you will use pages 16, 26, 36, 46, 56, and 66, depending upon the first name. Using Figure 2-1 page 17, look for Lott Robb. Note that it would be on page 36. All would not fit on one page—there will be multiple pages probably marked as 36-1, 36-2, etc. or 36-a, 36-b, etc. Find

36 1	GRANTOR [key] INDEX						
	All Names contained in this section are arranged in these columns. The number following a name indicates the page of this section where all entries of that name may be found						
Powe	1	Quick	6	Rowe	6	Read	11
Paye	1			Roe	6	Reid	11
Pope	1			Raub	7	Rhoads	11
Pease	2		➜	Robb	7	Rhodes	11
Pare	2			Reeves	7	Reckhow	14
Peck	4			Roush	7	Rezeau	14
Pike	5			Rush	7	Resseguie	14
Peabody	6			Roach	7	Resseguie	14
Paddock	6			Ross	7	Resseque	14
Paddick	6			Rose	8	Ridgway	14

Figure 2-3. In using the Russell index, do not use only the charts shown in Figures 2-1 and 2-2. Once you have determined the page you need, it is important to check the initial page of that section as explained to the left.

the initial page (likely 36-1 or 36-a) and note that at the top of that page (as shown in Figure 2-3 above) some surnames have been assigned *their own page.* To the right of the name Robb is a 7. You must now go to page 36-7. Some areas created an individual page for each surname. Others only did so if that surname had many entries; if not, they were just entered in that section (in this case 36) chronologically as they were recorded. The search for names on the initial page is not limited to those which fell into "Misc." It applied to all the key letters. Make it a practice to examine that initial page of any section the Russell index directs you to, or you may miss your family's entries.

THE CAMPBELL SYSTEM AND OTHER "FIRST NAME" INDEXES

Some indexes are not alphabetical by the surname, but by the first name.[3] This can help you find your ancestor's listing immediately if you are only looking for a specific name. But if you are checking all listings for the surname (which is the best strategy), it can be cumbersome.

In using any index, be aware that when there were more entries than could be entered on a single page, the pages were assigned the same page number but marked with the addition of "a" or "1." Therefore, if the Bell surnames or B surnamed were assigned to page 375, and needed more than one page, they are likely "375-a," "375-b," etc., or "375-1," "375-2," etc.

---

[3] This is somewhat similar to the soundex index of the United States federal census, except that in the soundex system, surnames are grouped together by sound, and then listed alphabetically by initial letter of the given name.

In this, find the index with the initial letter of the surname on the spine. *All* the surnames starting with that letter are listed in it, with no effort to list them alphabetically. They alphabetized instead by the first name, and even then, not in strict alphabetical order. If you are looking for Allan Johnson, go to the pages with the "A" *given* names. Allan Johnson will be intermingled with others whose surnames start with J, and first names starting with A. If you are looking for Thomas Johnson, look for the section of "T" given names. Usually 2-4 letters are combined. Perhaps all the A, B, C, and D first names, then E, F , etc.

It is essential to know nicknames when using a first-name index. If you don't know that "Gus" is a nickname for Augustus, and are looking only under A, you will miss him as "Gus" in the "G" section!

It quickly becomes apparent that this is a slow system when searching all entries for a surname. You can't even have it photocopied, for the entries will span many pages, depending upon the time period. It should be noted, however, that the entries are chronological. Therefore, you can limit the search to the years pertinent to your particular problem in each of the sections.

COTT INDEXES

There are a variety of Cott indexes. One variation is to break down the surname by the first two or three letters of the surname, as shown in the following:

Don't know that Patsy was a nickname for Martha, that Fate was used for Lafayette, and that Sandy was used for Alexander? You may be missing records! (See p. 57.)

Ri Rhi			Roa to Ron Rho			Roo to Roy		
A B 125	I J Xcept Jo 152	R S 181	A B 204	I J Xcept Jo 223	R S 246	A B 261	I J Xcept Jo 280	R S 303
C D 132	Jo 161	T U V 188	C D 209	Jo 230	T U V 251	C D 266	Jo 287	T U V 308
E F 139	K L M 171	W Y Z 192	E F 214	K L M 238	W Y Z 253	E F 271	K L M 295	W Y Z 310
G H 145	N O P Q 177	Cor. or Firm. 198	G H 218	N O P Q 243	Cor. or Firm. 257	G H 275	N O P Q 300	Cor. or Firm. 314

Figure 2-4. In the above version of Cott, surnames starting with Roa to Ron, and also those starting with Rho, would fall into the second column shown. The initial letter of the given name would determine the page number—Lemuel Roane would be on p. 238. Note the variant spellings of the surname when you use this type of index. In the above example, Edward Roane would be on p. 214, while Edward Roone would be on p. 271 (third column above).

First two Letters of Surname.		
Ep to Ez		
First Letter of Given Name and Page.		
A ...76	H ...85	P Q 97
B ...78	I ...86	R .. 98
C ...79	J ...86	S .. 99
D ...80	K L .92	T ..101
E ...81	M ...93	U V 102
F ...83	N ...96	W ..103
G ...84	O ...96	Y Z 105

Figure 2-5. In a variation of the above, the illustration at the left shows the range of surnames along the top of the column, but the letters of the given names are arranged differently. Alexander would be on p. 76, Harold on p. 85.

GRAVES TABULAR INITIAL INDEXES

In Figure 2-6, the large initial to the left/top is the first letter of the surname. The second letter is beneath the initial letter, along the left. The third letter of the surname is out to the right of the first. In the example shown, the surname Garvin would be on page 308. The surname of Gleason would be on page 286. There is no division by the first name in this index; only the surname.

DIVISION TABLES TO GRAVES' TABULAR INITIAL INDEXES.

Entered according to Act of Congress, in the year 1866, by W. H. GRAVES, in the Clerk's Office of the District Court of the United States for the Northern District of N. Y.

G	A	B	C	D	E	F	G	H	I	J	K	L	M	N	O	P	Q	R	S	T	U	V	W	X	Y	Z
A	278	283	285	285	285	291	291	292	292	295	295	296	302	302	304	307	307	308	313	314	315	316	316	316	317	317
E H	“	“	“	“	“	“	“	“	“	“	“	“	“	303	“	“	“	310	“	“	“	“	“	“	“	“
I	“	284	“	“	“	“	“	“	“	“	“	298	“	“	“	“	“	“	“	“	“	“	“	“	“	“
L M N	“	285	“	“	286	“	“	“	“	“	“	301	“	“	“	“	“	“	“	“	“	“	“	“	“	“
O	“	“	“	“	“	“	“	“	“	“	“	“	“	“	305	“	“	311	“	“	“	“	“	“	“	“
R	279	“	“	“	287	“	“	“	293	“	“	“	“	“	307	“	“	313	“	“	316	“	“	“	“	“
S U W Y	283	“	“	“	291	“	“	“	295	“	“	“	“	“	“	“	“	“	“	“	“	“	“	“	“	“

Figure 2-6. In the Graves index above the first three letters of the surname are used. This example is for G surnames; the second letter is along the left beneath it, and the third letters are along the top to the right of the large initial letter.

ADDITIONAL INDEXES

Some indexes have been described here; there are others. Take the time to grasp whatever indexing system is used in that particular office. If it still is unclear, ask for assistance from the clerk.

CAN'T FIND A NAME IN THE INDEX?

Look for variations of the surname, and also of the given name. Also consider the following.

DID THE INDEX ERR?

If you find an entry for Book 1 page 232 in an index and cannot find the entry on that page, try the following:

- Recheck your note–did you miscopy the entry? Could the book be Book I instead of Book 1? J instead of I?
- Make sure you understood the index. Take another name from a record book (a grantor, grantee, name of the decedent, etc.), and check the index to see if it is on that page of the index. If not, perhaps you are not using that index correctly.
- Look for an index in the original record book itself (instead of a later consolidated or general index). It may show a different page number.
- If it is a deed and you can't find the entry indexed under the grantor, check the grantee index to see if the same page is assigned. If it is a marriage under groom and it's not on that record page, check the bride index to see if the marriage is listed as a different page. The clerk may have erred.

LOOKING FOR GEORGE WASHINGTON PELLIER?

Check every possible variation. He may be:

Washington G. Pellier

G. W. Pellier

W. G. Pellier

George W. Pellier

- Examine a few pages before and after page 232. If that doesn't work, try checking 132 or 332 to see if the first digit was entered in error. Or, the second digit may be wrong, try 212, 222, 242, etc.

- Check to see if that series of numbers was repeated. It's possible the clerk went from 230 to 239 and then inadvertently restarted with 230 again.

(More strategies involving specific types of records are present-.ed in the individual chapters involving deeds, probates, civil court records, and vital records.)

DID YOU MISS SOME ENTRIES?

Watch for columns in the index which show at the bottom that the entries have been continued to another page. This happens frequently with common surnames. If the S section has been allotted only a prescribed number of pages, the S surnames may exceed that figure. At the bottom of the last column of the S surnames, look for a note "continued on page —" or "See page —" or even, "See the Q section." (Occasionally, the section has been continued more than once.)

WHAT'S MISSING IN THE INDEX?

When using an index, note its limitations. Does the marriage index include both grooms *and* brides? Does the index to a civil register list only plaintiffs and not defendants? Make a note in your records indicating the scope of the index you used.

USING THE INDEX FOR MAXIMUM RESULTS

Indexes offer multiple clues even before you examine the documents. A deed in which John Williams deeded land to Richard Williams will infer a probable relationship even without examining the deed. If Jonathan Hawks deeded 23 acres of a tract on Indian Creek, and 25 years later he is omitted from the index but Gustavus Hawks deeded 23 acres on that creek, we may infer a probable relationship from the index. An indexed probate proceeding in which Richard Martin was bondsman for Mary Martin implies a relationship between them. Three different people of the same surname deeding land over a five year period to the same person suggests the possibility they are selling an inherited tract and are related. They are clues to follow.

List all the items from the index for the surname you seek, in the appropriate time period. Do this even if time does not permit an examination of all the documents. If the listings of the surname all appear on the same indexed page, you may be able to photocopy the page to conserve time. If photocopying is restricted, then copy it by hand. Note all the pertinent data. If it is a lengthy list, and time will not permit you to take all details,

"Indexes offer multiple clues even before you examine the actual documents."

note at least the names of the parties, the book and page reference, date, and type of document. Condense anything else which appears. You will probably personally examine at least some of these documents, but once you get back home, if you find that others look promising, you have the indexed list to pursue it. You can borrow microfilm for those entries from the Family History Library of the LDS Church (if those records have been microfilmed). Or write to the courthouse giving them the type of document, names of parties, and book and page reference. Ask them to quote the fee for a photocopy. (See more on the Family History Library in Chapter 11.)

AFTER THE INDEX IS EXAMINED

The indexed entries will refer to a record book and page[4] (or folios, which can consist of more than one page). Once you have obtained the indexed listings, make some decisions as to what to examine first, as time may run out. Then go to the shelves and locate the book. Find the page and examine the record. If warranted, abstract it. If you think that it absolutely has no connection to your search (do not be hasty in that judgment; later you may find it's important), at least make a notation that you did examine that record. If you think it is important, after you abstract it, photocopy it too. In later chapters we will discuss in more detail the records you will find.

BROUGHT YOUR COMPUTER?

Mentioned previously is my own preference not to use the computer in the courthouse. But that does not mean it doesn't have a place in your onsite search! If you are not "dead tired" from the day's research, use the evening to type the notes you gleaned that day. Type everything you took—your log, your indexes, and your abstracts. Now, while it is fresh in your mind. While doing so, you may suddenly realize the significance of a name in one of the records and can pursue the lead while you are still in the area. Or, you may notice that you missed a name or date and can perhaps follow up the next day.

Once you have typed the notes into your computer, you can use your word processor's "find" or "search" feature to run some of the names for similarities. You note that "Benjamin Johnson" came up in more than one record. Enter his name in "find." You note that he not only witnessed your ancestor's deeds on three occasions, but he also witnessed the deed of two others by the same surname. Might he be related? Was your ancestor's wife a Johnson? It's worthy of further investigation. And, it will suggest that those of the same surname who used him as a witness could all be related to each other.

Computers can be a handicap in the courthouse unless there is a table available for that purpose. Even if you do find a spot, you probably will not be permitted to plug into the courthouses' electricity.

_____

[4] The index may also refer to a loose packet or file, discussed in Chapters 5, 7 and 8.

(There is, of course, the possibility that Benjamin Johnson was an attorney, but the earlier the record, the greater the possibility that he was a relative or close friend. And, as we know from our other genealogical research, friends often traveled together from old neighborhoods and are worth pursuing, too.)

LEGAL AGE

Keep in mind that the legal age for males usually differed from females. For most activities a male did not reach the "age of majority" until he was 21, while a female reached it at 18. The legal age varied in different states for different purposes, and changed over the years.[5] In some cases a male had to be sixteen to be added to his father's poll list for taxes; in other others, 18 or 21. A male could inherit property at any age, but normally had to be 21 to convey it without a guardian. Marriageable age was generally 21 for males and 18 for females, but this too varied. In some areas females especially could marry at a younger age.

To be certain, the state statute needs to be examined.

THERE WAS A FIRE!

Beware! The busy clerk may try to dissuade you with "There was a fire here." Should that stop you? Not until you ask more questions!

First, ask "What year did the fire occur?" After all, if the fire occurred in 1840 and the records you need are from 1860, it won't matter.

Second question, "If any records survived, where would I find them?" The fire may have affected only the civil court records—the probates and deeds may still survive. Or, the fire may have destroyed only a portion of the records. Surviving records may still be in the courthouse or may have been transferred to a state archives, state library, or other repository. Ask questions!

Also, if records were destroyed, there may have been an effort to reconstruct some of them. Those who held original deeds and still had a vested interest in the land may have brought those originals to the courthouse for re-recordation. Those words, "There was a fire," should be only a signal to do more investigating.

Legal age varies from area to area, and often for males and females. It can also vary in different time periods, and for different legal transactions.

There was a

FIRE

Don't let that deter you. Ask questions!

---

[5] Some cases have been reported where a male conveyed property under the legal age, but the deed had no force until he arrived of age.

THOSE OTHER RECORDS ON THE SHELVES

Take time to look around. Study the spines of the books. Unfamiliar with a particular type? Take a few minutes to study it. This is how you amass experience. Looking at a book that does not name an ancestor is not wasted time. Your pool of knowledge increases with each venture into something new. And with knowledge comes confidence.

In the next chapter, we will enter the Recorder of Deeds' vault and start examining records.

CHAPTER POINTS TO PONDER

✓ Study the posted directory to ascertain the office in which you want to start your search.

✓ When approaching the clerk, ask about the location of indexes rather than recite your genealogical problem.

✓ Good work habits include speaking quietly, returning all books to the proper shelf, and not taking up too much counter space.

✓ A variety of indexes will be used from area to area.

✓ Keep a log of all the records you examined, whether you had positive or negative results.

✓ List all the items indexed for your surname in the pertinent time period.

3 PROPERTY MATTERS

IMPORTANCE OF LAND OWNERSHIP

Our ancestors toiled to obtain land. That purchase was among the most important events of their lives. When we visit and walk the ground on which they lived, we are moved. Standing where they once played, grew up, and perhaps are even buried, fills us with a deep sense of family. It's worth every bit of effort it takes to find the tract.

The records generated with land ownership help us "know" those we never met. A deed may disclose that great-great-grandfather George Washington Stewart was called "Wash," and that he was a tollkeeper. His siblings may be revealed through the division of the property they jointly inherited. Even his wife Hannah's identity might surface when her father George Baker signed a gift deed to her. Leads materialize when we take the time to probe.

Land records are among the most reliable records for genealogists. If an error occurred—perhaps in the property description or other clause, a subsequent document should correct the error. Years may have passed, but when the error was discovered, it normally was rectified. Not uncommonly, that later record will furnish details on who owned the property originally and subsequently, providing you with at least a partial chain of title.

The local register of deeds office holds diverse land records[1] of which the deed—the conveyance of real property by the owner (the "grantor") to the buyer (the "grantee"), is the most common. Deeds and related land records provide one of our best sources for identifying families if we understand their use and interpretation.[2]

In some states the tracts were named. The custom was prevalent in Maryland—we can share a bit of their joy and humor - *Anna's Delight, Jonathan's Folly*, and *Poor Habitation*.

Was the land located in a state-land state or a federal-land state? It matters!

---

[1] There are state and federal records involving land that are not in the courthouse— grants, patents, military bounty records, and others.

[2] It should also be noted here that the records in the local recorder's office may not all concern land. This will be further discussed in Chapter 8.

STATE-LAND STATES vs. FEDERAL-LAND STATES

Did your ancestor acquire his property from another individual, or was his first purchase from a governing body? We need to understand the "first purchases" before we can fully digest the facts within the land records.

State-Land States. Connecticut, Delaware, Georgia, Hawaii, Kentucky, Maine, Maryland, Massachusetts, New Hampshire, New Jersey, New York, North Carolina, Pennsylvania, Rhode Island, South Carolina, Tennessee, Texas, Vermont, Virginia, and West Virginia—the thirteen original colonies and seven others, are called "state-land states." In these states the first title to land came from the colonial or state government (or a proprietor)[3] to individuals. These first purchases, called grants in some states or patents in others, are not local records. In state-land states those documents were issued by a land office of the state or by agents of the proprietor, and are usually now available at the state's archives. In some states, once the state had issued a grant or patent, the purchaser also had that patent recorded locally in the county or town, but this was not consistent.[4]

Federal-Land States. Thirty states are "federal-land states" or sometimes called "public-land states." These are generally classified into two groups. 1) The eastern federal-land states (east of the Mississippi river and one tier of states west of the river), that is: Alabama, Arkansas, Florida, Illinois, Indiana, Iowa, Louisiana, Michigan, Minnesota, Mississippi, Missouri, Ohio and Wisconsin. 2) The western federal-land states: Alaska, Arizona, California, Colorado, Idaho, Kansas, Montana, Nebraska, Nevada, New Mexico, North Dakota, Oklahoma, Oregon, South Dakota, Utah, Washington, and Wyoming.

In federal-land states, the first transfer of land came from the federal government to an individual (or group of individuals). The process generated a number of papers, including important case files.[5] Upon completing the required process, the entryman was issued a patent by the federal government. The original patents for the eastern states and the serial patents from July 1, 1908 for all states are in the custody of the Bureau of Land Management-Eastern Division.[6] Pre-1908 patents for western states can be obtained from the land office of the western states.

FEDERAL LAND PATENTS
To start your search for the initial land patented from the federal government to an individual in the federal-land states (formed after the Northwest Ordinance of 1785), go to the website of the General Land Office at <http://www.glorecords.blm.gov>. Images of many patents and good background information are available at the site. Though these are not courthouse records, the initial purchase from the federal government may furnish the long sought answer as to how your ancestor obtained his land.

---

[3] In Virginia a grant was by the colonial government; a patent by the proprietor of the Northern Neck area.

[4] Check with the state archives to see where the grants or patents are available in your state of interest. They are likely located right at the archives. They may also be available on the state archives' websites or in book form.

[5] Land-entry case files are in the custody of the National Archives. See Kenneth Hawkins, *Research in the Land Entry Files of the General Land Office. Record Group 49* (Washington, D.C.: National Archives and Records Administration, rev. 1998). This free publication may be obtained from the National Archives, and is also available online at <http://www.archives.gov/publications/general_information_leaflets/67.html#intro>.

[6] Many are also available online at <http://www.glorecords.blm.gov>.

SURVEYING DIFFERENCES

In general, the property description in state-land states was given in "metes and bounds" using compass points, trees, creeks, and other natural markers.[7] Or, a tract was subdivided into lots, a map filed, and the land sold by lot number. In federal-land states, the land was normally surveyed according to a prescribed rectangular six-mile survey.[8] The tract is described by section,

---

THE PROCESS TO OBTAIN A LAND PATENT OR GRANT.
STATE-LAND STATES.
APPLICATION. A request for a warrant to have a survey made. Few of these applications exist, and if they do, usually they are not easy to use.
WARRANT. A certificate authorizing a survey.
SURVEY. The surveyor's sketch of the boundaries of a tract of land, together with details of acreage, adjacent landowners, waterways, etc.
PATENT (called a GRANT in some states). The official deed from the government to the private owner.

FEDERAL-LAND STATES.
The land was generally already surveyed. From that point:
CASE FILE. In this file were papers to fulfill the requirements of the particular act under which the land was sought. As an example, if it was preemption, appropriate affidavits showing the length of time the person had resided on the property, and improvements made, were filed. Other acts generated other required affidavits, all maintained in the case file.
PATENT. Issued after the process was completed and all requirements met.

These case files are federal records available at the National Archives (in Washington, D.C.) in Record Group 49. The federal patents for eastern states are available from the Bureau of Land Management, Eastern Division for eastern states. The serial patents from July 1, 1908 for all states are also available there. The patents for western states before July 1, 1908 can be obtained from the state land offices. See also the website at < http://www.glorecords.blm.gov>.

The above process was for individuals applying for government patents/grants. Federal land was required to be surveyed (with some exceptions) before an entryman could make application; in state-land states it was surveyed after the process was initiated.

---

township, range, baseline, and meridian. A tract described as "SE ¼ of the NW ½ of Sec. 10 Twp 9 Range 20 East" in most cases would indicate it lies in a federal-land state.

Once the land had been "patented" or "granted," either in a state-land state or a federal-land state, subsequent transfers by the owner were local records. Understanding this process clarifies why the researcher is often unable to determine from the local records how the land was obtained. Your ancestor may have been the original private owner—in other words, your ancestor

---

[7] There are exceptions. For instance, in the Virginia Military District in the federal-land state of Ohio, the land is described by metes and bounds. In other instances a particular tract in a state-land state may have a rectangular survey, but not identical to that of the federal government.

[8] There are exceptions to this too. As an example, the United States Military District in Ohio is in five-mile surveys (instead of six), as are some other surveys of Ohio.

A state-land state description by metes and bounds might show a description such as this one from a deed: Beginning S 68 degrees E 80 poles thence S 10 degrees West 10 poles to a branch ...

6	5	4	3	2	1
7	8	9	10	11	12
18	17	16	15	14	13
19	20	21	22	23	24
30	29	28	27	26	25
31	32	33	34	35	36

Figure 3-1. The above illustrates a township in a federal-land state, consisting of 36 sections, as numbered by the act of 1796. The pattern for numbering pre-1796 started with 1 in the lower southeast (bottom right) corner (see Figure 3-2 below). Section 16 was reserved for the benefit of schools.

36	30	24	18	12	6
35	29	23	17	11	5
34	28	22	16	10	4
33	27	21	15	9	3
32	26	20	14	8	2
31	25	19	13	7	1

Figure 3-2. The above numbering pattern for the federal land survey, set up by the Northwest Ordinance of 1785, started in the southeast corner. This numbering pattern was changed in 1796. (See Figure 3-1.)

may have obtained the land from a government or proprietor. In that case, to find that first record necessitates an exploration of the state or federal record books, which is beyond the scope of this courthouse book.[9]

LAND SURVEYS

In federal-land states, the original rectangular survey system was first designated in the Land Ordinance of 1785. The survey called for six-mile square townships comprised of 36 sections, each one mile square.[10] (See Figure 3-2.) In a later act of 1796, the numbering pattern changed (see Figure 3-1) and has been in effect ever since. Using guides (see Source References page 201) to understand the rectangular survey property description, and Figure 3.1 on this page, it is easy to identify adjoining property owners[11] by the legal description of their land as recited in the land records. Those property owners with land in close proximity to your ancestor and carrying the same surname are probably related. Even those bearing other surnames could be related, and should at least be scrutinized for the possibility that they are members of the family, or friends who traveled to the new location together.

In state-land states, the original surveys appear in survey books of those various states, normally held now by the states' archives. To determine those whose properties adjoin in state-land states you'll need to examine the property description of the deed, which often includes the neighbors. Some researchers take the additional step of platting a neighborhood.[12]

INDEXES FOR LAND RECORDS

The most common type of local land indexes, located where deeds are recorded, include:

Grantor Index and Grantee Index (or sometimes called **Direct Index** and **Indirect Index**). These are separate index books for the sellers (grantors) and the buyers (grantees).

General Index to Deeds. In this, the grantors and the grantees are in the same index book. The organization of these indexes varies. 1) The grantors and grantees may all be on the same page,

---

9 See Source References page 201.

10 These dimensions can vary depending on curvature of the earth.

11 See Patricia Law Hatcher, *Locating Your Roots: Discover Your Ancestors Using Land Records* (Cincinnati, Ohio: Betterway Books, 2003). See also Dr. George W. Knepper, *The Official Ohio Lands Book* (Columbus, Ohio: The Auditor of State, 2002).

12 Platting a neighborhood furnishes clues by proximity to other families. Researching these other families can lead to relationships, and to former residences.

separated by a column designating "to" or "from" to show who was deeding to whom. 2) There may be a grantor index in the front of the book and a separate grantee index in the back of the book. 3) The grantors may be assigned the left hand pages while the grantees appear on the right hand pages. With this latter type of index it is easy to get to the end of the grantees (those on the right hand pages) and not notice that there may be more pages of grantors (those on the left hand pages). Keep going until you are sure you have come to the end of both.

Mortgagor Index and Mortgagee Index. In most areas, the earliest of the records combine mortgages with deeds, and they are, therefore, in the Grantor and Grantee indexes. The dates in which they made the separation differ from area to area. However, some areas (such as New York) separated these documents from the beginning of the county records. In those cases, it is important for those doing early research not to limit the index search to Grantor and Grantee, but to also examine the Mortgagor and Mortgagee indexes.

Consolidated Index. This is an overall index to a variety of records. In using it for land records, remember that a consolidated index (as discussed in Chapter 2) was usually prepared many years after the original indexes were created. So much time had passed in the interim that it was tempting for county officials to eliminate certain documents they deemed no longer important. One of their favorite omissions was the personal property deeds. The reasoning—"Who cares if someone mortgaged his household furniture 150 years ago?" But of course, we genealogists do. This possible omission is an important one. Personal property deeds are one of our richest sources of clues. This is especially true when parents deeded all their personal property to a child in exchange for life care and specified the relationship in the body of the document. To determine if personal property deeds have been excluded from a consolidated index, check the "type of document" column for a number of surnames for several years. If you don't find *any* mention of personal property deeds, they were probably omitted, and you'll need to resort to the original indexes[13] to find them.

Devisor and Devisee Indexes. The devisor index lists wills in which real property was transferred. Though helpful, that information would also be available through a testator index listing wills. The devisee index is a different matter. What joy it would bring to researchers if every state had this type! This index includes those who were devised real property in a will, that is, the testator left some land to those persons (the devisees). Let us say that George Johansen devised a plantation to his brother-in-law, your ancestor Augustus Williams. But, you didn't know that

When writing to the courthouse, address your inquiries about land to "Recorder of Deeds." Even if it is called something different in that county, they will understand the nature of your inquiry and direct it to the proper office.

---

[13] Original indexes are discussed in Chapter 2.

your Augustus had a brother-in-law named George Johansen. Therefore, you had no clue to examine the Johansen will unless you used a devisee index. In the latter, while searching the Williams name, you find Augustus Williams listed as a devisee of George Johansen, and it provides the book and page number of the Johansen will. You can now examine it. In many a relationship will be mentioned—granddaughter, son-in-law, a married sister, or other.

Unfortunately, not too many states maintained a devisee index. North Carolina did, and some other states had scattered volumes of a similar nature, perhaps called "Heirs of Descent" or some such name. Watch for these in the register of deeds' office.

Tract Indexes. These federal records for federal-land states are normally not at the local level. However, some courthouses do maintain tract indexes. If the county does have such an index, use the legal description[14] you have for the property, (that is, the section, township, and range), and locate the book and page which matches that description. You will be amazed! All the owners over time of the tract should be listed on that page. It may even include helpful remarks, such as "by will of father" (to indicate an inheritance) or other explanatory note. The tract index (and tract books) can help resurrect the history of the land when deeds have been lost or were never recorded. It may also suggest inheritances that might not otherwise be ascertained. Only a few areas have such tract indexes available locally–they are not generally available in courthouses statewide, but are enlightening.

In federal-land states, the tract index leads to the tract books. These large ledgers are organized by baseline and meridian, and then by section, township and range.[15] The page devoted to a particular section includes the names of owners, notations about payment, and other important details.[16] The tract books are federal government records. Some are available at the National Archives, at the Bureau of Land Management, and copies at other scattered locations. Microfilmed copies are available through the Family History Library and its branches.[17]

Lot and Block Indexes. There are a few counties (usually in heavily urban areas) in which the indexes for the transfer of

---

[14] That legal description can be in a deed, or even in some of your family's papers.

[15] See Hatcher's *Using Land Records* previously cited.

[16] Though federal land records are not local courthouse records, those researching their ancestors will find that a study of federal land, and use of those records, will solve many problems. Besides the books here mentioned, there are study courses, lectures, and other material available. Especially, check for lectures at national conferences by going to Repeat Performance's website at http://www.audiotapes.com and entering "federal land."

[17] Not all the books are available on microfilm.

land are based on Lot and Block, instead of grantor and grantee. If they did have a grantor and grantee index, it may be retired to a storage facility. Such is the case with Chicago. You need to know either the Lot and Block or the address of the property to request a search for Lot and Block. If you do request the grantor/grantee indexes for an earlier period, it will take days to retrieve them from storage (if they still exist). The record book page matching the Lot and Block will contain a history of the land from the first extant deed on record. A few counties throughout the country use this system, as does the District of Columbia. (In some areas these records are called "registry" records.)

ENTRY BOOK INDEXES

In some state-land states, separate "Entry Books" contain transfers of property under various occupancy laws of the state. These transfers are usually not included in the deed indexes and, thus, are often overlooked. When you are in a register of deeds office, poke around and explore any books which seem unfamiliar. You may find such records in the state of your interest.

PECULIARITIES OF DEED INDEXES IN LAND RECORDS

If your search for a deed of sale of your ancestor's property is unsuccessful, consider that the land may have been sold for debt or taxes by the sheriff or other county official. If so, it may be indexed under "S" for Sheriff, "C" for Commissioner, "T" for Tax Sale, or even indexed under the sheriff's own name rather than the name of the owner. In one case in Limestone County, Alabama, no record could be found of the sale of Nancy Rose's land. Finally, in a slim volume on a courthouse shelf marked only as "Tax Lien Sales," the puzzle was solved. The state had a tax lien on the 60 acres, and subsequently, the state sold it at public sale. Nancy had lost her land.

If you can't find the deed transferring land out of your family, but you know the name of one of the later owners, start from that point. Look at the grantee index and find the deed in which that later owner purchased it. Next, using the name of the grantor from whom he bought the land, in an earlier grantee index find how that person had obtained it, until you work it back to your ancestor's time period. In this manner, you can often reconstruct the chain of title back to your ancestor's era.

If you are trying to determine the name of a later owner, see if the land department has plat maps for a later period. If so, this should assist in identifying a new owner.

Sometimes when there was a string of grantors, the clerk only indexed the first name of that string in the grantor index. For instance, if the grantors were Jonathan Abbott and his wife Nancy formerly Gordon, Mary Gordon, Martha Gordon, Alexander Gor-

RECONSTRUCT THE CHAIN OF TITLE.
Know the name of a later owner?
* Find that owner in the grantee index and note the name of the grantor from whom he bought the land.
* Find that grantor in the earlier grantee index book to see how *he* acquired it.
* Keep following it back until you find when your ancestor purchased it.

Figure 3-3. Below, a typical general deed index. It shows one column with entries of "F" for from (grantor), and "to" (grantee). Thus, it is indexed chronologically both for grantors and grantees. It includes Vol., Page, Acres, Sec., Twp., Range, Lot, Dollars, and Remarks. The columns for Sec., Twp. and Range give us a clue that this is a county in a federal-land state, using the rectangular survey system described earlier in this chapter.

don, William Gordon and Joseph M. Gordon, the clerk may have only indexed it as "Jonathan Abbott *et al*" (*et alii*, and other persons). If the clerk picked up only the first listed name, it would be easy to miss the deed entirely unless you checked the spouses of the married daughters.

Make it a practice to look at every "et al" deed that you note in the index. Consider these as "must see" items to determine who those additional people were.

To save yourself some research time, as you are copying the indexed items, note whether any are duplicates. The clerk may have diligently indexed every grantor in the document, including all spouses. In that case, you'll have multiple entries for the same deed. Note this in some manner on your listing so you don't lose time looking up the same deed several times!

WHAT DO DEED INDEXES INCLUDE?

As with your search in other departments at the courthouse, you will want a record of all indexed transactions of the surname you are researching in the pertinent time period. List them all from both the grantor and the grantee deed indexes.

The index usually consists of several columns and normally include:

- Name of grantor
- Name of grantee
- Date of document
- Date of recordation
- Acreage
- Location
- Type of instrument
- Record book number and page number

If the indexed entries are all grouped together, you'll save time by photocopying those index pages if it is permitted. Otherwise, hand copy, taking all the essential details including the location of the property. Sometimes the column with property location is quite detailed. If that is the case, when time is limited abbreviate the location if necessary. You can acquire these details as you later abstract the documents.

Once copied, examine the index listings you took for names of those known to be members of your family, and make a note to examine those in their entirety. They are your first priority.

Date of Deed	NAME			NAME		Vol.	Page	Acres	Sec.	Twp.	Range	Lot	Dollars	Remarks
Feb 30-1832	Rose	Geo	F	Rose Peter		P	21	StClairsville	10-11				450	✓
Sept 5-1832	Rose	Geo	F	Norris Mary B.		P	335	StClairsville	10-11				1	
Jan 5-1836	Ring	Geo	to	Owings Hezekiah		J	286	801	18	5	4		300	

Next, study the column designating the type of record. Note particularly any that mention a gift deed, partition, power of attorney, personal property, quit claim, or *et al.*[18] These documents (discussed later in this chapter and in the next) are particularly significant genealogically and often reveal relationships. Add them to your priority list in case time does not allow you to examine all the listings.

Using the book and page reference, locate the record book, and abstract[19] the documents you've tagged as priority. As you abstract each, note on your list that you have done so. (My own system is to use a check mark beside the indexed document reference to indicate I want to examine it, and an asterisk (*) beside it to indicate that I did. (I can then quickly note from my copied index what has been examined and abstracted. And, the asterisk is easy to type and include when I enter my notes on the computer.)

INDEXES PREPARED BY OTHERS

Occasionally, you will find that the county did not prepare an index to the early deeds. This is highly unusual, but did sometimes occur. In one Virginia courthouse I visited, the index had been prepared and kept by a law firm for many years, though a copy was later donated to the courthouse.

Title companies (those who insure the title to the property) usually have their own prepared indexes, though normally those are not open to the public.

TYPES OF DOCUMENTS

Specific types of deeds and other instruments found in the deed department include, but are not limited to, the following.[20]

Bill of Sale. Written evidence of the sale, usually of personal property, showing the parties, consideration, and the property being transferred. Often recorded among the deeds

Cemetery Deeds. These deeds are to cemetery lots for certain cemeteries. They can be valuable for identifying the original purchaser and the date. The "deed" may be only a license for burial, rather than the conveying of the actual plot of land. Some cemetery deed books are for the conveyance of the land for the whole cemetery; the owner then grants privileges of burial.

Deed of Heirs. One of the best records for proving relationships is the deed of heirs. The heirs inherited a tract, and were

---

[18] *et alii*, and other persons.

[19] See abstracting in Chapter 1.

[20] The very brief definitions provided are based on more complete definitions in *Black's Law Dictionary*. This should be consulted for full meaning of these terms and the exceptions that occur.

now deeding their interest in that tract. It often mentions how they acquired that interest ("that descended to us through our father Wilson Jackson, deceased …") Such a document often includes the names of grandchildren, who stood in place of a deceased mother or deceased father who was an heir.

Deed of Lease and Release. In early Virginia (and a few other areas), title to land was sometimes made by dual documents. The first, a Deed of Lease, usually specified a nominal amount such as 5 shillings. It was followed (a day or more later) by a Deed of Release, which conveyed the property to the grantee. A typical example of a Lease and Release, this one from Berkeley County, Virginia (now West Virginia):

In this form of conveyance the deed of lease is often misinterpreted as a traditional lease. Check the following documents for several pages to see if there is also a release.

> On 1 May 1778, Deed of Lease, Jonathan Rose of County of Berkeley to John Champion of same, for 5 shillings, conveyed 319 acres, on both sides of Mile Spring branch, last granted to Peter White by Lord Fairfax on 3 October 1766. Signed: Jonathan Rose. Witnesses: Edward Beeson, Paul Hulse. Acknowledged: 19 May 1778.
>
> FOLLOWING THE ABOVE RECORDING: Deed of Release, 2 May 1778, Jonathan Rose and Ann his wife of Berkeley County for £100 convey to John Champion of same, 319 acres. Signed: Jonathan Rose, Ann Rose. Witnesses: same as above. Personally acknowledged: 19 May 1778.

Note that the Deed of Lease is signed only by Jonathan Rose, (his wife was not required to sign a lease), and specifies a nominal consideration of 5 shillings. One day later, the true story is revealed. Jonathan and Ann (his wife now joining since she has a dower interest) release the land for £100. Through these tandem transactions they conveyed the land to John Champion.

Discharge (military). This is a non-land document. The practice of recording military discharges usually started after the Civil War, but significantly increased after World War I.[21] Discharges are typically found in a separate set of books in the Register's office, marked on the spine as "Discharges." Normally each book has its own index, though there may be a general or consolidated index. (In earlier records the discharges were often indexed and recorded in the same books as deeds.)

If the wife did not sign a release, she was still entitled to her dower even though her husband had sold the property. It therefore encumbered the tract until her death or remarriage, assuming she outlived her husband. Occasionally we see a deed in which land is being sold "subject to the dower of ..." which is a lead to the former owners. This is especially valuable when the property was inherited. The dower of the wife ceased at the end of her widowhood.

Dower Release. In most cases a man's wife had a one-third dower interest in his real property. (This could vary. If they had no children, she probably was entitled to one-half. Sometimes she received one-half by law if there were only one or two children.) The husband could not sell or otherwise dispose of her dower interest without her release. She usually came into court and gave that release, after

---

[21] In more recent times, a Veteran's Form DD214—the separation paper, is recorded.

being questioned whether it was her free will to do so. If she could not physically attend, the court appointed an official to visit and personally question her at home. This dower release usually immediately followed the deed in the record book, but there are many cases in which the wife did not give her release until a later date, thus creating a separate record. (For curtesy, the rights of a husband to a portion of his wife's real property if there was a child born alive, see Terminology page 72 in Chapter 5.)

In some states the wife normally did not join the husband in the deed. If she did, it was usually an indication that the land had descended to her, probably through her own family. After marriage her husband acquired his right to her property. In Maryland, although customarily the wife did not join her husband in signing the deed, she did release her dower interest in the acknowledgment. It's important to understand the customs of an area so that the records can be properly evaluated.

Gift Deed (or Deed of Gift). A deed in which the grantor (seller) makes a gift of a tract or some personal property. The grantor was not deeding everything; he still retained other property. Usually the consideration was for a small amount (5 shillings or $1.00 was common) to ensure its legality. The grantor may have included the relationship, as in one where the grantor gave "to my son Bernard Schneider, for love and affection … and the further consideration of $1.00 …." (A specific relationship, however, may not be stated.)

Also common was a gift deed in which the grantor gave *all* his land and personal property to a son or daughter in exchange for the maintenance of the grantor (and spouse) during their natural lives. Such gift deeds can sometimes explain the lack of a probate proceeding. Having disposed of everything, no probate was necessitated.

Indenture. In property transactions, a deed in which two or more people enter into reciprocal obligations towards each other.

Lease. An agreement between a landlord (the lessor) and the tenant (the lessee), for real or personal property. (See also Deed of Lease and Release.)

One interesting variation of a lease was the "three-life" lease used for a time in some areas. These leases often state specific relationships, as did the one recorded in Cecil County, Maryland, in which "Eph Aug't Herman" leased to Sarah Rose, widow, a tract for her natural life, after her decease to go to William Rose, eldest son of Thomas Rose deceased, and after William's decease to Thomas Rose "son of the aforesaid deceased." It was not to be sold by Sarah, but to descend "for three lifetimes." Three-life leases were sometimes used to circumvent an entail-

It has crossed my mind, when reading dower releases—did a wife ever balk when she was questioned, and admit that she was *not* doing this freely?

ment on the property (see later). Though the owner could not sell because of the entail, he could give a lease on it.

Marriage Contract (sometimes referred to as a Prenuptial Agreement). Though not common, they do exist in the early records, particularly when the wife was to inherit property from her side of the family. Her father, in order to protect property he intended to give her, might require her to enter into such a contract to preserve the land on the maternal side of the family, or to protect it from possible debt of a son-in-law.

In the following abstract of a deed from King George County, Virginia, the circumstances and recording were a bit different. It is a Deed of Trust, and instead of preserving the property in the female's family, it acts as a marriage contract, but gives the property to the husband when Nelly dies.

Marriage contracts can be made for a variety of reasons: the bride is a widow with property before her marriage; the father of the bride wants to protect property on his side of the family; the intended groom is in debt and the contract is to protect what the bride brings to the marriage, etc.

> King George Co., Va. Deed Book 13 pp. 190-191, 22 February 1830, Nelly Rose of King George County, and Thomas Bernard of the same county, make over land "I now live" on bought of N. H. Hooe and small tract "inherited from my father" and all personal property upon trust, Nelly Rose anxious to give her property to Loval Rollings but fearing she might "come to want" makes the conveyance in trust for their mutual benefit. It was agreed that if Nelly Rose outlived Lovel Rollings the indenture was to be null and void. Nelly Rose and Loval Rollings were to enjoy profits of the property. Thomas Bernard was to see that the property was used by Rose and Rollings and no other. Should Rollings outlive Nelly he was to inherit the property. (It was signed by Nelly Rose and T. Bernard; the signature of Loval Rollings was not required.)

Marriage Contracts were sometimes used for widows, to protect property the widow was entitled from her deceased husband.

A mortgage recorded in the record books will often have a notation in the margin indicating that the mortgage has been "satisfied." Or, the marginal note may note a record book and page number on which the satisfaction of the mortgage has been recorded. These notes indicate that the mortgage has been "paid off."

Mortgage (and Chattel Mortgage). An instrument in writing in which the mortgagor gives security to the mortgagee, usually for repayment of a debt. (A *chattel* mortgage was used as security specifically for personal property.) Mortgages may be mixed with the deeds in the deed books, or may appear in separate mortgage volumes with their own indexes. If they were recorded among the deeds, they may read almost identical to a deed except that the mortgage contains a clause that the document is to be void if the obligation is repaid by a certain date as stated in the document. If this mortgage is misinterpreted as a deed, it can mislead the researcher as to the dates his family lived in the area. Do look for mortgages—if you can't find a deed for your ancestors, the mortgage books may list them. (Abbr.: Mtg., or Chattel Mtg.)

Oil and Mineral Lease, or Oil and Gas Lease. This is a lease for the right to extract oil and the minerals only (or oil and the gas). It is not a lease for the land itself.

Partition Deed. A deed for the division of property between several co-owners. The partition deed is always valuable in a search if the property was being divided among joint heirs. The court action preceding the deed should also be sought.

Personal Property Deed. A deed of personal property, household furniture, horse and buggy, farm implements, etc. Before slavery was abolished, this usually included slaves. (There are exceptions. For a time in the 1700s in Virginia, slaves were considered real property. As real property, the slaves could then be entailed.) See also "Entail" (page 41). (Abbr.: Pers. Ppty. or sometimes PP.)

Petition for Sale of Real Estate. This is a request asking the court for some action specified in the petition. In the Register of Deeds' office, one of the most common petitions is for the sale of real estate in an estate, sometimes recorded among deeds.[22]

Power of Attorney. An instrument in writing in which one person or group of persons (the principal) appoints another as agent to perform either all acts or specific acts on behalf of the principal. Powers of attorney may be recorded in a separate set of books, with their own indexes. Or, they may be intermingled with other land records and indexed as part of the general deed index. This type of instrument is often of considerable genealogical interest. (Abbr.: P of Atty., P of A, P.A. and PofA.)

The value of powers of attorney can be readily seen in the following 1833 document recorded in Greensville County, Virginia, which furnished the names of heirs, married names, new residences, locations of heirs in Tennessee, and connections to three estates from which they inherited.

> Abner Sammons and Susan his wife formerly Susan Dunn, Thomas Dunn, Patsey Dunn, Walter Sammons and his wife Lucy formerly Lucy Dunn, Nancy Dunn, Jane Dunn, James Dunn, Richard Sammons and Polly his wife formerly Polly Dunn, all of State of Tennessee and residing in counties of Williamson and Rutherford [Tennessee], appoint William Lyell of Rutherford County, Tennessee as attorney to go to the State of Virginia, Greensville County, to collect money, negroes, personal estate, etc. inherited from estates of Lucretia Dunn, Drury Dunn and Nancy Dunn, deceased. Dated: 22 Oct. 1833. Ack.: Rutherford County, Tennessee, 22 Oct. 1833.

Quitclaim Deed. A type of release which passes any claim or interest that the grantor may have in a piece of land (without claiming that such interest is valid or contains any warranty) to the grantee. Quitclaim deeds very often suggest that the grantor had an interest in the land through an inheritance. For example, Lucy Carlisle of Washington County, Maryland, widow and relict

---

[22] The petition may appear only in the office where the suit was initiated, usually the probate office.

of Walter Bond late of the same county, deceased, conveyed to Joseph Wheeler and Edward Bond of the same county; whereas Lucy Carlisle had a dower in the lands in the county aforesaid, of which the said Walter Bond "died seized" [that is, he owned the land at death], for $500 she quitclaimed her dower in the land.[23]

Right of way deed. The right of a person to pass over the land of another. [Railroad rights of way include the land itself.] A right of way may be granted for various reasons—`to bring utilities to a home, to grant access to a neighboring lot, etc.

Trust Deed (sometimes called Deed of Trust). In some states this was a type of mortgage in which the land was deeded in trust to a trustee to secure the property. It consists of three parties—the owner of the property who is mortgaging it, the person who is lending the money, and a trustee who is holding the property until the mortgage is paid. (Abbr.: Trust, or TD, D of T, or DT)

Warranty Deed. In this, the grantor warrants a good, clear title. This is the most common type of deed. Often the clerk only entered a designation in the "type" column of the index for those documents which were other than warranty deeds. In that case, anything in the type column unmarked can be assumed to probably be a warranty deed. (Abbr.: War. or WD)

TERMINOLOGY

Above we discussed some of the types of records. Before proceeding further, let's discuss some terminology you will encounter while working with land records. The following are very basic definitions for words and phrases involving deeds and other land records. For fuller meaning and alternate definitions, see a law dictionary.

Abutting owner (or abutter). The owner of land which adjoins where no land, road or street intervenes. Thus, the abutting owners' property touches the specified land.

Acknowledgment. A statement that either the person signed an instrument personally or that he witnessed the signing.

Affirm. To make a solemn and formal declaration that an affidavit is true, that the witness will tell the truth, etc. Substituted at times for an oath, especially by Quakers.

Agreement. A meeting of two or more minds; a coming together of opinion or determination. Not exactly synonymous with a contract; an agreement might lack one of the essential elements of a contract.

Alienate. To convey; to transfer the title to property.

---

[23] The widow could not sell her dower interest—that was an interest only for her life, but she could quitclaim her dower. Note also that the quitclaim suggests the widow's remarriage (later proven by other papers in the estate).

Anno domini, A.D. In the year of our Lord.

Appertaining. Belonging to or relating to.

Appurtenance. That which belongs to something else; an appendage. Something annexed. This would include a right of way, an outhouse, barn, garden, easement.

Assign. To transfer, make over or set over to another.

Assigns. Those to whom property is, will be, or may be assigned.

Caveat. Let him beware. Warning to be careful. For example, in 1778 in Surry County, North Carolina, William Breeden entered 100 acres on the East side of Fishers River adjoining John Allen and Elijah Thompson, including the improvements that formerly belonged to Bennett Rose and Elijah Thomson. The warrant was granted 8 December 1778, but caveated by Barzalia Harrison. Harrison was giving warning that he believed that he had an interest in the property. With that clue, a search should be initiated to determine how Harrison acquired that interest. He may have been an heir of Bennett Rose, or perhaps the interest emanated from some other source.

Chain carriers or chain bearers. Those people who carried the measuring chains used by surveyors. (Two were usually required. They were often related. Their names appear on the survey.)

Congressional township. See township.

Consideration. The cause, motive, price or compelling influence which induces the parties to enter into a contract. In a deed, this is usually monetary; however, it can be for "love and affection," the exchange of property, or for other considerations.

Convey. To transfer or deliver to another.

Curtilage. Originally, a place enclosed around a yard, such as the land and outbuildings around a case, or a courtyard. Now, any land or building immediately adjacent to a dwelling, usually enclosed by shrubs or a fence.

Dower. The provision the law makes for allotting a portion of land to a widow. Usually one-third, but can be one-half in some circumstances.

Entail. This limits the succession of real property.[25] It alters the rules of inheritance to lawful issue, going in a line of descent as prescribed by the entail. It may be limited to males, and commonly to the eldest son of each succeeding generation creating a "male tail." It could however be set up for the benefit of females, too. Though entails were most often established by a will, many were established by a deed. (For more discussion, see Chapter 7 pages 99-100.) An example:

In Fauquier County, Virginia, on 16 July 1733, Edward Curd of Henrico Co. deeded "for love and affection" for "my lawful daughter" Elizabeth Williams, did grant to "said Elizabeth Williams and to ... heirs of her body lawfully begotten forever one certain piece or parcel of land containing two hundred acres ..." [The important clause here is "heirs of her body lawfully begotten forever." This particular entail differed from most entails in that it was not limited to males—it was to descend to "heirs," male and female. Most entails specified "male heirs" or particularly, to the eldest son and then to his eldest son, then to his eldest son, and continuing in that manner. The entail limiting Elizabeth Williams effectively restricted the sale of the Curd land until Virginia abolished entails in 1785.]

---

[25] In Virginia for a period of time in the 1700s, slaves were considered real property, and could be entailed.

Escheat. The reversion of property to the state when there was no individual entitled to inherit. For example, in Westmoreland County, Virginia, an 800-acre grant to Edward Hart of that county escheated to the state in 1690 after Hart's widow Margaret married Henry Cossome, who died without heirs.

et al, *et alii.* And other persons.

et ux, *et uxor.* And wife.

et vir. And husband.

Fee simple. These words, when used alone, convey an absolute estate with no limitations or conditions. The owner is entitled to the entire property unconditionally.

Fee tail. See entail.

Feoffment. The grant of lands as a fee, commonly accompanied by livery of seizin (*q.v.*).

Folio. A leaf of a page or manuscript. It was the custom to number the leaves, and thus folio included front and back. Where each folio or sheet is separately numbered, it is usual to refer to the front as *recto* (right), or the folio number followed by R, and the other side as *verso* (turned), with V following the folio number.

Foreclosure. To shut out, to bar, to terminate. Often used when a debt is not repaid.

Freehold. This is an estate held for life or an estate in fee (which includes fee simple and fee tail.) Those appointed to juries and county offices were required to be freeholders.

Gavelkind. Common in Kent, England, and used in some parts of the American colonies. The land descended to all the sons equally and could be disposed of by will. (This is sometimes referred to in documents as a conveyance in the manner of East Greenwich, County of Kent, England.) Usually, this particular type of tenure was established in the first royal deed or grant, and restated in succeeding ones: "to be held as of our [royal] Manor of East Greenwich in the county of Kent."

> Don't let a mention of "in the manner of East Greenwich, County of Kent, England" mislead you into thinking your family had to be from that location. That clause refers to the manner of inheritance.

Grant. In land, a grant refers to a particular type of transfer, that is, the conveying of a tract of land from a colonial or state government to an individual. Some colonies and states called these patents, as did the federal government.

Grant, bargain and sell. Terms used to convey real estate; the whole phrase was often used.

Grantee. One who receives property.

Grantor. One who transfers property.

Habendum clause. *Habendum et tenendum.* Portion of a deed starting with "to have and to hold ..." This determines what estate or interest is being granted by the deed.

Have and to hold. A common phrase in conveyances derived from *habendum et tenendum* (see above) of the old common law.

Heirs and assigns. A standard clause normally indicating that there are no restrictions.

Heirs lawfully begotten of his body forever. A clause in a will (or deed) which establishes an entail.

Hereditament. Things capable of being inherited, whether it is real, personal or mixed.

Homestead. The dwelling house and adjoining land where the family dwells. Can also refer to the Homestead Act of 1862, in which land could be obtained from the federal government at no cost if certain requirements were met.

Homestead Exemption. A law passed to allow a householder or head of family to protect his house and land from creditors.

id est; *i.e.* That is, that is to say. As an example: I convey to my daughter my remaining personal property, *i.e.*, my kitchen chairs and table, and my cupboard.

In witness whereof. The initial words of the concluding clause of deeds.

Inmate. In early times, married or widowed; landless, living in the same house as another or in another building on the same property.

Interlined. The addition of a word or words to a document, between lines or words already written, so that the document did not have to be rewritten. The clerk, in transcribing the document into the record books, usually noted at the end that certain words or sentences had been interlined.

Jurat. Usually means a clause or certificate indicating when, where, and before whom an affidavit was sworn. However, in wills and deeds, the addition of the word "Jurat" after a witness's name indicates that the witness did later go into court to acknowledge his or her witnessing.

Lien. A claim, encumbrance, or charge on property for payment of a debt.

Livery of seisin (also seizin). A common law ceremony transferring the land. It was a livery *in deed* when the parties went onto the land to perform the ceremony, or livery *at law* when the ceremony was not performed on the land but in sight of it. The document usually mentions this ceremony very briefly, as in the court of 1730 in Goochland County, Virginia, when Edward Curd acknowledged his deed to William Walker with Livery of Seizen endorsed by himself to Walker. In many cases the document will show only "Memorandum of Livery." See also: Turf and Twig.

Male Tail. An entail which descends to males only, usually set up as the eldest. See also Entail.

Manor house. A house, dwelling, or seat of residence.

Mesne conveyance. An intermediate conveyance between the first grantee and the present holder. A term for deeds, especially used in South Carolina.

Messuage. Dwelling house with the adjacent buildings. Formerly the term had a more extended meaning, *i.e.* dwelling house with the adjacent buildings and curtilage.

Metes and bounds. A way of describing land using compass points, natural points (a tree, river, etc.) and distances.

Mineral right. An interest in minerals in land, with or without ownership of the surface of the land.

Moiety. The half of anything, but sometimes an equal part of three co-owners.

Partition. See pages 39, 73, and 125.

Patent. See grant.

Peppercorn. The reservation of a nominal rent was expressed by the payment of a peppercorn.

Plantation. In American law this refers to a farm, or a large cultivated estate. The term, used chiefly in the southern states, refers to a large farm on which crops were grown.

Plat. A map of a specific land area such as a town, section, subdivision or piece of land showing the location, boundaries and, usually, legal descriptions. See also *plot*.

Plot. A synonym for plat, but in common usage refers to a small piece of ground, generally used for a specific purpose, such as *a cemetery plot*.

Processioning. A survey and inspection of boundaries practiced in some of the colonies by the local authorities or those appointed by them.

Quiet Title. An action to remove any possible clouds on the title of the property.

Quitrent. Rent paid annually by a tenant to the government.

Quod vide, *q.v.* Which see. It is used to direct a reader to another location in the writing where further information will be found.

Real property. Land, and generally whatever is erected or growing upon or affixed to land.

Reversion. In deeds refers to any remnant left to the grantor.

Scilicet. In that place. See ss Figure 3-4 this page.

Sealed and delivered. These words are usually followed by the signatures of the witnesses.

Seisin, seizin. See Livery of Seisin.

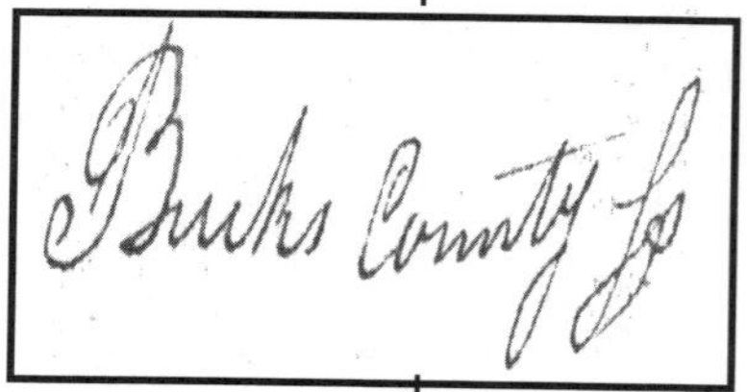

Figure 3-4.
Bucks County ss—see the explanation at the right. (See also Chapter 1 for the "tailed s.")

ss. (Often written as an old styled double s which looks like an inverted f.) The clause starts with the locality followed by ss, and indicates that the signing took place in that locality. *Black's Law Dictionary* states that it is "supposed" to be a contraction for *scilicet*. The location followed by "ss" is used in many documents when a notary public or an officer of the court prepares a statement that someone appeared before him to sign.

Tenement. Commonly applied to houses and other buildings.

To wit. That is to say; namely. As an example, in a gift deed: "I give to my three children, *to wit*, John, Joseph and Mary…"

Township. 1) In federal government surveys this is a township six miles square, a part of the rectangular survey. It is also referred to as a congressional township. 2) In some states, townships are civil and political subdivisions of a county.

Turf and twig. A ceremony in which a piece of the turf and a bough or twig was delivered by grantor to the grantee in making a livery of seisin (*q.v.*).

Waters of. Land that drains into a particular creek, river, or other body of water. Does not have to adjoin the named body of water.

Widow's third. A widow's one-third dower.

CHAPTER POINTS TO PONDER

✓ Land records are one of the most accurate sources for genealogists.

✓ Federal-land states differ from state-land states in methods of the transfer of land to an individual.

✓ Surveying systems differ among states, and sometimes within the same state.

✓ Land records have indexes which may differ from indexes in other courthouse offices.

✓ There are a variety of different land documents which can help genealogists.

Using the background this chapter provides, in the next chapter we'll actually search for some of those land records and see what they can tell us!

4 SEARCHING FOR PROPERTY RECORDS

Armed with a foundation on the first ownership of land from the last chapter, and with that chapter's fresh look at indexes, let's see what the records hold. Digging for land documents in the courthouse is bound to infuse your search with renewed excitement and viable leads.

THE OFFICE FOR LAND RECORDS

The name of the courthouse office you'll use for local land searches varies. It may be the Recorder of Deeds, Register [or Registrar] of Deeds, County Recorder, Register of Conveyances, or something similar. It may even be a part of the County Clerk or Circuit Court Clerk's office. Once in that office, finding the documents your family left is the first step. Squeezing every clue from them is the next.

TYPES OF RECORD BOOKS

The Register of Deeds office will hold a variety of record books. Though varying from area to area, some of the most common record books you will find follow.

DEED BOOKS

These books hold the recorded transfers of property from grantors (sellers) to grantees (buyers). In the early times, when the county first began functioning, the deed books may have been the only record book available. The deed books could include other sundry recorded documents, even wills. As other offices were established in the courthouse, they started separating the books or files and we see the emergence of these separate books for powers of attorney, military discharges, and various others.

SURVEY BOOKS AND WARRANTS

Federal land was surveyed as a result of the Land Ordinance of 1785 passed by our new government. It was not necessary to

The survey may also contain a clue by specifying whether the original warrant was based on military service.

issue individual warrants authorizing the survey because the federal surveys were structured by the requirements of the 1785 ordinance. (See also Chapter 3.)

If the property was in a state-land state (as discussed before in that same Chapter 3), an individual applied for the land and paid any entry fees. Then a warrant was issued by the proper authority which authorized the survey of the property. The warrant included the name of the purchaser, the acreage, and other pertinent details.

Some surveys were the result of special later acts such as the occupancy acts in Tennessee. If so, the warrant specified under which act the survey was to be made. For example, in 1842 Hardin County, Tennessee, a warrant ordering the survey designated that the warrant was issued under the Occupancy Law of 1840. It resulted in the survey of 44 acres for Abraham Parsley/Passley

Plats are created for a variety of purposes:

- An original survey in a state-land state, the survey being made as the result of a warrant ordering the survey. (A patent or grant would follow.)
- A partition action (to divide property).
- A resurvey.
- Sometimes accompany actions for sale of real estate in a probate proceeding, an action involving debt, etc.

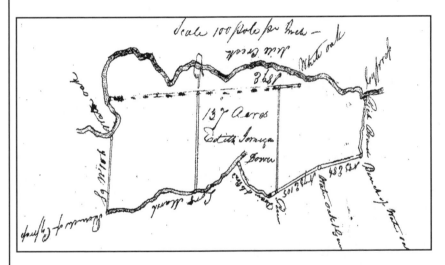

Figure 4-1. Plats such as the one shown above are accompanied by a written legal description. The document also will give details on the purpose of the plat.

on the waters of Indian Creek. Included were the property description, date, and neighbors.

Even after the property was transferred from the federal or state government to an individual, additional surveys might be made. For example, a new survey could be necessitated to correct a previous survey, or to divide the tract into smaller parcels.

The survey includes a plat of the land and is signed by the surveyor or deputy surveyor. If the survey is the result of a specific act or statute, the survey usually recites the title of the law or authority under which the warrant to survey was issued. The survey also includes acreage, and perhaps the name of the waterway and names of adjoining property owners.

Importantly, the survey also includes the name of chain carriers (CC) or chain bearers (CB). These are the males who carried the surveyor's chains. Opinions vary as to whether there was a legal minimum age for a chain carrier. In many cases, the age was based on common law or custom. The male had to be old enough to handle the awkward chains. Always note the names of these chain carriers. If the surname is the same as the warrantee who is having the land surveyed, it implies a relationship. (Even if the surname is different, there might be a relationship.)

For federal land, the surveys and field notes are in a variety of locations, mostly scattered among the National Archives (Cartographic Branch in College Park, Maryland), the various regional archives, and the Bureau of Land Management-Eastern Division in Springfield, Virginia. Colonial or state surveys in state-land states are now usually in the state's archives. For surveys made after the initial transfer of the land from either the colonial, state, or federal government to an individual, the survey books should be in the courthouse (or in some areas the town hall).

Figure 4-2. The chains used for surveying were cumbersome. And often trails had to be cleared before the surveying could continue.

PLAT BOOKS AND PLAT MAPS

Plat books in the courthouse vary. They usually show the plat of the land (including legal description and boundaries) and identify the present and perhaps previous owners. If it is a federal-land state, you need to know the section, township and range, as the plat book will be arranged by that legal description. For plats in state-land states, you may need to know the address of the property in order to identify the legal description. Ask the clerk's assistance if you have difficulty with their system.

POWERS OF ATTORNEY BOOKS

Though some counties recorded this type of document with other land transfers such as deeds, in some areas they were entered in separate record books even from the earliest times. These important records have been described in Chapter 3, and an example is given in that chapter (page 39).

MORTGAGE BOOKS

These books record mortgages involving real property and personal property. Documents called Deeds of Trust (or Trust Deeds), given to secure repayment of a loan, are normally recorded in the Deed books, not in the Mortgage books. (Deeds of Trust can be distinguished from a Mortgage for the former are three party documents. A Trustor (the person owing the money) deeds to a Trustee (who will hold the property until the money is repaid) for the benefit of the Beneficiary (who is due the money).

WHAT A DEED TELLS US

A deed has several bits of information:

- Date of deed.
- Name of grantor (and possibly residence and occupation).
- Name of grantee (and possibly residence and occupation).
- Consideration (what was exchanged for the property: money, "love and affection," another tract, etc.).
- Acreage (usually included, but not always). May refer only to a lot number, a tract name, or a previous deed or grant.
- Type of deed and conditions of the transfer, if any.
- Description of the property or some other identification such as a lot number on a specific map.
- History of the property. This was prevalent particularly up to early 18th century deeds. It is often the only record of a chain of title when the land has been inherited.
- Perhaps the names of adjoining property owners. (Those adjoining owners are especially apt to be shown if the description is by metes and bounds rather than the rectangular surveys of federal-land states.)
- Conditions, restrictions, and easements. These can be significant in establishing how the land was used–farm, woodlot, mill site, urban house, etc.
- Signature or mark of grantor.
- Witnesses who may be related.

Acknowledgment or Proof. If the deed was recorded, either the grantor, if available, or the witnesses "acknowledged" their signatures, or the grantor went into court to personally acknowledge his own signature. The clerk usually added this information at the end of the recorded deed when transcribing the document into the deed book.[1] (In some areas the acknowledging clause was customarily stated as "proving" the deed. Strictly speaking, however, "proving" relates to the *probate process* where the proof goes to the testator's testamentary capacity as being of "sound mind and memory," not just to his signature.)

Of particular value is the location where the acknowledgment took place. This can help document the migration of the grantors. If the property was in Hancock County, Illinois, but the deed was personally acknowledged by the grantor in Sacramento County, California, the grantor had probably moved there or may have had family there. The same clues exist for the witnesses who had moved and then acknowledged the deed, revealing their new locality in the clause.

In some cases there are several acknowledgments. Multiple grantors may have moved to various different locations and personally acknowledged their signatures in those localities. Or, one

---

[1] The clerk usually wrote the date of the recordation and the book and page number of that recordation on the original deed, which was returned to the grantee.

or more of the witnesses may have moved, necessitating an acknowledgment in each of the areas in which they lived when signing the acknowledgment.[2]

Also, some states have types of record books not routinely used elsewhere. In Tennessee, for example, separate "Note Books" were used to record the acknowledgment or proving of a deed when the witnesses or the grantor came into court.

History of Property. In the body of the deed, the history of the property may be recited, starting with the original patentee or grantee and continuing to the time of the new deed. This custom was prevalent in some areas, for instance, in parts of Pennsylvania, until the late 1800s. These important details should be added to your abstract. Many enigmas regarding transfers of land have been solved by a later deed with that history. An example of one informative deed appears in 1830 Allegheny County, Pennsylvania. It would have been difficult to reconstruct the history of this land without this deed, summarized as follows:

> Ebenezer Arskin McClellend, of Allegheny County and Sarah his wife convey to John Rose of same, whereas by patent dated 5 July 1804 granted to Andrew McFarland and David McFarland in trust for heirs of James McFarland, recorded in Patent Book 50 page 368, called Friendship Tract, which James McFarland held in partnership at the time of his decease with Robert Cochran as tenants in common. Heirs of McFarland & Cochran by indenture dated 3 November 1806 granted to William McClelland the above tract of 377 7/10 acres. William McClelland conveyed to John Rose 10 August 1811 land to contain 45 acres, being part of the above patent. William McClelland died and in his will he devised the above to Ebenezer Erskine McClelland ... etc.

THE RECORDING PROCESS

Understanding the steps in the recording process allows us to formulate a plan for the search. Keep in mind however that recording was not mandatory, and it wasn't necessary to the validity of the transfer. It did offer protection to the buyer who had his deed recorded before someone later showed up with a deed from the same grantor for the same land.

The process:

- The deed was drawn up, probably by an attorney. The grantor usually signed it before at least two witnesses.[3] If he planned to personally acknowledge it in court, witnesses were not necessary. The deed may have been recorded immediately after

---

[2] When an acknowledgment was taken in a different area, there may be an additional "certificate" following the recordation attesting to the fact that the person before whom the acknowledgment was made was legally authorized to furnish such documentation. For example, the county clerk of that county may attest that the Justice of the Peace who signed the acknowledgment officially held that position in the county.

[3] If more than two witnesses were present, it implies some concern. Some problem may have been expected and they wanted extra witnesses.

The grantors could acknowledge the deed personally in court. In that case, witnesses were not required.

signing, years after signing, or not recorded at all.

- The deed was presented in court before it was ordered recorded. Usually, the wife relinquished her dower interest at this same time. On that day, at least two of the witnesses appeared to state that they saw the grantor sign the deed. Or, the grantor personally appeared in court to acknowledge his own signature and deed, in which case it was not necessary for witnesses to appear. If witnesses were required for the acknowledgment and only one witness appeared, the judge may have ordered the matter continued for further proof. This necessitated one of the other witnesses (or the grantor himself) to acknowledge at a later date. If the grantor or witness had moved from the area, the acknowledgment was probably taken in a different county or state before a public official—a Justice of the Peace, a judge, or other official. The deed was not recorded until there was sufficient proving of the deed. When the court considered the deed sufficiently proved, the deed was recorded, and this was entered into an appropriate order book.

- If one of the witnesses died before the proving, or his whereabouts were unknown, the court could accept the testimony of someone who knew him personally and testified that the signature was the handwriting of the witness. (Or, in some cases, the court could accept one witness's testimony.)

- If the deed was properly acknowledged or proved, the Court then ordered it recorded, and the clerk made an entry to that effect in the court order book and/or the court minute book.

- After the deed was ordered recorded, the original deed was left with the clerk for recording. The clerk (as he had time) transcribed the complete deed into a deed book and followed the entry with a notation of the date and location that the acknowledgment or proving took place. When copying the information into the record book, the clerk usually ended with the recordation date, though sometimes that date is at the beginning of the document. It must be emphasized that the deed books in the courthouse are *copies* of the deeds as transcribed by the clerk, not the originals which were returned to the grantee.

- The clerk next made entries in the indexes under the name of the grantor(s) and the name of the grantee(s).

The courthouse often has a box or file of original deeds that no one ever retrieved. It may take some time to go through these loose unindexed documents. But it's like striking gold when you come up with the original deed to your ancestor's farm!

- After the deed was transcribed into the record book, the clerk usually wrote the book and page number and the date of acknowledgment on the original deed.

- At this point, the original deed was returned to the new owner[4] or his representative, who came to the courthouse to retrieve it. Some of the originals are still in the possession of descendants. Others were never picked up by the grantee and remain in the courthouse to this day.

---

[4] This is in contrast to what happens with a will. The original will is retained in the courthouse even after a copy is recorded in the will books.

If the deed itself cannot be found, look in minutes or order books of the time period. There may be proof that the deed existed by the clerk's entry of the acknowledgment. In Court Minutes of April 1784 in Wilkes County, North Carolina, the proving of two deeds by one of the witnesses, Benjamin Herndon, was entered. One was for the deed of John Rose Sr. to "Ozee" Rose, and the other for John's deed to John Rose Jr. Neither of the actual deeds is indexed in the index books, nor have they been found in the deed books. If it hadn't been for the proving of the deeds with the subsequent notation in the minute book, this valuable evidence of the deeds' existence would have been lost.

CLUES IN THE DEEDS

So, you do all this work—stand at that counter for hours, lift heavy books until your arms ache, and write until your fingers are ready to drop off. Will it be worth it? What might you find? For starters:

1   The names of the grantors. If they were husband and wife, usually that relationship will be specified, *i.e.*, "Benjamin Ferguson and his wife Mary..."

2.   You might learn residences. When a person moved to another area, his first deed in that new location might refer to him as "lately" of his previous county and state. This could provide the only proof of earlier residency. Or, if he still owned land in the previous area after moving, he may later have sold the land in the previous county, designating himself "now of" the new residence. For example, from the deeds of Burlington County, New Jersey, in 1872, Theodore F. Rose and Isabella his wife, "now of Barnegat" in Ocean County, New Jersey, deeded land they still owned in Burlington County.

3.   Occupations revealed in deeds are not only of interest in building the life history of your ancestor, but help separate individuals of the same name. In large cities, the addition of the occupation of the parties in legal instruments was common. In 1786 David Rose of Northern Liberties, county of Philadelphia, "Brickmaker" and Abigail his wife deeded to William Lavergne of the same place, "Apothecary ..."

4.   The dates mentioned, i.e., the date of the deed, the date the deed was acknowledged, and the date it was recorded, are all significant. A lengthy span of time between these dates may indicate some change in family status—a death, a move from the area, or other event. Perhaps the mother held a dower interest in the land, which was to descend to her son after her decease or at the end of her widowhood.[5] During her lifetime, that son may have signed a deed disposing of the land, but since the mother retained her dower interest during her life,

Some caution is advised, for it is always possible that a man changed his occupation during the years. Nonetheless, in most instances those shown with different occupations are different people.

---

[5] Her widowhood ended when she remarried.

the deed may have been held until her death. In those cases, the date of acknowledgment can assist in suggesting a time frame for the mother's death. Other family-generated scenarios could have caused the delay. Though we can't be certain a lengthy lapse of time was significant, it is always worth investigating.

5. The consideration paid can be revealing. It may be "for love and affection ..." implying a high probability of a relationship. Often the exact relationship is stated in such a deed—"to my daughter ..." Or, perhaps the consideration was not a specific monetary amount but for the maintenance of the grantor (and possibly the grantor's spouse) for life.

When a monetary amount is included, it can also be used for comparison with the value of other tracts bought and sold in contemporary times to help assess the family's prosperity.

6. The property description is of special significance. The land may be in close proximity to other land owners of the same surname, implying relationships. Or the neighbors mentioned may be friends who moved from another state with the grantor's family. (It was uncommon in the early times for people to move alone. They usually traveled with family and friends, especially if the move was of some distance.)

If the name of your ancestor was common, i.e., John Smith, it may be impossible to identify where he lived previously if you only know the state and not the county. But, if he had a neighbor by the name of "Zachariah Collins" and they had traveled together, that neighbor could be the key. Find the uncommon name of Zachariah Collins in the previous state and you may find your ancestor's earlier residence, too.

Property descriptions can have other clues. Your ancestor may have owned 40 acres of what was described as originally a 160-acre tract. Locating the names of the owners of the other 120 acres may lead you to relatives. Even if the surname of those owners were different, they could be the married females of the family.

Copying the full property description is ideal. Unfortunately, sometimes there are just not enough hours on your trip to hand-copy the full property description. If faced with a long list of deeds and little time to really evaluate the importance of each, you need to institute some shortcuts. Reduce your abstract time by noting only the essential property description details such as the names of waterways, towns, townships, lot numbers, or other identifiers. Include any adjoining property owners. You'll need this description and neighbors to determine the proximity of the land to others of the surname. If it is a federal-land state in the rectangular survey system, note the section number, township number, and the range. Compare that description with your other abstracts to determine proximity to others of the surname.

7. Look for special clauses in the deed. If it mentioned that the property "was willed to me by my father in his will dated August 3, 1845 ..." or some other similarly meaningful statement, include that in your abstract. (I always quote such clauses so there's little chance for misinterpretation later.)

8. Signatures are always significant—the man who could sign his name might be distinguished from another in the area by the same name, but who always signed with an X mark.[6] The clerks were supposed to copy the name or mark as it appeared. Technically, there would be a difference between an X mark and a + mark. Practically, however, the clerks often did not distinguish between them when writing in the deed books. However, if the mark was other than an X, the clerk usually represented it as it was in the original, attempting to copy it as it appeared. Some chose to use the initial of their given or surname (or both) as a mark; others varied.

See an example of initials for signatures in Figure 6-1 page 84.

9. The names of witnesses, and their residences if given, are important. They were often relatives or neighbors. Unfortunately, one myth is that a witness is *always* related. This is not so, but the possibility does exist of a relationship. Further research on the names of the witnesses may disclose the connection if one exists.

10. Always note if there are two or more people of the surname owning the identical acreage in fractions. As an example, William Smith may be listed in the index with 112 ½ acres, and in another transaction George Smith may be listed with 112 ½ acres. Possibly these were joint heirs, and the property was divided between them. Another way to locate joint heirs is to use the index to determine all the people of the same surname who sold to the same grantee, even if the transactions were at different time periods. Those grantors may be joint heirs who were selling their portion of inherited land to the same person. Reading those deeds may confirm that supposition.

OTHER CONSIDERATIONS

PHOTOCOPYING

Photocopy any deed or other document you consider essential to your search. It's usually not possible to photocopy every document. Not only can the cost be prohibitive, but copying large numbers of documents ties up the photocopy machines (or the clerk's time if there is no self-service machine). Thus, the importance of making detailed abstracts. Even when you do photocopy the record, abstract it while onsite so you can glean clues and follow potential leads while still there. Add the citation immediately, and check to be sure the whole document was copied.

Ask whether the photocopier is self-service. Bring coins with you in case you need them. Be sure to mark your copies with the citation. And check them to see that you didn't lose words along the sides, or at the bottom or top.

---

[6] Always remembering, however, that a man who could sign his name when younger might fail to when he is older because of infirmity or other causes.

SR. AND JR., ELDER AND YOUNGER, 1ST AND 2ND

Sr. and Jr. did not always mean father and son. It could indicate another relationship, perhaps uncle and nephew, cousins, etc., or no relation at all. Also watch for instances where "Sr." died and his son "Jr." then became "Sr."

Another way of keeping two people with the same name separate was "the elder" and "the younger." Perhaps a grandfather was "the elder."

If there were no close relationship between two men of the same name, the townsmen may have found yet another way to keep them separated. In Onondaga County, New York, the man called "Nathan Rose 1st" in the records was in the area early. Later, an older Nathan Rose arrived, and was dubbed "Nathan Rose 2d" to distinguish between them.

Another distinction was customarily used in some areas when two people bore the same name—this one of key importance. In Somerset County, Maryland, this custom helped identify John Goslee when the 1849 deed of George Price and his wife Zepporah conveyed land to John Goslee "of Joseph." This effectively established the name of John's father and separated him from another John Goslee in the area.

ABSENCE OF RECORDS

One of our biggest problems as researchers (aside from burned courthouses!) is the lack of recordation. Often there were no requirements (and may still be none in some areas) to record the deed. If the family was poor and the title remained within the family, deeds among the relatives were often just put in a "safe" place to avoid the recording fee. Years later, when the property was sold outside the family, the deeds were then brought to the courthouse. (In the present day, it is virtually unheard of not to record because the title companies would be unwilling to insure the title to the property.)

Other circumstances may cause the absence of recorded transfers. If the land was inherited, it passed to the new owner through the probate proceeding rather than by deed. If the land was en-

> The Courthouse office housing land records also records some non-land records such as personal property deeds, mortgages, leases, discharges, bonds, and others.

> Always check the indexes for many years beyond the time your ancestor died. The deed could be recorded more than 100 years after the fact. In some instances a deed involving a minor was held for several years until the minor attained the age of majority (legal age).

SOME REASONS WHY DEEDS MIGHT NOT BE FOUND
- The grantee couldn't afford the filing fee.
- The land was inherited; perhaps even through primogeniture (land to eldest son in some states).
- The land was entailed.
- It was lost for taxes.
- It was sold at a Sheriff's sale.
- The clerk failed to enter it into the record books.
- The clerk lost it.
- It wasn't sufficiently proved or acknowledged, so the judge didn't order it recorded.

---

tailed (see later in this chapter, and also see Chapter 6 pages 99-100), no deed was necessary. The indexes may be bereft of recordings of these so-called "silent transfers" for many years, even generations. But don't despair– supplement your land search by examining related tax records, warrants, and other records discussed later in this book.

STRATEGIES FOR SEARCHING LOCAL LAND RECORDS

When using an index, search for the ancestor under a variety of spellings of the surname. Be alert to variations in first names, too. Benjamin Franklin Adamson may be listed as Benjamin F., as B. F., as F. B., or as Franklin B. Adamson. Alexander McDonald may be listed as such, but also might be listed as Sandy McDonald, using his nickname.[7]

Can't find the deed you are looking for in a consolidated index? Go into the specific individual deed book of the time period where the deed was recorded. That record book may have its own index. If it did not, then search through the courthouse shelves to see if you can locate the original indexes used in the preparation of the consolidated index. Those preparing the consolidation may have inadvertently overlooked the entry. They may even have purposely excluded a whole category of records (such as personal property deeds already discussed).

Always examine a few deeds immediately preceding and following the deed of your focus. Those contiguous entries can be instrumental in providing new information. Several family exchanges may have taken place on the same day. The deed recorded one or two pages before the targeted entry, even though involving parties of another surname, could actually be one of the females of the family who is now married and deeding her portion of the property with her new husband. If so, you now have more leads on your family.

Make a list of your ancestor's land and the tracts of others of the surname in the vicinity. List dates when your ancestor bought, acreage, description etc., and list similar data on his sales. Enter the person's name, i.e., George Jackson, followed by each of his purchases in chronological order. Then examine the sales and add the sale of each tract immediately after the purchase of that tract. This will readily account for his acquisitions or you can spot sales of land on which purchases weren't found. This too is of vast importance. The lack of a purchase deed may indicate that it was a patent from the colony, state, or federal govern-

---

[7] See Christine Rose, *Nicknames: Past and Present*. 4th ed. (San Jose, Calif.: Rose Family Association, 2001). Though knowledge of nicknames is important in any index, in some, such as the Campbell index described in Chapter 2, it is especially important since the entries are indexed by the first name.

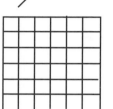

Put the township and range at the top.

Make a similar chart to use while you search.

Figure 4-3. The above is a blank chart of the 36 sections in a one mile township of a federal-land survey. Study the two illustrations, Figures 3-1 and 3-2 in Chapter 2 page 30 for numbering before and after 1796. Make yourself a large blank chart as above, and photocopy several copies so you can use one for each township as you study the deeds you collected. On one chart insert numbers for pre1796 and on another insert numbers after 1796. Enter the names you are searching into the proper section on the chart as you locate their deeds. You can then readily determine that if your ancestor in 1811 bought land in section 14 which had been patented in 1804, and another person by the same surname was in section 23 of the same township, they were actually neighbors and very possibly related.

ment, so you can then pursue that angle. Or, as discussed elsewhere, the lack of a purchase may point to inheritance or entail.

After I have entered my abstracts on the computer, I prepare the mentioned list by using the abstracts, arranging them in the order just described. I then have all the details readily available.

CONNECTING FAMILIES THROUGH THEIR DEEDS

If you can't examine every recorded deed, you can still effectively use the "location" column in the index for clues. That column should contain a brief property description (perhaps township or waterway), or a lot number, or section, township and range. (See Figure 3-1 page 30 in Chapter 3.) Make yourself small blank charts of a township with its 36 sections. Photocopy them, and keep them handy while you are searching. Use one chart for each township and range you find mentioned in the family's deeds. After writing the township and range along the top of the chart, enter the names of the property owners of interest to the section number on the chart. Make sure that the township and range match—Section 5 in Twp 2 N of Range 5 would not be on the same as Section 5 in Twp 3 N of Range 5. Double-check your work. These charts will allow you to quickly visualize who were near neighbors. Without such a chart it may not be readily discernible that the owner of Section 2 Township 4 South of Range 3 East was a neighbor to the owner of Section 11 in the same township and range.

Identifying those of the surname who were near neighbors is essential in making inferences on kinship when you have no document actually stating their relationship. Using varied indirect evidence helps in building a solid case.[8]

RECORDS NOT A PART OF THE LOCAL LAND RECORDS

A few additional words about records beyond the scope of this courthouse book:

> *NEW YORK:* Some large blocks of land held by land companies, such as the Holland Land Purchase. Check other states, too.
>
> *FEDERAL MILITARY BOUNTY LAND.* From the Revolutionary War through the last act in 1855, federal land in the public domain was given to soldiers (and officers in the Revolutionary War) for military service.[9]
>
> *STATE MILITARY BOUNTY LAND.* In addition to bounty land granted by the federal government, in the revolutionary war the states of

---

[8] A solid case can be built using the Genealogical Proof Standard. See Christine Rose, *Genealogical Proof Standard: Building a Solid Case,* (San Jose, Calif.: Rose Family Association, 2001). See also Source References page 201.

[9] See Source References on page 201.

Georgia, Maryland, Massachusetts, New York, North Carolina, Pennsylvania, South Carolina, and Virginia gave varying amounts of bounty land to their own soldiers. These records are generally available at the state archives.[10]

FEDERAL CASE FILES. Cash and credit files, homestead files, preemption and a variety of others connected with the purchase of federal land are part of Record Group 49 housed at the National Archives in Washington D.C.[11]

COLONIAL RECORDS. Some of the early land records of various states were not on the county level. They may be found in town records, or state records, before the formation of counties. Some states have transferred their colonial county land records to the State Archives. In addition, check for military bounty land for colonial wars at that state's archives.

PRIVATE RECORDS OF SURVEYORS. Often you will find in manuscripts scattered through a variety of repositories in the United States, private collections of surveyors. If you know the name of the surveyor, it may be well to pursue that possibility by using the *National Union Catalog of Manuscript Collections.* This multi-volume set is available in most medium to large sized libraries, and is partially available at <http://www.loc.gov>. The latter is the website of the Library of Congress. (See Chapter 11 pages 178-179 for further information on this source.)

LAND RECORDS ARE CRUCIAL TO RESEARCH

One of the reasons that land (and related) records are so important is that they provide connections—connections over time, over places, and between individuals—connections that often are not "permanently" recorded (or even implied) in any other record. And, barring disaster of some sort, they will go back to the very beginnings of a given county. Few other potential genealogical sources can make that claim.

The researcher should always keep an eye out for leads to other records. When perusing the land records at the local level, note whether the document might lead to records at another government level (such as state records for state land grants, federal records for federal patents and case files, etc.). Or even to other records in another office at the local level such as tax records in the assessor's office, or a file containing the petition for division of property in the circuit court of the county, etc. Let the records in the land office point you to the possibility of related records. There can be more involving the property than just the deed.

"There can be more involving the property than just the deed."

---

[10] See also Lloyd Bockstruck, *Revolutionary War Bounty Grants Awarded by State Governments* (Baltimore: Genealogical Publishing Company, 1996).

[11] Anne Bruner Eales and Robert M. Kvasnicka, *Guide to Genealogical Research in the National Archives of the United States* (Washington, D.C.: National Archives and Records Administration, 2000).

The best advice? When you are personally onsite poke around the shelves. Open that nondescript book with a blank spine— you may discover an important land record that other researchers missed, unfilmed and "hidden in plain sight." It will be a thrill. Finds like that keep you coming back to the courthouses to rummage its shelves, dust and all.

In the next chapter, we will start our search among the multitude of records in the probate department and discover some incredible treasures.

CHAPTER POINTS TO PONDER

✓ Records concerning land ownership are one of the most reliable of sources.

✓ There are various and assorted types of land documents.

✓ There are a number of non-land documents in the Recorder's office.

✓ Land records are full of clues on relationships, occupations, and other details.

On the next three pages you will find a fully transcribed deed, with all its errors in spelling and punctuation. Under each line explanatory remarks have been added.

THE FOLLOWING IS A DEED TRANSCRIPTION, WITH COMMENTS FOLLOWING EACH LINE OF THE ORIGINAL.

Surry County, Virginia Deed Book 12 1783-1787 p 241, 242

THIS INDENTURE made this 8th day of January Domini one thousand seven

> *Indenture in the line above means, in this case, a deed.*

> *Domini refers to Anno Domini; year of our Lord.*

hundred and eighty Seven in the twelfth year of the Commonwealth, Between Samuel Rose of the County of Hallifax in North Carolina of the one part and William

> *Samuel Rose is the grantor; the person conveying the property. The term "of the one part" refers to the first person in the action. In a deed, that is the grantor.*

Lamb of Virginia Sussex County of the other part. Witnesseth that the said Samuel

> *The term "of the other part" is the second person in the action; in this case the grantee, the person to whom the property is being conveyed.*

Rose for and in consideration of the Sum of ten pounds Current Money of Virginia to

> *"Consideration" in this case is what is being paid. (Consideration could refer to an exchange of property, or goods, or a consideration not tangible such as "love and affection."*

him in hand paid at or before the ensealing and delivery of these presents the Receipt

> *This refers to the payment of the amount at the time the deed is signed or before the deed is signed.*

whereof he doth hereby acknowledge hath Bargained and Sold, and doth by these

> *The grantor is acknowledging that he did sell the land.*

presents grant Bargain and Sell according to due form of Law unto the said William

> *The grantor states he is selling it as the law prescribes; that is, following the procedure of the law.*

Lamb his Heirs Executors or Assigns forever all that tract of Land lying and being in

> *By stating "Heirs Executors or Assigns forever" the grantor is stating that it is being sold with no restrictions; that is, it is not an entail, or a life estate, etc.*

the County of Surry containing by estimation seventy five Acres, be the same more

> *By stating "estimation" seventy five Acres, the wording protects the seller if it should prove not to be quite that quantity. Another way of putting this is "more or less" which in the above follows the "estimation" clause.*

or less and bounded as followeth viz beginning at Colliers line a large pine a corner

This document has been transcribed just as it appeared, spelling (such as Hallifax), punctuation, and all else.

Figure 4-4a. To the left and on the next two pages is a fully transcribed deed, with remarks under each line.

Tree thence along the said line South, to a corner tree a pine on Jordans line a corner
Here we have the name of a neighbor. Potentially, an important clue.

Tree thence along the said line to a corner tree a Scrub white Oak of Nathaniel
More neighbors.

Sebrell, thence along Sebrells line to a Corner Tree, thence North up the great Branch
to the Beginning also the reversion and reversions, and every thing belonging to or
Here the grantor is stating that should any remnant of title be still in the grantor's possession, that too is being granted.

appertaining to the said Land unto the said William Lamb and to his heirs forever
The grantor is granting anything that is part of this land.

(reserving the right of dower of Agnes Briggs) which said Land described unto the
This is important. Even though an explanation is not included, somehow Agnes Briggs has a dower interest. It is up to the researcher to determine why.

The clause involving Samuel as heir-at-law of his brother William Rose is important. In this deed, the relationship was clearly stated. In many other deeds, it might only refer to one as the "heir-at-law" of the other, and it would be up to the researcher to find what the current law was at the time of the document in order to identify the relationship.

said Samuel Rose as Heir at law of his Brother William Rose late of the County of
An important clause identifying Samuel Rose as a brother of William Rose. Further research would reveal that at this time in Virginia, the eldest brother was heir-at-law of a man who died single and with no children. (The father was not the heir and didn't come into the line of heirship until an act in the 1790s.)

Surry. TO HAVE AND TO HOLD the said Land and all the Appurtenances (except
This is called a Habendum clause, starting with the words "To Have and to hold ..." followed by a defining of how the land is being conveyed. These and the next few lines are conveying the land to William Lamb and his heirs forever (thus, it is not an entail). However, clearly, the dower right of Agnes Briggs is in force against the property.

as before excepted) unto the said William Lamb and to his heirs forever, and the said
Samuel Rose doth further Covenant and agree to and with the said William Lamb and
with his heirs forever that the right title claim and property of and to the said land
shall descend by these presents unto the said William Lamb and to his heirs forever
Against the right, title, claim, demand of every person or persons whatsoever, and the
said Samuel Rose doth according to the full meaning and intent of these presents

Figure 4-4b. Second page of the transcribed deed.

give the said William Lamb possession of the said land accept [*sic, except*] the dower before

> *The dower right of Agnes Briggs is again mentioned so that there is no misunderstanding that though the land is conveyed to William Lamb and his heirs and assigns, it is subject to that dower. William Lamb cannot dispose of that dower right without consent of Agnes Briggs. She will retain that dower right until her death (or her remarriage if the law so states). She cannot sell that dower interest to another. She can release her interest, with or without a fee, to whomever was designated to get it after her remarriage or death.*

mentioned. In Witness whereof the said Samuel Rose hath herunto set his hand and

seal the day and year above written.

> *This is the date at the beginning of the document. The "seal" was sometimes a waxed seal, but more commonly added in writing, to legalize the document.*

Samuel Rose   Seal

> *Samuel Rose signed and his seal is included. Since this is a transcribed copy and not the original, we can't tell if the original had an actual waxed seal.*

Signed Sealed Delivered
as his Act and deed
in presence of
Robert Lamb
John Lamb
Agnes (her x mark) Briggs
Edmund Stasey
Thomas Lamb

> *In the list of witnesses above, it is notable in the number. This implies that there is caution being exercised; possibly some difficulty is expected and the extra witnesses will help in preventing it. Note too that Agnes Briggs (who held a dower interest) was a witness.*

AT A COURT held for Surry County February the 27 1787 the within written Indenture of Bargain and Sale from Samuel Rose to William Lamb was proved by the oaths of Robert Lamb, John Lamb, and Edmund Stasey three of the Witnesses thereto and by the Court ordered to be Recorded

> *This clause indicates that the matter was proved in court by three of the witnesses. The deed could have instead been acknowledged personally by the grantor, or it could have been acknowledged or proved by the witnesses before an officer of the court such as a Justice of the Peace.*

Examined and delivered per order
        Teste Jacob Faulcon C.C. Clk

> *Jacob Faulcon was the County Court Clerk, and attested to the proving of the deed in court.*

Samuel Rose signed his name. If he used a mark, it would be transcribed in whatever way the original showed—Samuel (his x mark) Rose, Samuel (his SR mark) Rose, etc., depending on what the document indicates.

Figure 4-4c, the third and last page of this deed.

5 Estates Galore

Estate records[1] are among the genealogist's best friends. An ancestor dies—normally the relatives inherit. The subsequent paperwork launches multiple opportunities for those heirs to be named and their relationships identified. Other details might be interjected—occupation implied by contents of an inventory, financial standing in the community through accounts of money due the decedent, prosperity by acreage owned, and even who inherited the family Bible.

The probate office usually includes estates (with or without a will), guardianships,[2] and related matters. Each of these proceedings spawns records. Petitions, bonds, accounts, inventories, relinquishments, renunciations, final settlements—these and more. If you limit your search only to wills, you miss the collective data within the walls of the probate office. In fact, the will may not be the most useful of that collection. If the father named only the daughter who provided for him in his last days, the will won't provide a list of children. An intestate proceeding in which there was no will and the estate descended to *all* the heirs at law can be more illuminating.

WHICH OFFICE HANDLED ESTATES?

The assorted probate records may be in an office called the Register of Wills, Surrogate's Office, or even under the control of the County Clerk, Circuit Court Clerk, or others. If you cannot pinpoint the location of the records from the posted courthouse directory, ask one of the courthouse personnel which office handles wills and estates. They'll direct you.[3]

A surrogate is a judge in New York and a few other states who has jurisdiction over the probate of wills and the settlement of estates.

---

[1] In this book the term "Estate Records" is being used solely in the American sense of "decedent estate records," to distinguish it from the United Kingdom and Irish usage, where it refers to the continuing business records of a landed estate. The latter business records often span multiple generations of owner and tenant families and are private records, although many are now in public repositories.

[2] Guardianships may be in chancery, family court, or other similar court.

[3] When states had separate equity or chancery courts, some of these matters might be found there.

If the state of your search is one of the few states with an Orphan's Court,[4] check both that department *and* the Register of Wills.

The Orphan's Court (OC) handled the sale and division of real property from estates, the confirmation and auditing of accounts, and the guardianship of minor children (who may not be orphans). Treasures are buried in these files! Always check the orphans' court if the state has one, when you are searching for family history. (They may physically be housed in the same department as the register of wills.)

WAS THE ESTATE PROBATED?

You've searched but cannot find an estate record for your ancestor. Why? Consider the possibility that the deceased, at the time of his death, did not have enough property, real or personal, to warrant the proceeding. The laws dictated the minimum amount necessary to initiate a probate, that amount varied depending upon the state and the time period.

Another possibility. Your ancestor may have transferred his property before death, to a son or daughter or other person, in exchange for lifetime support for him and his spouse. This was common and not only guaranteed his and his wife's support, but avoided the necessity to probate his estate after death if he had transferred all his possessions and not just a portion.

Your ancestor may even have gifted his property to one or more of the children for the specific purpose of avoiding probate. In this case he probably remained on one of the parcels until death, but the gift deeds reduced the value of his estate and avoided the need for probate.

Another possibility, especially in the twentieth century, is that the property may have been part of a trust such as the modern "living trusts." Some of these trusts eliminate the need to probate the will.

And remember the caveats presented elsewhere among the pages of this book. You may be looking in the wrong place. The record may be in an independent city (see Chapter 1). Or the estate may be a colonial record before those actions became the responsibility of the county, or they may now be housed in the state archives, local library, or historical society. The records could even be in the jurisdiction of a second courthouse if the county had two.

SOME OF THE REASONS AN ESTATE MAY NOT HAVE BEEN PROBATED.
- There was not sufficient estate.
- The property was transferred or sold before death.
- The property was gifted to others before death, perhaps in exchange for life care.
- The property was in a special trust.

---

[4] Alabama, Delaware, Maryland, New Jersey, Pennsylvania, and perhaps a few others.

WOMEN AND WILLS

If a woman was unmarried or widowed, she could leave a will. In early times, if she was married, her property came under the control of her husband. She could not will it without his permission unless by an agreement. (Or unless there was a law which governed her particular circumstance, which rendered the property as her own.) Her dower (her legal interest as wife) in the real property was only for her lifetime or widowhood—she could not dispose of it even after her husband's death unless her husband had specified the land was to be hers outright. Even if her husband gave her property in addition to her dower, he usually designated to whom both the dower and the additional property should descend at her death or remarriage. If he did give her the dower or other property outright to do with as she pleased, she then could dispose of it during her life by deed or by her own will.

States were slow in changing their laws concerning women, but eventually women gained the right to control and handle their own property.[5]

Women's rights were severely restricted in the earlier times. Any property she had became the property of her husband except under certain circumstances.

KINDS OF ESTATES

Probate is a legal process by which a will is proved to be valid or invalid. It evolved to include the process established for a decedent when there was no will.

Basically there are three kinds of estates which particularly interest genealogists; testate, intestate, and guardianships:

Testate Proceeding. When the deceased left a will, and someone initiated a probate of the will, it is a testate proceeding. Usually, the estate was handled by an executor named by the testator (person making the will) when the will was written. Exceptions exist, among them:

- There was a will but no executor was named.
- The named executor died before the testator.
- The named person refused to qualify or give bond as an executor.
- The named executor moved from the state.
- The court did not accept the named person as executor.
- The named executor could not find anyone to post his bond.
- The named executor was too young to serve.

In the above instances, the court named an administrator to handle the estate. (See also Chapter 6.)

---

[5] See also Marylynn Salmon, *Women and the Law of Property in Early America* (Chapel Hill, N.C.: University of North Carolina Press, 1986).

Intestate Proceeding (Administration). If there was no will, or the court did not accept the will as valid, the estate of the deceased went through an intestate proceeding and descended to the "heirs at law" according to the contemporary law. In an intestate proceeding, also called an administration, the court appointed an administrator to handle the estate. (See Chapter 6.)

Guardianship. The most common types of guardianships you will find in your search are those for minors and incompetents, though there are others. In these estates, the court appoints a guardian. (See Chapter 6.)

THE PROBATE INDEXES

Each department in the courthouse has some variance in their indexes. The probate office is no exception. Its indexes have some differences from those in the deed office previously described.

Figure 5-1. To the right is a consolidated estate index. Often called "general" indexes, consolidated indexes for estates, land records, and other court records became popular because the sheer number of individual indexes created over a span of time became time consuming to use.

General Index to ESTATES—Bucks County, Penna.

General Index or Consolidated Index. In the probate office this type of index combines references to wills, administrations, the original file packet, and perhaps others such as inventories or accounts. The availability of such an index will reduce your search time considerably. If there is no general index, hopefully the court at least has an index to wills spanning several years, and a similar index to administrations. Lacking those, it will be necessary to examine each record book individually, relying upon the indexes in the front or back of each book. Related records —bonds, inventories, accounts, etc.— may also be individually indexed.

Figure 5-2 . Shown above is the estate index for the surnames beginning with X, Y, and Z. Beneath it are Proceedings docket books 1 and 2.

List everyone of the surname in the index for the time period of your search. Include the type of record (will, inventory, or otherwise), and the book number, page reference, and if given, the file or box number. You need this information to locate the estate files. If necessary, consult the clerk to determine their location. The clerk may need to retrieve those files personally.

Proceedings Index. This type of index is used in a few states, for example, Pennsylvania, Delaware, New Jersey, and Maryland. It involves the use of two books—the estate index, and the "Proceedings" docket book. (See Figure 5-2 on the previous page.)

The first is an estate index with the initial letter (or combination of initial letters) of the surname on the spine. If searching Adams, go to the index marked with an A; if searching Young, go to the book marked Y. Once you have the index book with the initial letter of the surname in hand, find the name you seek. Once found, note that the indexed listing includes a *book, page and block number*. Now look around the shelves for a set of record books with the word "PROCEEDINGS" on the spine. Using the book number you found in the first index you used, (the estate index with the initial letter of the surname), find the proper Proceedings docket book, and then go to the appropriate page number. That page will be divided into several numbered blocks—usually nine or twelve of them. Go to the block number (illustrated in Figure 5-3) which matches the entry you seek. For example, if the listing in the first book showed Book 3 page 85 Block 5, go to Proceedings 3, then to page 85, and then block 5 on the page.

The "block" will be titled with the name of the estate, the name of the person who handled the estate (normally executor, administrator, or guardian's name), and place of the deceased's last residence or where he died. In a guardianship, it will include the place where the minor or ward resides. The block should also show the estate file number so you can locate any original papers which exist. Next in the block is a listing of the major documents recorded. Each includes the year, and the book and page reference,[6] which will enable you to locate the actual documents. This block in the Proceedings docket is actually an inventory of the important recorded documents. Using the given references, go to the corresponding record books. The transcribed documents will be there. For example, if the block shows WB 3 p. 10, go to Will Book 3 page 10.

Only a few states use this combination of an estate index and proceedings docket, and usually only for probate matters.

Devisor and Devisee Indexes. If your ancestor was the recipient of a devise (that is, the recipient of real property through a will), the land passed to him through probate proceedings. Deeds were not required to be recorded.[7] Many years could pass without

Block Number

File number

Figure 5-3. The above is one of the "blocks" in a Proceeding Docket. It inventories the major papers in an estate file, and directs the user to the book and page where the transcribed documents can be located. In the example, the file number shown should enable you to access the original estate papers. The block entry further provides the filing date of the inventory, and references and filing date for the will and letters testamentary. (The originals of the will, letters, and inventory, should be in the file; transcribed copies in the given references.) Further, the entry discloses that Saml Gummere and John Spencer were executors.

---

[6] For example, it may show "Will, 1858, WB 5 p 90: or "Inv. Min. Bk B p 5 1802." These are entries that lead you to Will Book 5 and Minute Book B.

[7] Now most states file a special document evidencing such transfers.

any trace in the land recordings.[8] If a tract passed down the family for two or three generations, it may even be fifty or one hundred years later before a deed was finally recorded, most likely when the property was conveyed out of the family. Recognizing that it would be helpful to have an index to track these inheritances, North Carolina handled that problem though devisor and devisee indexes.

DEVISOR INDEX. Lists the name of the devisor (the testator who devised land). This index is somewhat redundant; the testator index would also turn up the same will. The difference is that the testator index would include all wills, while the devisor index was meant to include only those wills in which real property was devised.

DEVISEE INDEX. The devisee is the person who was the recipient of a devise of real property through a will. What a treasure this index will be in your search! A relationship almost impossible to otherwise detect may surface. If Susan Baldwin inherited a tract from her grandfather Jonathan Walters, and you knew nothing of a Walters connection, how would you know of the Walters will with all of its important familial details? With a devisee index you'd readily find it. You would search under the BALDWIN name with which you are familiar. Under "B" Susan Baldwin would be listed as a devisee. After her name, the name Jonathan Walters would appear as testator, with the will book number and page of his will. This leads you easily to that will naming Susan. Many unsuspected relationships have been disclosed because of these indexes. The devisee index was not prevalent except in the state of North Carolina, but other states occasionally have a similar volume. If in the register of deeds office or the probate office you spot an index labeled "Heirs of Descent" or some similar designation, take a look.

Estate File Indexes. "Loose" papers in an estate are normally the originals. The file may include one paper or many. If there was an inventory taken of the estate, the appraisers drew up a document listing the inventoried items and the value of each. The appraisers signed it, as did the executor or administrator. It was brought into the courthouse for the court's approval. Any account for the estate was signed by the executor, administrator, or guardian who then brought it into court. If the law required a newspaper publication of any of the court proceedings, that newspaper prepared an affidavit of "proof of publication" with the notice attached and sent it to the courthouse to be filed.[9] These and other original papers, such as receipts and petitions, are what make up the "estate file" or "estate packet."

[8] He should, however, be listed in tax records if those are still extant. Assessors and tax collectors frequently noted who was actually in occupancy or paying the taxes, although nothing in the deed records, or readily accessible from probate records, confirmed the change. See Chapter 10.

[9] The newspaper identified in the "proof of publication" can be a clue that may lead to an obituary. This can be particularly helpful in rural areas where there were no local newspapers.

Each original document was folded in thirds and inserted into a cover titled[10] at least by the name of the estate and the year the proceedings were initiated.[11]

The estate file index will state the file number, and the type of proceeding, i.e., will,[12] administration, etc. Using that number, you should be able to retrieve the original file. If you can't find it, ask the clerk.

There may be a separate index to estate files. Or the file number may appear in the consolidated index or the proceedings index (both previously discussed).

Published Indexes. Also important are published statewide indexes. In a few states, compilers have attempted to list all the wills (and possibly other key estate records) for a specific time period. One such example is that of Clayton Torrence's *Virginia Wills and Administrations, 1632-1800.*[13] Included in it are references to wills, administrations and inventories up to 1800, listed by surname and then by county. The value of statewide published indexes cannot be overestimated. You may be searching

A number of compilers have published statewide probate indexes. Look for these as you access the catalogs of genealogical libraries.

VIRGINIA WILLS AND ADMINISTRATIONS—1632-1800

AARON	*Halifax*	*Spotsylvania*
Amherst	Joseph 1788.	Dannett 1732 w.
Danl. 1765 a.	*Middlesex*	ABNUTT
ABELL	Saml. 1779 i.	*Frederick*
Shenandoah	*Northampton*	James 1798 w.
Joseph 1772 w.	Wm. 1678 w.	ABRAHAM
ABBAY	Jno. 1655 i.	*Northampton*
Northumberland	ABDAIL	Jno. 1677 w.
Eliz. 1796 w.	*Northampton*	*Princess Anne*
Jno. 1791 i.	Hancock 1774 i.	Richd. 1702 w.
ABBETT	ABDEEL	*Westmoreland*
Culpeper	*Northampton*	Thos. 1754 i.
	Thos. 1750 i.	

Figure 5-4. Clayton Torrence's index above illustrates the usefulness of published indexes.

for the estate in the wrong county—perhaps your ancestor moved during later years to live elsewhere with a son or daughter. The statewide index will help overcome this problem.

---

[10] Another option was to bundle them and tie them with red tape, then store them on open shelves, or in whatever containers were available.

[11] This was usually the year the estate commenced.

[12] It is important to note that the original estate files, or "loose" papers, should have the original will, though in modern times some clerks have removed all the original wills and created separate "wills only" files to preserve them.

[13] Clayton Torrence, *Virginia Wills and Administration, 1632-1800* (Baltimore, Md.: Genealogical Publishing Co., 1930, 1990, 2000).

TERMINOLOGY

Following are some terms specifically regarding probates. These are abbreviated—see *Black's Law Dictionary* or other law dictionaries[14] for more complete definitions.

Administrator (-trix). A person appointed by the court to handle an intestate proceeding, that is, an estate without a will.

Administrator cum testamento annexo (administrator *cta*). This indicates that there is a will. Either an executor was not named in the will and the court was appointing an administrator to handle it, or the executor died, refused to qualify, couldn't qualify, moved from the area, etc. In many areas this term has fallen into disuse and instead the administrator cta is referred to as "administrator with the will annexed" and abbreviated as "w/w/a."

Administrator de bonis non (administrat or *dbn*). A person appointed by the court to handle the remainder of the estate. This situation might arise if the administrator died before the estate was settled, moved from the area, was judged incompetent to continue to administer, or various other causes. More modern usage in many areas is "successor administrator."

Beneficiary. One who will benefit through the will.

Bequeath. To give personal property by will.

Bond. The court required two or more bondsmen (or "securities") to guarantee the performance of the executor, administrator, or guardian. The bond is the written evidence of that obligation.

Bondsmen. See Bond.

Brother-in-law. The husband of a married sister, sometimes the husband of a married sister-in-law. In early times could be a stepbrother, or occasionally an adopted brother. (See also Sister-in-law.)

c.t.a. See administrator cum testamento annexo.

Committee. Usually a group of people, some of whom may be related, delegated to a particular duty such as advisors or managers of an estate of an incompetent person.

Contest (will). To oppose, resist, or dispute a will.

Coverture. The status of a married woman under common law.

cum testamento annexo. See Administrator cum testamento annexo.

Curtesy. An estate by which a man was entitled, on the death of his wife, of the lands and tenements which she owned. For the husband to be entitled to curtesy, they had to have had lawful issue born alive (even if the child subsequently died). It is an estate for the term of the husband's natural life only.

de bonis non; *dbn*. See Administrator de bonis non.

Devise. To give real property by will. A devisor is the giver (the testator) while the devisee is the recipient.

Executor (-trix). A person named by the testator in a will to handle the estate.

---

[14] There are also a number of online law dictionaries. For example, try *Bouvier's Law Dictionary*, 1856 edition, available at <http://www.constitution.org/bouv/bouvier.htm>. It also includes a number of archaic terms which may not be found in the modern law dictionaries.

Guardian. A person lawfully invested with the charge of another person. Appointed to handle either the person, the estate, (or both) of a minor, incompetent, or one otherwise incapacitated. A guardian ad litem is invested with that charge for a specific purpose (perhaps, as example, to transfer a specific piece of property).

Heir. See Heir at law.

Heir at law. One who inherited real or personal property in intestacy cases.

Imprimis. In the first place; first of all.

Infant. A person under the age of legal majority. (Remember, a 19-year-old male is an "infant" in the eyes of our legal system if the law says you need to be 21.) See also: Majority.

Intestate. A person who died without a will. The resulting court proceeding may be called "intestate" proceeding or "administration" proceeding.

Inventory. A detailed list of articles of property, and their estimated or actual value.

Letters. When the court approved the appointment of an executor, administrator, or guardian, "letters" were issued by the court making that appointment. Letters Testamentary, Letters of Administration, or Letters of Guardianship are commonly seen in estate matters.

Lineal. That which comes in a line, such as a direct line, parent to child.

Locus sigilli (L.S.). In place of the seal.

Majority. Full age; legal age at which a person is no longer a minor. The age at which, by law, a person is capable of being legally responsible for all of his or her acts. (This will vary for certain actions, depending upon the laws of the time, and the state.)

Next Friend. A person acting for the benefit either of an infant (i.e., under the age of majority) or of another person unable to look after his or her own interest. For example, in an 1831 partition in Oneida County, New York, Court of Common Pleas, there was an allotment among heirs of Walter Cone late of Westmoreland decd, including one of the grandchildren, Hannah Palmer Cone of Versailles, Ripley County, Indiana. She was under 14 and represented by her "next friend" Edmond Cone. Following this, a guardian was appointed for her to act in her interests in a sale of the property.

Orphan. A person who has lost both (or sometimes one) of his parents. Usually used with a minor.

Partition. The dividing of land (or personal property) by co-owners, usually resulting from an inherited parcel. This division may be voluntary, or compulsory through a judicial action.

Primogeniture. Firstborn or eldest son. In states that practiced primogeniture, any estate not disposed of previous to death or by will succeeded to the eldest son. (New England never practiced primogeniture, except for Rhode Island—instead, the eldest son usually received a double portion of the estate.) In some areas, the eldest son could challenge his father's disposition of the land to others, as a denial of his "birthright."

Receipt. Written acknowledgment of receiving something.

Relict. A widow or widower; the survivor of a married couple.

Sine prole, *s.p.* Without issue.

Sister-in-law. The wife of a married brother; sometimes wife of a married brother-in-law. In early records could be a stepsister, or adopted sister.

Son-in-law or Daughter-in-law. The husband of a married daughter, or the wife of a married son. In early times often meant stepson or stepdaughter, or occasionally could refer to an adopted son or daughter.

Surrogate. In some states, a judge handling probate proceedings.

Testament. Under early English law, a written instrument that disposed of personal property after death. Today the words "will" and "testament" are equivalent, and the single writing may devise real property and bequeath personal property.

Testamentary. Pertaining to a will or testament.

Testate. A person who died leaving a will is said to have died "testate," and the subsequent proceeding is often referred to as the "testate proceeding."

Travail. The labor of childbirth. Example: "I give to my wife Dorothy who is in travail …"

Videlicet, *viz*. A contraction for videlicet; to wit, namely. (See page 44.)

Widow's allowance. The amount which a widow may claim (usually set by law) from her husband's estate, free of claims, for her support and maintenance and that of minor children.

Widow's election. A widow may take what is allowed her in the will of her husband, or may choose to take what the law allows which is usually the amount that she would receive under intestacy laws. (Sometimes used to designate what the widow chooses to keep as dower from personal property of the estate.)

Will. An instrument which disposes of a person's real and personal property after death. Often titled "Last Will and Testament." See Testament.

Witness. Usually a person who declares or affirms that he was present and personally saw an event, that is, an eyewitness.

UNDERSTANDING THE LAW

In order to interpret what is found in the records, we need to understand the law at the time of the event.[15] The law may have been based on common law or a statute enacted by a legislative body. A good law dictionary should get heavy usage as you transcribe and evaluate the documents. We need to constantly keep in mind that the law differed from colony to colony and later from state to state. And, in fact, in different time periods within the same jurisdiction. We can spend years on a fruitless chase because we were unaware of a contemporary law that could have explained seemingly conflicting data.

NAMING CHILDREN IN THE WILL

Children were often omitted in a will because naming them was not required.[16] The testator may have left his estate only to a

---

[15] Source References page 203.

[16] Sometimes the testator did give to "all my children" without specifically naming them. That is one of the most frustrating clauses of all!

specific child who had tended to him during his last years. Or perhaps he had settled with one or more of the other children before his death by giving money, personal property, or tracts of land. To avoid possible legal entanglements, the testator usually named all the children, specifying only $1.00 or five shillings or other small amount to children with whom he had previously settled. Though it is possible that such a small sum to certain children indicated the father was disinheriting them, usually it implies that he had already given those children what he considered their share. If he were truly disinheriting a child, it is more likely he would make a stronger comment "I give my son John only $1.00 and desire that he has nothing more to do with my estate," but even that is not proof that the testator was actually disinheriting that son out of displeasure. We cannot know for sure, unless the wording is such that there is no way to misunderstand the testator's intention.

Sons normally got the land, but if there was sufficient, daughters and their husbands often received tracts too, though usually of less acreage.

PRIMOGENITURE OR DOUBLE PORTION

Primogeniture was based on the common law of England.[17] If the law of primogeniture was still in effect in those states which practiced it when the will was made,[18] the eldest son inherited any real property not otherwise devised. Thus, the eldest son might not be specifically named in the will. The father who owned 250 acres might devise 100 acres among five sons but omit mention of additional acreage or the name of the sixth son who was the eldest. Unless the father designated specifically who was to obtain any remainder, that remainder would normally descend entirely to the eldest son by intestate succession (not covered by the will) and primogeniture.[19] It can explain why your ancestor's name was omitted from a will though still alive. If the testator by will disposed of all his land to others and left none for the eldest son to inherit, some areas allowed the eldest son to resort to a court action to restore his "rightful inheritance." Any such actions would be left to a court of equity to decide. (See Chapter 8).

Not all states practiced primogeniture. The southern states, New York and Rhode Island did, and it was not abolished until 1777 by Georgia, 1784 by North Carolina, 1785 by Virginia, 1786 by Maryland and New York, 1791 by South Carolina, 1798 by Rhode Island,[20] and other states at varying dates.

Contrary to common belief, not all of New England rejected primogeniture. Rhode Island, except for a brief period, did use this system of succession.

---

[17] Primogeniture was practiced in England, with the exception of Gavelkind (see page 42) in Kent. The latter provided that all the sons would inherit equally.

[18] The date primogeniture ended varies for each state which practiced it, but it was shortly after the end of the colonial period. Check state statutes for the exact date.

[19] There are always exceptions. In some jurisdictions it may be possible that the prevailing custom was to mention all land in the will. It is also possible that under certain circumstances the land would escheat to the state if not mentioned. Check state statutes.

[20] In Rhode Island for a ten year period, 1718 to 1728, the law specified that the estate would descend to all the children with the eldest son receiving a double portion. In 1728 it reverted to primogeniture.

Following the Revolutionary War, Pennsylvania and New England states abolished their system wherein the eldest son received a double portion of the land as his birthright. In these states, until such time as they may have abolished double portions, if the estate were divided into ten parts, and John received two parts, you know that John was the eldest son (though not necessarily the eldest child).

Primogeniture is a complicated study, for laws differed and methods of abolishing it varied. Normally it applied only to real property, but as discussed elsewhere,[21] there are exceptions. For example, for a time slaves in Virginia were considered real property.

DAUGHTERS

Did the daughters inherit land? In the states which practiced double portions to the eldest son, the law varied as to whether the daughters equally inherited. For example, in the Plymouth Colony charter, the descent was in the manner of East Greenwich, county of Kent in England, providing for descent to the sons equally to the exclusion of the daughters.[22] But the rest of Massachusetts early adopted a more equitable distribution, dividing lands among all the children, sons and daughters alike, except that the oldest son received a double portion.

As to the father's wishes, usually it depended upon his holdings. If he had sufficient property, he was likely to also give his daughters and their husbands a tract, though usually not in the same quantity as the sons. If the quantity of his holdings did not permit such a division, the land normally went to his sons or even to only one son. Daughters may have inherited some part of the household furniture and perhaps some livestock. Very commonly daughters were given a "bed and bedding" upon their marriage, or in the father's will. Any amounts advanced to them while the father was alive were carefully deducted from any portion they received upon his death.

Unmarried daughters were provided for by their fathers—in addition to any bequests, he usually designated that they could remain in the home place until marriage.

These of course are all generalities—the father could provide for daughters in any way he saw fit, and if a daughter had taken care of him, she was likely to inherit a major part of the estate. A daughter very commonly also inherited the family Bible.

Provisions for daughters usually depended upon the wealth of the father.

---

[21] See Chapter 3.

[22] This was not changed until 1685 when it was provided that all the lands should descend to the sons equally, except that the oldest son would receive a double portion.

INTESTATE DIVISION *PER STIRPES* OR *PER CAPITA*

Per Stirpes refers to a method of dividing an intestate estate where the children of a deceased legal heir divide the share which their deceased parent would have been entitled to had that deceased parent lived. For example, if a person died leaving three children who were each to inherit 1/3 of his estate, and one of these children had died leaving four children, those four children would inherit the 1/3 part of their grandparent's estate to which their parent would have been entitled.

In a *Per Capita* distribution the estate is divided among the number of individuals, share and share alike. In the example given above, counting two surviving children, and four grandchildren representing the deceased child, there would be a total of six individuals. The estate would therefore be divided into six portions. The grandchildren in this case would receive more in the *per capita* distribution. The two children would receive less; their *per capita* share would be 1/6 each instead of 1/3.

The contemporary law would dictate by which method the distribution was to be made in an intestate estate.

HEIRS AT LAW, SONS-IN-LAW, AND OTHERS

Common law or statutes of the time and locality dictate the interpretation of the records. Search the laws for the period of your interest. For instance, in Virginia when a man died intestate, unmarried and without children, his eldest brother was his heir at law. It was not until the early 1790s that a statute was enacted putting the father in line as his son's heir at law. Misunderstanding of the term "heir at law" until that enactment has caused the misidentification of a number of Virginians. If there is some problem of relationship in your family, evaluate the documents with the prevailing law in focus.

Another misunderstanding stems from the term "son-in-law" or "daughter-in-law." Beware! This was often used to mean stepson and stepdaughter. "Brother-in-law" or "sister-in-law" could, and often did, refer to step siblings.[23]

Did your ancestor mention a "cousin" in his will, one whom you have never been able to identify? That term was used loosely and should not be taken to mean a first cousin without further confirmation. It could be a more distant cousin or even a great aunt or other relative. In a few instances the term has even been given to a dear friend who was as close to the family as a relative.

---

[23] Occasionally the term was used for a "relationship" based on adoption.

PROBATE COURT MINUTES AND COURT ORDERS

During the court process for testates, intestates, and guardianships, various entries were made in the court minute books as well as in the separate court order books. (The minute books will be more explanatory; the court order books[24] contain only the order that was issued.) The minutes include notations made when the documents were brought into court, when the witnesses testified, when the court appointed the executor or administrator, and the other steps along the way. They are a record of what happened in court each day the court was in session. Though the transcriptions of the main documents were usually entered in their own record books (wills in will books, inventories in inventory books, etc.), in the earliest of times the clerk may have entered them all in the same minute book.

Minute books may or may not have an index. If they do, the index will be limited, usually indexing only the name of the decedent, minor, ward, or principal party of the entry. If there are no indexes, research must be conducted page by page. If you are lucky, someone may have abstracted and published the information. The index in the publication should be of tremendous value since the published book's index will include *all* the names appearing in the abstracts. Don't depend on the book for accuracy of the actual abstracts, though. Using the book's published index, locate the entry in the original minute books and read the document yourself. Errors can creep into published abstracts, in spite of great care taken by the compiler.

Figure 5-5. From a court order book, an order to accept the inventory and appraisement which had been returned to the court. The above 1739 document again demonstrates the difficult early handwriting. The whole passage reads: "At a Court held for Prince William County March 24.th 1739. William ffoster [which we will transcribe as Foster] returned this Inventory & Appraisement and it was Ordered to be Recorded." Did the letters "e" and "d" trip you up!?

Court Order Books (sometimes abbreviated as COB) usually do have an index to the main subject, such as the deceased. If there was no index or the index is now missing, you will need to search each page.

The hunt for the death of Thomas Wells is an example of what might be found "buried" in the court order books. The various estate indexes of Lunenburg County, Virginia did not disclose any listings for his estate, though the evidence *suggested* that he died in the mid 1750s. A page-by-page search of the court order book revealed in September Court of 1755:

> In an action of Robert Hannah vs. John Wells and Thomas Wells, on a petition, the deft. John having been duly summoned and he not appearing, and "as to the Defendant Thomas he having departed this Life, therefore this suit as to him abates ..."

---

[24] Court orders were required by law to be recorded. That may explain why in some areas court minute books were discarded during the years, while court order books were retained.

Some work was involved, but it resulted in establishing at least a date by which he was deceased.

THE ESTATE PACKETS

Original estate records are marvels! They are referred to as estate files or estate packets, and sometimes as "the loose estate papers." They include testate, intestate, and guardianship matters, and others not as common. They can provide many leads. And, there is always the thrill of finding actual signatures. Even if your ancestor only made a mark, you know that he actually held that piece of paper in his hand. And, though only selected documents are transcribed by the clerk into the record books, the packet itself should be full of additional gems.

The packets often solve a discrepancy in the records. The clerk could have erred in the transcribed will—a momentary slip in copying the names of only five of the six children named in the original will, and proof of your ancestor's status as a child is gone! Even the signature might have been miscopied. In the 1853 will of Sarah Rose, filed in the Will Book in Hardin County, Tennessee, it shows that Sarah Rose signed her name. Yet the original will shows that she signed by an X mark.

Estate packets were often filed in tin boxes,[25] each containing a number of packets, and may still line the office walls. Using the indexed entry, try to match the entry with one of the file boxes. The boxes may be labeled by the initial letter of a surname, or perhaps by a box number or other file designation. Importantly, each set of boxes *may* hold only a specific type of file. Wills may be in one set of boxes, administrations in another, and guardianships in a third set. Stay alert for the type of document as well as the file number when using the indexes and hunting for the file. Otherwise, if you are looking for the probate of a will marked as file No. 35 in the administration box instead of the will box, you won't find the correct file. In other areas they may be intermingled in the same box, with perhaps only the word "Estates" on the outside, or a range of file numbers, or the initial letter of the surnames in that box. (For example, William Posey's estate would be in the P box.)

In some courthouses, the packets are stored in the attics or basements or offsite.[26] Unfortunately, during the years through the carelessness of both researchers and clerks many packets have been lost, misplaced, or even stolen. If you do not find the packet

The file or box reference might be a number, such as 45. Or, it might be a letter, Box S (for surnames starting with S), or any other combination that made sense at the time.

Be careful when trying to retrieve the metal boxes that are high along the courthouse walls. The courthouse may have a loose ladder to use, or they may have a ladder which slides along a rail. In some courthouses there is a pole which fits over the box handle, allowing you to pull the file out and lift it down. Don't try it though unless you have the strength to handle the weight. Call for the clerk's assistance if you must.

See Figure 1-3 page 4 for a photograph which includes file boxes along the top.

---

[25] It is also possible that the old file boxes have been discarded, and that all the loose estate papers have been unfolded, inserted into manila files, and are now stored in traditional filing cabinets. Smoothing these old and fragile documents helps to preserve them, for they deteriorate rapidly along creases.

[26] If stored offsite you may have to wait 1-3 days for the retrieval of the file. If you are able to ascertain ahead of time which original files you need, and know they are offsite, phone before you arrive to request that those files be retrieved so they will be available when you arrive. (Some areas may charge a fee to pull the files.)

where it should be, look around. You may find stacks of packets that were previously pulled and never refiled.

In some instances, the clerk will discourage (or even refuse) the use of the original files, asking you to use the record books instead. If you are required to use only the record books, you will likely miss a number of items the clerk did not copy into them. For example, the clerk did not usually copy receipts and newspaper notices, both valuable to your search.[27]

The packets may have been microfilmed, and if so, help to preserve the originals by using the film. Many of the fragile originals are literally falling to pieces; if you do use them, handle them with care.

Not all states have early probate packets. It may be a state in which they were not kept or a county whose records were burned, lost, or destroyed. Some states have especially good probate packets. An example is New York. A law passed in the 1820s required a petition in either a testate or intestate proceeding, and further required that the petition name all the next of kin and residences. Even if the will did not name all the children, the petition names them all (or their heirs if one or more of the children were also deceased). The petitions therefore provide more information than the will, with the added benefit of knowing where the heirs moved.

BUT KEEP IN MIND

We need to constantly be aware while working in courthouses, town halls, and probate districts, that earlier records for the colonial period may have been at the state (colony) level rather than the local level. For example, probate courts did not exist in Connecticut until 1698. Prior to that time, wills in the New Haven Colony were filed with the Secretary of the Colony. In the Connecticut Colony, estates were administered under the "Particular Court." Many of the early Connecticut wills have been transcribed or abstracted and are accessible in that form. Looking for those early originals among the records of the probate district would, however, be unsuccessful.

Other colonies at times also maintained their records with their own colonial government before they established a system to process them in the counties. The state websites are helpful in determining whether that is the case in the state of your interest.

---

[27] Receipts can disclose the name of heirs or relatives, and newspaper notices often name all the next of kin and their last known residence, and may lead to the newspaper in which the obituary was published.

CHAPTER POINTS TO PONDER

✓ A decedent's estate was only probated if it was valued above a certain monetary figure determined by law.

✓ Primogeniture was practiced in some states and abolished at varying dates within a few years after the end of the colonial period.

✓ New England (with the exception of Rhode Island) and Pennsylvania did not practice primogeniture but instead gave double portions to the eldest son.

✓ Women generally did not leave wills unless they were widowed or single, though exceptions exist.

✓ A bequest of $1.00 or 5 shillings does not prove the person was disinherited.

✓ Estates can be accessed by a variety of diverse indexes.

Without a doubt, estate records infuse our research with ways to help enhance our knowledge of every aspect of our ancestors' lives. In the next chapter we will delve into more details involving probates so we can better understand and evaluate the use of those records.

6 ESTATE DOCUMENTS

> In the Name of God Amen
> I John Gorman of the City of Philadelphia, innkeeper ...

The preceding chapter pointed us to the indexes to locate estates, and terminology to understand the clauses and the participants in the actions. Let's now zero in on the actual documents, and the variety available. This mass of related probate records forms a pool in which you will dip many times.

We'll start with estates which include wills—that document which can hold many answers to our puzzles. Perhaps the name of a wife, mention of a father or mother, or the names of the children. The will may not give us the answers we need—the wife may have predeceased her husband and therefore was not named. The father may have made his home with a daughter in his elder years and left everything to her and therefore not named other children. But the wills in the estates are only one of the collective documents. This chapter is sure to surprise you with the many opportunities for your family to be mentioned in related estate records.

And, what if your ancestor did not leave a will? Is it even worth looking for any other papers? Indeed yes. Records in what is called an administration (without a will) can provide even more family details than a will. In an administration the deceased did not pick who was to inherit—it was determined by contemporary law. A succession was set out in a certain order—first the spouse, the children, (or if a child is deceased that child's children), perhaps father and mother, perhaps siblings when there are no children, and it goes on. The law did not remain static—changes were constantly made on the order of succession. Sometimes it becomes important to seek out the existing law of the time period in order to evaluate the record.

When a person died, he may have left minor children. If the deceased had sufficient property for the family to initiate a probate proceeding, guardians would be appointed to protect the children's rights. There are other reasons a guardianship might be instituted. Guardians could be appointed to protect the estate of an aged person who is incompetent, and for other reasons. Guardianship proceedings in those instances could also provide clues on families; details often include ages, relationships, and residences.

Within the pages of this courthouse guide you will learn not only how to locate these records during your courthouse search; many tips on using the records are also included. If there were five witnesses was that important? If an executor refused to serve, what might it indicate? Could a wife advantageously choose not to take what her husband gave her? Leads abound on the pages of those faded old documents—we need only to understand what they are.

WILLS (Testate Proceedings)

A will was either written by the testator or written on his or her behalf, usually by an attorney. The testator signed or made a mark[1] and affixed a "seal."[2] The will was witnessed by two or more persons.[3]

EXECUTOR, ADMINISTRATOR CTA AND DBN. Normally the testator named one or more people as executors to handle the estate. It is likely (especially in early times) that the executor was a relative or a trusted friend.

The court *did not name* an executor—that could *only* be done by a testator. The court can, and usually did, confirm the person named by the testator if there were no objections and a bond was posted.[4] The court did name *administrators* in estates without wills and sometimes even when there was a will.

If an executor was not named in the will, was unable or unwilling to qualify, or for other reasons there was no executor, the court appointed an administrator *cum testamento annexo* (*cta*, with the will annexed).[5] The administrator *cta* acted in the same manner as an executor and was required to follow the will.

If the executor did not serve until the estate was closed, the court appointed an administrator *de bonis non* (*dbn*) to handle the re-

Figure 6-1. Some used the first initial of their first or last name, or even both, as above.

---

[1] The most common was an X mark (or + mark), but sometimes the mark represented the initial of the name or other variant.

[2] The seal may be an actual waxed seal or a written form such as "Seal" or "L.S.," an abbreviation for *Locus sigilli*, the place of the seal.

[3] The exception is a holographic will, discussed later in this chapter. This will was written wholly in the testator's own handwriting, and though witnesses were not required, two people familiar with his handwriting had to testify in court.

[4] Sometimes the testator specified in his will that no bond was to be required. The judge or probate office may still require a bond since the purpose is to protect creditors as well as the estate assets and the heirs.

[5] In more modern times most areas use "with the will annexed" instead of "cum testamento annexo." This may be shown as "w/w/a."

mainder of the estate until it was closed.[6] Among the reasons for such a replacement: the executor may have died before completing his duties, moved from the state, had his bond withdrawn, or been unwilling to continue.

CODICILS TO WILLS

Codicils (additions or changes to a will) were dated, signed and witnessed. A codicil may have been added immediately after the initial signing—perhaps the testator forgot a bequest, and added a codicil rather than having the whole will rewritten. But most commonly the codicil was added at a later date.

A codicil often reflected a change in family status. A son moved west and was advanced his portion to help with his move. The codicil reflected this by reducing his portion to only a token amount. A daughter married and was advanced her portion to help in setting up her new home. Or maybe the intended recipient died and new provisions were made for that share. And, of course, one of the children could have evoked the father's displeasure, so he decided to disinherit that child. All these reasons and more could precipitate the making of a codicil after the initial will was signed. If changes were to be extensive, a new will would probably be written, but for changes in a clause or two the codicil was an easier process.

MORE THAN ONE KIND OF WILL

Normally wills are drawn by an attorney, and witnessed by friends, neighbors, or others. Two less common wills may surface during research.

HOLOGRAPHIC WILL. This is a will written entirely in the handwriting of the testator. Witnesses did not have to be present at the signing, but later at least two people who knew the handwriting of the testator were required to testify in court that the handwriting was indeed his.

NUNCUPATIVE WILL. An oral will,[7] sometimes referred to as a "deathbed" will, was usually made when there was imminent threat of death—wartime, an accident, or other circumstances. It was made before at least two witnesses, sometimes three depending upon the law. Additionally, it was to be reduced to writing within a certain number of hours (perhaps 48 or 72 hours), and usually restricted by law to personal property. (Any real property would descend through the state's laws of descent in intestate proceedings as if there were no will.)

---

[6] Now many areas have abolished the term administrator *de bonis non* and use instead the "successor administrator."

[7] A nuncupative will is invalid in some states.

THE PROBATE PROCESS

If your ancestor died leaving a will, the law specified a time period in which the will was to be produced in court.[8] After the testator died, someone, (usually the person named in the will as executor though at this point he was not yet officially confirmed as such), petitioned the court to accept the will. A hearing date was set to prove the will. A notice of the hearing was issued to the potential heirs to advise them of the hearing date. The notice was usually in the form of a citation (an official summons calling someone to court). The law may have also required a published notice in a newspaper, especially if the residence of one or more of the heirs was unknown.[9]

On the day of the court hearing anyone challenging the will appeared. The witnesses to the will also appeared and attested that the testator signed and declared it to be his last will, that he did so freely, and that he was of sound and disposing[10] mind at the time. If the witnesses' testimony were accepted, and no one contested, the will was proved, admitted to probate, and a bond posted for the performance of the executor. The issuance of a document known as "Letters Testamentary" (the official evidence of the court's order) confirmed the court's appointment of the executor.

Usually shortly thereafter the clerk indexed the will and transcribed a copy into the will record book. The clerk included a clause stating the date the will was proved, which witnesses appeared in court to prove it, and the judge's order.

It is important to note that the original will *was retained in court records.* This was in contrast from an original deed which was returned to the buyer after the clerk transcribed the deed into the deed books. An original will was never to be returned—it was retained as part of the court records even though the clerk transcribed it into the will books. This is advantageous to you; as a genealogist you can compare the clerk's transcribed copy with the original will to be sure there were no errors in the transcription. Clerk's grew tired as they wrote those long documents— errors were easy to make.

See Figure 6-2 for an illustration of the process, starting with the will taken to the courthouse.

Some families have discovered original wills among their family papers. These are likely earlier wills dated before the last will was made, or wills for which there was no reason to probate. It is rare that a descendant will find the original of a will still in the family if that will had at one time been taken to the courthouse for probate, even if a newer will replaced it. The will, even unprobated, was normally retained in the courthouse.

---

[8] There are always exceptions to every rule. In one estate I found that the will of the husband was not probated until almost forty years after he died—filed for probate only after his wife died.

[9] In present times usually a Notice of Hearing is mailed.

[10] "Sound and disposing," meaning that the testator knew what he had and what he was doing with it.

WHEN THERE WAS A WILL: SUMMARY OF PROBATE PROCESS

WILL: Taken to the courthouse. Petition to probate the will filed. Hearing date set.

CITATION (or hearing notice) issued: Notifies potential heirs of hearing date. Served or mailed to potential heirs so they could appear in court to contest if they wished. Usually also published; definitely published if residence of some of the heirs was unknown.

COURT HEARING: The witnesses appeared. If no one contested, the will was proved. Executor posted bond; if accepted, the court issued Letters Testamentary. Exceptions: if no executor was named, or the named executor was not confirmed, the court appointed an administrator *cta. (cum testamento annexo*, with the will annexed).

INVENTORY: Usually three responsible and disinterested people were appointed by the court to inventory and appraise the property. The inventory was signed by the appraisers and the executor, and the document returned to court for recording.

WIDOW'S SUPPORT: Commonly the widow was allowed a year's support out of the estate and a paper was drawn up to confirm what she was to receive. Her dower interest may have been set aside at this time, though often it was later in the probate proceeding.

SALE BILL (or Account of Sale): If there were to be a sale of personal property, a sale date was set for public auction. Every item sold was listed with amounts received and the buyer's name. This Sale Bill was "returned" to court for confirmation.

ACCOUNT: One or more accounts filed during the probate process, showing sums received, notes due, amounts paid for estate expenses, or paid on notes, etc. In other words, an accounting of monies in and out of the estate.

REAL ESTATE SALE: If real property were to be sold, the executor petitioned the court for permission to sell unless the will gave that specific permission. Sale date set, usually for a public auction at which time it was sold to the highest bidder. The sale was confirmed by the court. After confirmation a deed from the executor to the buyer was recorded in the Recorder of Deeds' office.

FINAL SETTLEMENT: May be a specific document or merely a notation in a minute or order book. In more recent times, is by a decree of the court.

COMMENTS: There are sundry other documents and many variations of the above depending upon time period, law, locality, and size of estate.

INTESTATE: The procedure was the same as testates except that there was no executor. Someone petitioned the court to administer the estate and if the court approved, Letters of Administration were issued. (The law usually dictated who had the first right to serve as administrator.)

GUARDIANSHIP: The main difference in the procedure in a guardianship: when someone petitioned to have a guardian appointed the court decided whether guardianship was necessary, and if so, a guardian was granted Letters of Guardianship.

"Disinterested" indicates that the person has no personal interest in the proceeding and would not gain monetarily.

Figure 6-2. To the left, summary of the probate process.

OTHER DOCUMENTS ASSOCIATED WITH ESTATES

Estate documents consist of much more than just wills. Every document associated with the estate you search should be examined. One document may add an additional clue not found in another—the name of the widow, the number of children, a new residence, a new husband.

PETITION

The process to probate an estate starts with a petition. This is true whether it is to probate a will, to administer an estate of a decedent who died intestate, or to set up a guardianship estate. The petition is normally signed by the person who is "praying" (asking) to be appointed.

The petition contributes to our understanding of what is transpiring. It can tell us what the petitioner (the person making the petition) is asking of the court, why he thinks the petition should be granted. If it is a petition in the matter of a deceased person, we know the deceased died before the date of the petition. In some cases, the actual date of death is included in that document, and perhaps even the place of death. (The matter of the date of death and locality of its happening seems to sometimes

Figure 6-3. To the right, a petition for the probate of a will. Note that residences are given in this 1897 document.

Probate of the Last Will and Testament

of Parker H. Rose _____ late of Parishville _____ deceased.

SURROGATE'S COURT, }
ST. LAWRENCE COUNTY. }

BE IT REMEMBERED, That heretofore, to wit: on the 14ᵗʰ day of July
A. D. 1897 Royal Dond and A. J. Rose
Executors named in the LAST WILL AND TESTAMENT,
of Parker H. Rose late of Parishville in
the County of St. Lawrence, deceased, applied to the Surrogate of the County of St. Lawrence to have the said
LAST WILL AND TESTAMENT
which relates to both real and personal estate, proved and recorded; and on such application the said Surrogate
did ascertain, by satisfactory evidence, who were the widow
heirs at law and next of kin of said deceased testator, and their respective residences, viz: Cynthia A. Rose
of Parishville, N.Y. A. J. Rose, Parker H. Rose, Myron J. Rose, Gertrude Kings-
bury of Stockholm N.Y. Barbara E. Dond of Parishville N.Y. John H. Rose
of San Francisco, Cal. Jehiel P. Rose of Nashua N.H. Arthur E. Rose whose
residence is unknown and cannot after due dilligence be ascertained
Emma H. Turner of Anita, Iowa, Harriet C. Culver of Audubon, Iowa,
Hosea B. Rose of Shelby, Iowa, Luther P. Rose of Shelby, Iowa, Daniel P.
Rose of Mattoon, Ills. John Rose, Luther Rose of Windsor, Ills. Elizabeth
Killigass of Providence, N.J. Dora Garrett of Bruce, Ills. Adelia Newell
of Ogdensburg, N.Y. Rose Allen of Potsdam N.Y. Myron Rose, Frank Rose
Edward Rose, Helen Rose, Harriet Rose of Mattoon, Ills.

and said Surrogate did thereupon issue a citation in due form of law, directed to the widow
_____ heirs at law and next of kin
by their respective names, stating their places of residence,
requiring them to appear before said Surrogate at his office
in the village of Potsdam in said
County, on the 7ᵗʰ day of September A. D. 1897
to attend the probate of said Will

be a matter of custom rather than law in some areas in earlier times. Later those details were often included by law.

The petition is important. In any type of estate they should be sought.

BOND

If the court approved an executor (or appointed an administrator or guardian), a bond was then posted for the performance of the duties and obligation. The amount of the bond depended upon the value of the estate.[11] The bond was a promise, under seal, to pay a stated amount to the state if the executor failed to perform faithfully. If the executor had real estate, he might be permitted to give his own bond. Otherwise, he would need a surety to guarantee his payment, or another person to be the principal or promissor on the bond. Often the other bondsmen were family members or good friends, though sometimes they were "professionals" who received a fee for undertaking the responsibility.

If it is a state which created estate packets for original documents, you should find the original bond in that packet. Or, the clerk may have created a file specifically for original bonds. A copy of the bond was transcribed into the record books.[12]

The text of the bond specifies whose failed performance triggers payment, who is promising payment, and whether a third party is guaranteeing payment as a surety. In an administrator's bond in Philadelphia the bondsmen John Rose of Germantown Road, John Ambler Jr. of corner of Green and Charham St., and William Wilson of 10th at Poplar gave a bond in 1850 for Jonathan Rose, as administrator of Edwin Rose dec'd. Jonathan Rose stated that "he is the father of the Deceased." This bond not only specified relationship but by adding residences provided other potential clues. Don't believe the myth that bonds aren't important!

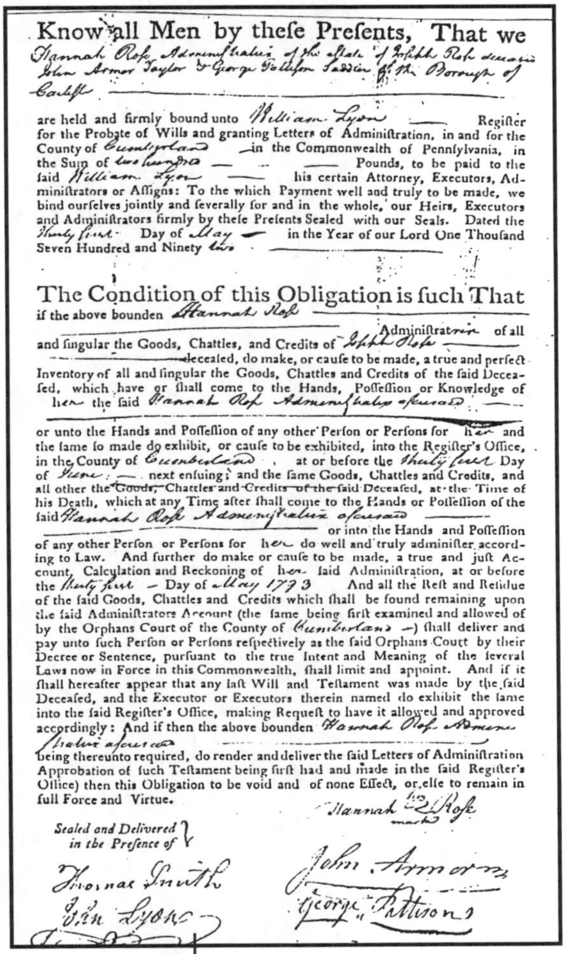

In the bond example shown in Figure 6-4, the duties of an administrator are designated.

Figure 6-4. A bond for the administratrix in an estate. The administratrix (as can be seen by the bond) is bound to certain duties including the making of an inventory, an account, etc.

---

[11] As noted previously, sometimes the will specified that the executor should serve with no bond required.

[12] Often a printed form was used for a bond, with space left to fill in the individual specifics. Special printed bound bond books with these printed forms were often used.

"LETTERS" ISSUED

After the petitioner posted bond and the court ordered the appointment, Letters Testamentary, Letters of Administration, or Letters of Guardianship were issued. These documents are the court's formal appointment granting that person the right to handle the estate.

The original "letters" should be in the estate packet. A copy was entered in the record books—perhaps not word for word, since the original was usually a standard form, but at least a notation was entered that the court ordered letters issued and to whom.

Sometimes the letters which were issued were noted in the same book in which all wills, administrations, and guardianships were kept, and most commonly titled "Will Records" or "Estate Records." Or, the letters may have been entered into separate books clearly marked as "Letters Testamentary," "Letters of Administration," or "Letters of Guardianship." Look on the shelves of the courthouse for book spines showing these designations. Compare the letters that were issued with the petition. Did the judge grant letters to the petitioner? Or perhaps denied the petitioner's request, and chose someone else instead?

In most cases we might assume that the person to whom the letters were issued was related—a widow, son, daughter, or even a son-in-law or other relative. Sometimes however when the deceased was in debt, one of the creditors applied in order to preserve his monetary interest in the estate. If no one applied for letters, the sheriff or other court appointed official, might have applied in order to assure the estate was properly distributed.

INVENTORY

Want to learn details of your family, other than just names, dates, and locations? Locate the inventory of the estate!

Once an executor or administrator was appointed to handle a decedent's estate, whether it was a testate or intestate proceeding, appraisers (usually three responsible and disinterested men) located and listed all real and personal property of that decedent.

The inventory itself is bereft of names, except for slaves mentioned by their given names, and the names of those who signed the document—the appraisers, and the executor or administrator. The inventory gives a glimpse into the decedent's home in a particularly intimate fashion. We see how many cups and saucers the family owned, how many spoons, knives, teakettles. Some measure of prosperity can be assessed by the amount of livestock and farm equipment. The listing of "three pewter dishes," "one bowl," "2 feather beds," "six teaspoons," "one cow," is bound to overwhelm us with an awareness of the sparse furnishings in their home. A listing of shoemaker's tools or the weav-

Inventory listings give us a wonderful sense of the family's status. And often, some of these precioius items survive as family heirlooms.

ing loom and many bolts of fabric will point us to the occupation. The total value of the inventory, when compared with others in the same time period, can provide some knowledge of our ancestor's status in the community.

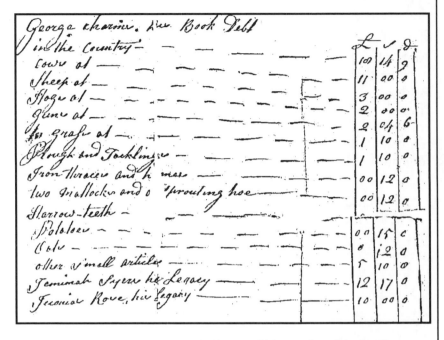

Figure 6-5. Part of the inventory in a 1772 estate. This was the original, and as can be seen, was torn and tattered but still survives.

Customs and laws in different areas, if understood, can help immensely. In Maryland, for instance, the major creditor signed the inventory, as did a relative. Identify which is the creditor, and you know the other should be related.

An inventory is one of the most powerful and personal documents to use when reconstructing your family's life beyond their names and dates. Through it you'll start to identify with the lives they led and see them as the people they were.

ACCOUNT

During the estate process, the executor, administrator, or guardian was required to file periodic accounts of the income and expenses. There may be only one account. In larger estates which continued for a period of time or guardianships which continued until the age of majority, a "First Account," "Second Account," etc. were filed until there was a "Final Account".[13] An account should not be confused with a Sale Bill, sometimes called an Account of Sale, described next.

---

[13] When there was only one account it is referred to as the "First and Final Account."

ACCOUNTS OF SALE AND SALE BILL

These are gems. Take a careful look at the buyers. These were the people who came to the estate sale and bought the contents of your ancestor's home and farm. The widow buying some of the very household goods she had used when her husband was living seems especially poignant. She received her dower, but any additional articles she wanted to keep, she had to purchase.

All the buyers with the same surname surely were related, making this document one of the most significant for family clues. Additionally, some of those with different surnames who purchased may have been in-laws, or otherwise related. Still others could be close friends or neighbors. Through their names, you might identify the area in which the deceased resided even before his arrival in the county.

PETITION FOR SALE OF REAL ESTATE

The will may have specified that certain tracts of land be sold and the proceeds used for family support, or distributed to various heirs. Or the debts of the estate may have exceeded the cash and the value of the personal property, necessitating the sale of real estate.

The process to sell real estate of a decedent can include:
- Petition for Sale of Real Estate.
- Notice of Hearing. Those opposing are given an opportunity to explain why.
- If the court orders the sale, notice of the date and location is posted at various locations.
- Public sale is held.
- The court confirms the sale by a document issued.
- A deed by the executor or administrator is recorded to the buyer.

Whatever the reason, when the executor or administrator petitioned the court[14] for an order to sell the real estate, the property to be sold was described and the reason for the necessity of sale was stated. Notices of the hearing were issued to the interested parties, usually by citations. If the court agreed to the sale at the hearing, a date was set and notices of that sale date posted in a variety of locations.[15]

Unless otherwise directed by the will, the sale was usually at public auction to the highest bidder. The court later confirmed[16] the sale and issued an order for the property to be conveyed. That order should also be among the original estate papers and a copy transcribed into the court order books.

The final document should be in the Recorder of Deeds' office—the deed[17] to the highest bidder signed by the executor or the administrator.

---

[14] As noted previously, the will may have granted the executor the right to sell real property without petitioning the court.

[15] Usually the notice of sale was posted on the property, at the courthouse, and perhaps other locations.

[16] There could be reasons why the court would not confirm the sale; the court may have decided that the price was insufficient, some of the heirs may have disputed the sale, or other reasons may have influenced the court to reject the sale.

[17] The sale may be indexed under the decedent's name, though Executor's Deeds are usually indexed under the name of the executor. Since the executor's name often differs from that of the deceased owner, the probate records are often the only way to locate that link in the property chain of title.

FINAL SETTLEMENT OR FINAL DISTRIBUTION

When the testate or intestate estate was ready to close, there may have been a document filed clearly titled "Final Settlement" or "Final Distribution." Or there may have been only a short paragraph entered in the record books to the effect that the estate was settled. In some counties these entries were in record books specifically marked as final settlements or final distributions. In other counties they may be mingled with wills, accounts, and other estate documents. If original estate packets exist, they should be there.

Often the final settlement or the final distribution included a listing of legacies paid to heirs, and perhaps the names of the heirs. Unfortunately, there are many times when no such document exists. Instead, only a mention in the court minutes or court orders indicates that the estate was settled. Or, the final settlement is there but (frustratingly!) only says it was distributed to "the legatees" without naming them.

You might also find an order to release the executor, administrator (or guardian if it was a minor's estate and the minor reached the age of majority) from the duties of that appointment.

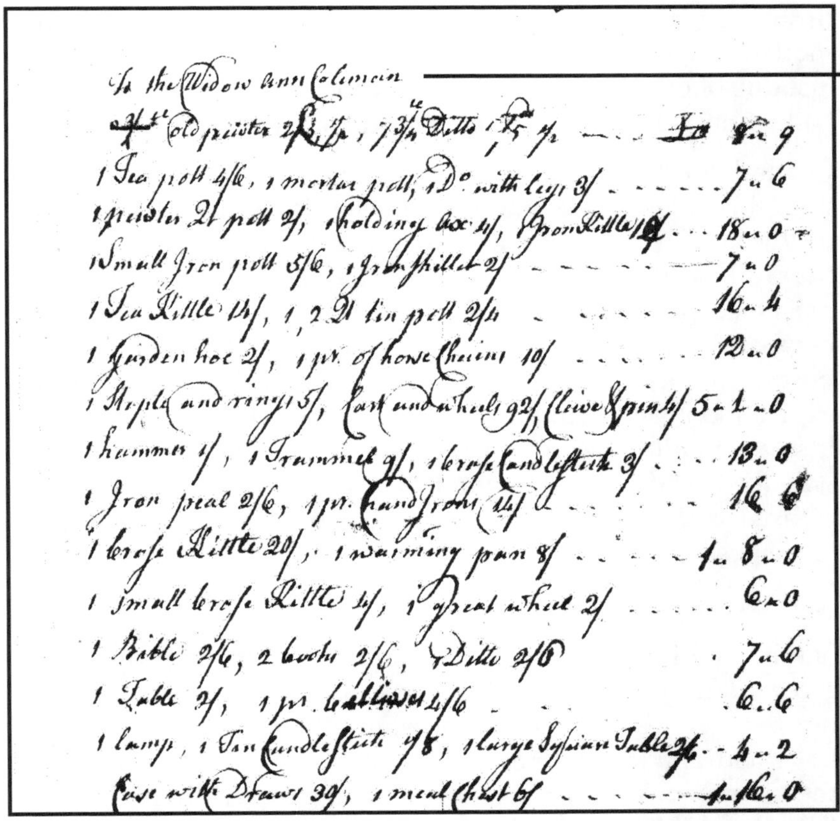

Note that the widow Ann Coleman was specifically named. Each of the other heirs was also named and their portions itemized.

Figure 6-6. The above is part of a final distribution; a portion of what was distributed to the widow. Also included in the same final distribution were similar listings of what was allotted to each of the children (and the heirs of the deceased children). The final distribution named them all.

RENUNCIATIONS

One of the interesting sidelights of the probate process are renunciations. They often have a hidden story. These documents can indicate family troubles, though there could be a benign reason for the renunciation.

In a renunciation the widow might elect not to take what her husband had allowed her under his will, choosing instead to accept what she would have received if he died intestate. Why would she do that?

Let's look at an example.

Ann Rose was given one third of the extensive estate of her husband Jonathan Rose by his will of 1779 filed in Berkeley County, (then) Virginia. That might appear to be generous since he left a large estate. We would wonder why Ann elected at the court hearing to take instead what the law would allow. In this case, the answer was simple. She and Jonathan had no children, and because of this, the intestate laws allowed her one half of his estate, not the one third he specified. Ann had done her arithmetic!

The opposite can happen. In one New York probate file the husband did not allow his wife the third dower she would have ordinarily received by law. Some of her children urged their mother to renounce his lesser provision for her and to claim her just due of one third. Her reply as recorded in depositions: "If he had wanted me to have it, he would have given it to me."

In another estate the husband made his will giving his wife one third, his eldest son two thirds, and specified that after his wife's death the eldest son was to receive her one-third dower in addition to his two thirds. The husband also directed that his wife *could* elect to receive a child's portion. And indeed, that is exactly what she did. But why, you might ask, would she take a child's portion (which was less than her one-third dower). Again, the explanation comes from the law. Rejecting the dower and taking instead a child's portion, she was not restricted to an interest only for her life or widowhood. She was free to do whatever she pleased with her child's portion—she could sell it, give it away, or dispose of it by her will.

And that is just what she did.

She lived with her younger son and later left the property she received from her husband's estate to that younger son. She could not have done so if she had accepted the dower, as she would have had only a life interest. (Her action was also beneficial to the older son, so much so that he agreed in writing to her election of a child's portion. He could then do what he wished with the property he had inherited, unencumbered by his mother's right of dower.)

ADMINISTRATIONS

Those proceedings which are intestate, that is, without a will, are often referred to as administrations. The procedure for administering the estate is much the same as when there is a will—see Figure 6-2 page 87 in this chapter. The process started with a Petition for Administration which often gave the relationship of the petitioner, and the relationship of next of kin. There are many instances where an administration proceeding offers more personal information than a testate proceeding when the decedendant left a will. For example, in one case the family had heard that their ancestor (named Francis) had run off to Iowa from Philadelphia with the family cook. As an old man in declining health, Francis was on his way back to Philadelphia to straighten out his affairs with his wife before his death. But he died intestate in a hotel in Dubuque before he could accomplish that task. His estate records included nine full pages describing how he had married the cook in Iowa without divorcing the Philadelphia wife, rendering all the Iowa children illegitimate. The ensuing dispute between the "widows" and the court's explanation of its findings enriched the reconstruction of this family's life.

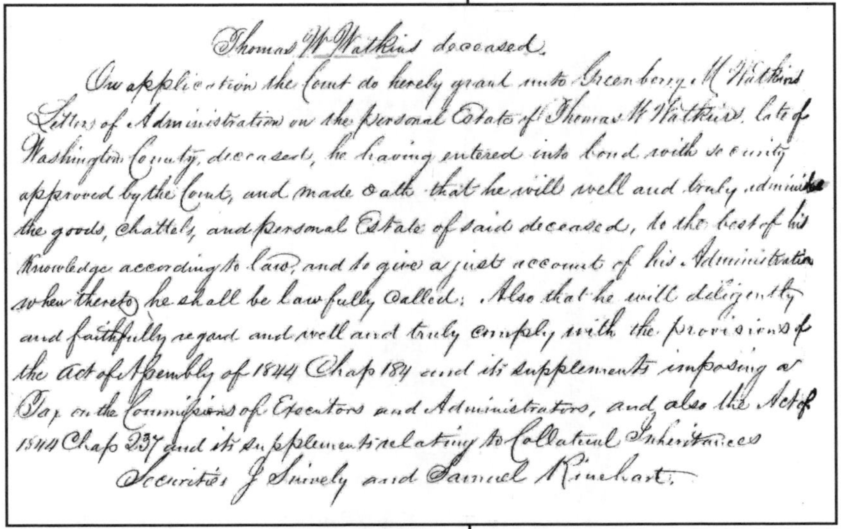
Thomas W Watkins deceased.
On application the Court do hereby grant unto Greenberry M Watkins Letters of Administration on the personal Estate of Thomas W Watkins late of Washington County, deceased, he having entered into bond with security approved by the Court, and made oath that he will well and truly administer the goods, chattels, and personal Estate of said deceased, to the best of his knowledge according to law, and to give a just account of his Administration when thereto he shall be lawfully called; Also that he will diligently and faithfully regard and well and truly comply with the provisions of the Act of Assembly of 1844 Chap 184 and its supplements imposing a Tax on the Commissions of Executors and Administrators, and also the Act of 1844 Chap 237 and its supplements relating to Collateral Inheritances
Securities J Snively and Samuel Rinehart.

Figure 6-7. The court ordered administration granted to Greenberry M. Wilkins on the personal estate of Thomas W. Watkins.

RELINQUISHMENT IN AN ADMINISTRATION

Often the widow, though having the first right by law to administer her husband's estate, chose not to do so. This signed relinquishment may be the only paper in the estate file giving her name. She could ask the court to appoint a particular person in her place (often a son), or she could ask the court to appoint any suitable person. In some instances the court appointed the major creditor as administrator.

The law generally designated who was eligible to administer, and in their order, i.e., a widow, eldest son, other sons, daughters, etc.

In the 1807 estate of Hannah Roosa of the Town of Shawangunk, in Ulster County, New York, a relinquishment by Isaac A. Terwilleger and Diannah Terwilleger state that the deceased had personal property, and that they, as her only surviving children, relinquished their right to administer. They recommend Joel Sparks, *a* "grandson." Thus, a valuable relationship was revealed.

Relinquishments often provided the relationship of the recommended person to the deceased.

PUBLIC ADMINISTRATOR OR OTHER PUBLIC OFFICIAL

If the decedent left no family, or none of the family wanted to administer the estate, a public official, especially the sheriff or constable, may have done so. For example, in Amherst County, Virginia, in the Law Order Book of 1890 it is stated that Sarah E. Rose died intestate, "more than three months ago ... no one has applied to administer" and therefore Jno P. Beard, sheriff, was appointed as administrator. (More recently, many counties have Public Administrators who serve in such circumstances. Check for such an office, especially for late 19th, and 20th centuries.)

GUARDIANSHIPS

The more common types of guardianship records used by genealogists are those involving minors. Others commonly used are guardianships for incompetents—those with mental illness, senility, disability, or other debilitating reasons.

GUARDIANSHIP OF MINORS

The court may appoint a guardian for several reasons. Your ancestor's wife may have died, but perhaps her children were to receive property from a relative on her side of the family. The existing law may have required that a non-relative be appointed as guardian of the minor children if the inheritance were from the deceased parent's family.

Figure 6-8. The above is a typical example of the appointment of a guardian. Often these entries are brief. In this: "Jacob Craig Guardian. On application It is ordered by the Court that Jacob Craig be and he is hereby appointed Guardian to Fountain Snively, he having entered into bond with security approved by the Court for the faithful performance of his bond." If either of these was connected to your family, you would want to investigate the possibility that Jacob Craig and Fountain Snively were related.

If the minor children are listed as "orphans," you need to exert some caution. That term may indicate that only one parent was deceased, usually the father. In other instances, it is meant to indicate that both parents are deceased. No conclusion can be reached without a study of the family.

Note too that a guardian might be appointed for the *estate* of a minor (in which case one of the parents might still be living) or for both the *person* and estate of the minor. In the latter instance, probably both parents were deceased.

If you find a guardian *ad litem*, it was a temporary appointment for a specific purpose.

BONDS FOR GUARDIANS

In estates of minors or in the case of incompetents, a bond was given just as with wills and administration proceedings. These can be informative—for instance, in a guardianship bond in Champaign County, Ohio, in 1846, William Davis was appointed guardian of Francis Elmira Davis, Joseph Davis and Sarah Elizabeth Davis, "minor heirs and legal representatives of Elizabeth Davis late of said county deceased."

ENTAILED PROPERTY IN THE HANDS OF MINORS
If the minor was the recipient of a tract of entailed land (see Chapter 3 page 41), normally under the laws governing entails, the guardian could not sell the land. There are exceptions.

Let us say the widowed mother remarried, and she and her new husband were moving some distance. Her two-year old son was the owner of a tract by virtue of an entail. It would make no sense to retain that land for him, so far from their new home. The court could grant permission to sell the land, but would normally require that the funds be used to purchase a tract in the new area, and the entail transferred to that new tract. This type of action can generate some informative paperwork, often reciting the history of the land and how the original entail was originally set in motion.

CHOOSING A GUARDIAN FOR A MINOR
Though the court appointed the guardian, the child at fourteen (if competent) was usually allowed to choose his or her own guardian. It is always a clue on age when you see a minor making the choice – it can be assumed that child was over fourteen, but still under the age of majority.[30]

NEXT FRIEND
"Next Friend" is a person acting for the benefit of an infant (under the age of majority) or a person unable to look after his or her own interest and needs a guardian. Knowing this term will help you in evaluating documents. The next friend could act on behalf of a ward, but did not have the power of a guardian. For example, in Cambria County, Pennsylvania, a petition was filed on behalf of John Rose, Polly Rose, and Jacob Rose by their mother and next friend, Elizabeth Costlow, "formerly Elizabeth Rose." They were minors, under 14, children of David Rose late of the county, deceased. Acting as "next friend," she requested the court appoint a guardian. These minors were likely expected to inherit from some source and thus, the petition.

The term "next friend" is often misunderstood.

GUARDIANSHIPS FOR INCOMPETENTS
There can be many reasons why a person was in need of a guardian. The following will demonstrate. In Montgomery County,

[30] Depending upon the state and the type of action, the age of majority (legal age) can differ for a male and female.

Ohio, in the year 1900, a man we'll call John, aged 65, was adjudged a habitual drunkard and a relative was appointed his guardian. During subsequent years various other relatives took on the guardianship. When the final account was filed eleven years later, we can presume that the ward had died.

Senility, mental disease, or other problems could render a person incapable of handling his or her own estate, necessitating the guardianship.

COMMITTEE (IN CASES OF INCOMPETENCY)

In some areas, when a person had been judged "insane," a "Committee," usually composed at least partly of relatives, acted on his or her behalf. In an estate in 1887 in Chester County, Pennsylvania, the widow was in an insane asylum at Norristown. She had as her "committee" a male (relationship unknown, though a possible brother), a son-in-law, and two daughters. Unidentified names on the committee are potential clues; examine them further for relationships.

GUARDIAN'S ACCOUNTS

The guardian of either a minor or an incompetent had to file an account of monies received and spent. Depending upon the value of the estate, the account may have been filed annually or more frequently. If it were a minor's estate, a Final Account was filed when the minor attained the age of majority. The filing of the Final Account for an incompetent may signify that the ward had died.

CHAPTER POINTS TO PONDER

✓ There are different types of wills.

✓ For sundry reasons an administrator might handle a testate proceeding instead of an executor.

✓ Wills can provide many clues—understanding the wording is essential.

✓ When the decedent left no will, his estate is "intestate" or "administration."

✓ The process in an administration is similar to the process when there is a will.

✓ Guardianships are usually for minors, but can be for other reasons, such as incompetency.

7 MILKING EVERY CLUE FROM ESTATES

If we look at estate papers with an eye beyond what's actually written on the papers, we will be learn much more of our ancestors and their family. Some understanding of their lives and the dynamics of their family will be our reward. How? The documents can point us to disharmony in the family by the terms of their wills or testimony when contesting, the spirit of adventure as they move, a measure of their prosperity by what they owned. These and more can create a window into the past.

LET'S CONSIDER

ENTAILS

An entail limited the succession of the land. The person to whom it was originally entailed could not sell or devise the land. It remained under the provisions of the entail until the law abolished this form of limited ownership or provided for alternate methods of conveyance. Watch for a specific clause in wills[1] giving land "to his heirs lawfully begotten of his body forever…"[2] Note that the clause does not say "his heirs and *assigns* forever …" The addition of the word "assigns" allows for disposing of the property to non-relatives and therefore is not an entail.

How can this knowledge provide evidence of identity?

Robert Rose by his will dated in 1698 filed in Norfolk County, Virginia, gave to son John a tract "to him and his heirs lawfully begotten of his body." Robert didn't stop there. He gave tracts to sons George and William with the same entailment. Robert was going to make sure his land remained in his family. As a result, you won't find any recorded deeds for the descendants until

---

[1] Entails could be established by deed—see Chapter 3. And, as mentioned in that chapter, in Virginia slaves were for a time part of real property and could be entailed.

[2] An entail is often created to preserve the property in male lines only, and is referred to as a "male tail." It can however be set up to include the heirs of daughters, too.

after entails were abolished (which, in Virginia, was in 1783). By this time, it was probably in the hands of grandchildren or even great-grandchildren. *Identify who owned the land in 1783 when entails were abolished and you have proof of descent from Robert.*

Starting at the end of the colonial period all entails were abolished at various dates or provisions were made that allowed the owner to sell in fee simple (without restrictions) or to sell in some other methods delineated by the new laws.

WERE THERE TWO WILLS?

Once in a while we are especially lucky. Instead of one will in the courthouse, there are two. Perhaps a family member brought an earlier will to the clerk, not knowing that a later will existed. The clerk did not return it, but kept it in an "unproved wills" file. Watch for such a file or box on the shelves. In the case of Randolph Rose of Schuyler County, Illinois, the clerk has his 1859 will and his last will dated in 1861, which was the one proved. By comparing the contents it is possible to determine some changes in family status which occurred during those two years.

Occasionally the appearance of a will in the "unproved" wills file is not a case of there being two wills. Perhaps after it was taken to the courthouse it was determined that there was no need to probate the will, for there was insufficient estate. There may even have been a problem with the witnesses proving the will.

Procedures have changed during the years. In some jurisdictions, wills can now be deposited for safekeeping with the Register of Wills before the death of the testator.[3] The law may also require that anyone who discovers what purports to be a will to file it with the Register.

WILLS OF UNMARRIED ADULTS

We need to be sure not to overlook the unmarried siblings of our ancestors. Their estates may be goldmines, providing details not available elsewhere.

For example, the 1859 will of John Rose was filed in New York City. It is a treasure. An unmarried millionaire, he left a large part of his estate to siblings. Then he gave every one of his first cousins $1000 with a year to present their claims by proving their relationship. It does not take much imagination to know what that estate file must hold. (A bonus: he declared in the will that his place of nativity was Wethersfield, Connecticut.)

A puzzle of two wills
In one unusual case, the will of James Rose in 1831 was filed in Hawkins County, Tennessee, which gives excellent information including mention of his pension for service as a soldier in the revolution. Problem? He didn't die until 1842 when his newer will made that year was probated in King George County, Virginia! You'll hear more of this man at the very end of this book.

Genealogy is full of interesting sidelights. In the case of John Rose, he was one of *ten* siblings. But neither he, nor any of his siblings left children even though some had married. John's parents, if they aspired to be grandparents, were sadly disappointed. Yet, this family provided abundant clues through their estates to prove relationships of many of their relatives.

---

[3] Lawyers used to hold wills for clients, and in some areas still do, but it often discouraged the executor from making an independent choice of an attorney for the estate. Changes were made in some states to allow the executor to more easily make his choice.

MAKING IT FAIR

Most fathers were scrupulous in keeping track of advances they gave to their children. Then, when making a will, the father equalized the children's inheritances. Timothy Rose of Woodbury, Litchfield County, Connecticut, in his 1769 will gave daughter Amie Sherwood 7 pounds 4 pence, daughter Mabel Rose 40 pounds 9 shillings and 2 pence, daughter Joanna Spaldin 10 pounds 13 shillings 6 pence, daughter Lurana Manvil 2 pounds 3 shillings 8 pence and to daughter Jerusha Rose 50 pounds. Can you visualize Timothy during the years, meticulously entering every shilling's worth of goods he ever advanced?

GLEANING CLUES FROM WILLS

The clues contained in a will are numerous. They can lead us not only to relationships, but to burials, religions, occupations, and a myriad of other interesting aspects of our ancestors' lives.

PREVIOUS RESIDENCE. Wills can indicate previous residences, and if we are exceptionally fortunate, previous countries. The 1794 will of David Rose of New London County, Connecticut, identifies that he is of the "islane of St. vincents, formerly of Scotland, now being in the City of New London in the State of Connecticut." The 1810 will of John Rose of King George County, Virginia, gives a tantalizing clue when he mentions that "having been advised that a certain interest or claim beyond the Atlantic Ocean has fallen to me by inheritance or the devise of a deceased relation ..."

ESTIMATING DATE OF DEATH. If the exact date is not given in the probate proceeding, you can estimate the decedent's date of death as between the day the will was signed and the day the will was presented or proven in court. Any narrowing of dates assists in locating related records. In an intestate proceeding you know that the deceased died at least before the day the petition to administer the estate was initiated. It might be even more closely calculated if you can find in the accounts of the estate the date the coffin was ordered, or the date the burial occurred.

DID HE MOVE? Sometimes it may seem that the testator moved, when actually he did not. The will of Zephaniah Dyson is dated in 1814 in Ohio County, Virginia (now West Virginia) but proved in 1816 in Tyler County. Did he move? Probably not. The county of Tyler was formed in 1814 from Ohio County—he no doubt lived in the same spot.

AFFIRMING. If the usual opening of the will "In the Name of God Amen" is omitted, it often indicates that the testator was a Quaker. If the witnesses affirmed their signatures, that, too, is a clue that you probably have a Quaker family and that you should pursue Quaker records of the area. Quakers did not "swear" but did "affirm." Knowing that, you can check other records to

The testator did not have to name all his children in his will, but a prudent man would do so. He would leave those to whom he wished to give nothing a nominal amount so that later it could not be said that he inadvertently forgot to include them. A nominal sum – 5 shillings or $1.00, could mean that he had already settled the portion he intended on that child.

In our compilation we could state the estimated date of death as, "he died between 12 March 1875 (date of his will) and 15 June 1876 (date his will was proved)." We would then add the citations.

101

confirm the religion, especially the monthly meeting records of the Quakers.

WIFE'S NAME AND DOWER. If living, usually the wife's given name is mentioned in the will. If it isn't in that document, you may find it in the bond, distribution, sale, or other related record.[4] Normally, the husband specified that the dower right of the wife in the land and personal property was to end upon her widowhood or when she died, and specified to whom it would then descend. He could, however, choose to give her dower to her outright, allowing her to dispose of it. The dower right could vary—if there were no children, the wife was normally entitled to one-half of both real and personal property. In some areas she also received one-half if there were only one, or only two, children. (Check the statutes of the state and time period.)

FORMER SPOUSE. Sometimes previous marriages are specified or inferred. "I give my 100 acre plantation to the children of my *former* wife ..." That is a clear indication of a previous marriage. Another term, not so clear, is a clause "to my *now* wife I leave all my household furniture and stock of cows ..." This should be treated with caution, for "now" wife can either be an indication of a previous marriage, or may just be used in a legal sense to cover a situation in which the "now" wife might die, and the testator remarries. Other clues exist: a man might mention a living wife in his will, and then include a bequest "to my daughter Sarah the bed and bedding *that was her mother's* ..."[5] A tenuous clue to a possible previous marriage but worth investigating.

GRAVESTONES AND RELIGION. Wills can even point the way to the location of gravesites. Deborah Rose of New Port, Cumberland County, New Jersey, in 1849 made a bequest to the Methodist Church of New Port, for "doing up the grave yard." She further directed her executor to put up a "good and warrantable" tombstone on her own grave. Now you not only know where she is buried, but also the denomination. A perusal of their church minutes and registers may produce more.

Church records can be very useful. Tombstones can also help, but dates on the stones cannot be relied upon without further documentation.

---

[4] Know nicknames! Many years ago in working with a will naming a wife Pattey, I found that when the will was probated, wife *Martha* Rose was named executor (executrix). I thought that the testator had remarried between the date of the will and the date he died. Imagine my surprise to later find that Pattey and Patsey were common nicknames for Martha! A knowledge of nicknames would have saved me two years of search. Additionally, if I had understood in those early years of my research that only the testator could name an executor I would have been tipped sooner that since a woman named Martha did serve as executor, she *had* to be the wife Pattey named as executor in the will. (For Christine Rose's *Nicknames: Past and Present*, see Source References page 201.)

[5] This wording "that was her mother's" often suggests a previous marriage. The testator may have married a widow who had some personal property from her previous union. There could however be other explanations— for instance, one possibility is that the mother could have been the recipient of a gift or inheritance from one of her own relatives and it was now being passed to her daughter. But the clue is strong and should be investigated to determine if the mother did have a previous husband.

APPRENTICESHIPS. Commonly, a testator arranged for the apprenticeship of his minor children through his will, especially if he were ill and knew he would not live to see those children grown. The 1749 will of James Rose of Cumberland County, New Jersey, directs his son James Rose "be put out to some Trade upon Long Island, Here, or elsewhere, at the discretion of my executors." A bonus–the inference to connections on Long Island.

Apprenticeships may also provide estimated ages. In Bute County, North Carolina, in 1769 Blackman Pardue, orphan, 14 years old next 14 October, was apprenticed to be taught the business of a "taylor." In 1804 Duplin County, North Carolina, Ancrum Shaw Everit, an orphan aged 16, was apprenticed to John Hunter to learn the trade of sadler and harness maker.[6]

THE EXECUTOR. Usually in earlier wills the executor was related, probably a spouse, an adult child, a brother, or other relative. Or, the testator may have named a trusted friend. (When a woman made her will, she often named her brother as executor, but that relationship cannot be assumed and needs further investigation.)

THE WITNESSES. The witnesses to the will may have be related, if they did not benefit under the will. Thus, they might be siblings, parents, uncles or aunts, or even a son who was not inheriting if his father had previously given him his share. The witnesses might be good friends or close neighbors. People moved from one area to another together, often with family or friends. Identify the friends of your ancestor and you can often identify the previous residence of your family.

There are very occasionally exceptions, when a witness to a will can be proved to indeed have received a bequest. But it is rare and was probably a situation in which the family members did not object, and the bequest was not substantial.

Also to be noted is that witnesses to a will usually cannot inherit under it (because they are not disinterested). This can sometimes be a clue to separating people of like names, for example a brother who witnessed and a son who inherited.

MORE ON PACKETS

We looked at estate packets in Chapter 5. The original will should be in that file packet;[7] the clerk's transcription is in the large will record book.

Is there any reason for us to seek the original will if we have access to the clerk's transcribed copy? Yes, for errors can appear in the clerk's transcriptions. Perhaps a name was spelled incorrectly, a name omitted in a long list of children, or other such

"*Examine the original*" does not mean that we literally have to do that. If the original wills have been microfilmed, or the clerk has made photocopies available to preserve the original, they are acceptable and help in preserving the originals. Compare that image of the original will with the transcribed copy. This is especially important when you have seen a transcript or abstract prepared by someone other than a clerk, but even clerks can err.

---

[6] Ancrum was apprenticed for 4 years and 9 months. We can therefore assume that he was aged 16 years *and three months*—the apprenticeship to last until he reached 21.

[7] Some clerks in the present day have removed the original wills from the estate packets and created a separate set of files holding only those wills. Access to those originals may be limited.

It's wonderful to find an estate packet with informative papers. But, we need to pay careful attention or they can lead us astray.

Let's follow this probate packet, and see what happens.

This is the estate of a Derick Roosa who died in 1827 or 1828, in Ulster County, New York. First, there is a will of "Dirck" Roosa which names his children. So far, so good.

After the will, and our initial excitement at finding that, we now have the newspaper notice. Hmm....the will was dated in 1797, but the newspaper notice is over thirty years later. Well, maybe he made his will as a young man. But no, at the end of the will, as shown on the previous page, it shows the will was proved 7 August 1797. What is going on?

Proceeding on to the petition, it too is in 1829. Further, it mentions the will of "Dirick" Roosa, But says that Dirick D. Roosa is a devisee under the will of his father Dirick Roosa. Yet, the 1791 will did not name a son Dirick D. Roosa.

Receipts are dated in the 1830.

Studying all of this, what accounts for the discrepancies? Human error. The will of "Dirck" Roosa, dated 1791, is in the wrong estate file. After investigation, an 1827 will (proved early in 1828) of the correct Derick Roosa was found, recorded in Will Book G in Ulster County. Clearly, the wrong Derick Roosa will is in the file.

This demonstrates that we need to carefully read and evaluate all the documents we find. Otherwise we could be led astray.

It also demonstrates that the original estate packets contain immensely useful documents to help us construct our family's history.

inaccuracy. Sometimes there are inexplicable differences. The will of Thomas Rose in Bedford County, Pennsylvania, dated in 1841, made a bequest to a grandson Alexander *Bell* Rose. When the clerk transcribed this will, he entered the name as Alexander B. Rose, losing a potential clue. It's always a good practice to not rely solely on the clerk's transcribed copy of the will—examine the original too when it is available. If the originals are on microfilm, that is an acceptable substitute.

VARIED DOCUMENTS IN THE ESTATE PACKET

An estate packet will demonstrate the value of examining all the papers in an estate, not just the few records the clerk transcribes into the record books. The following documents were obtained from a packet filed in Ulster County, New York, and are abstracted here to demonstrate the variety of documents in a packet.

File titled: DERICK ROOSA. died 1838, Nov. 30. Box 33

WILL of Dirck Roosa of precinct of Shawangunk, yeoman, to two sons Peter and Richerd the farm on which I now live in precinct of Shawangunk, to son Peter the westernmost moiety, from De*va*shill? [etc.], Richerd the easternmost part, to son Aldert 100 pounds, to son Cornelius 140 pounds, residue to four sons Peter, Richerd, Aldert and Cornelius. Appointed the four sons executors. Dated: 4 August 1791. Signed: Dierck Roosa. Witnessed: William Gillispy, Matthew Gillespy, Mary Gillespy. Proved: 7 Aug. 1797.

NEWSPAPER NOTICE: Sale of estate of Derick Roosa, deceased, lot in the Town of Shawangunk, contains lot in a certain division lately of part of estate of Derick and Aldert Roosa, deceased, which was allotted Derick Roosa Jr., [etc.], also lot in No. 3 of Beckman Patent, as devised by Derick Roosa to Derick Roosa, along line of John and Anthony Crispell, [etc]. Dated 19 September 1829.

PETITION: 23 July 1829, personally appeared Dirick D. Roosa, a devisee under will of Dirick Roosa deceased, who is under 21, and Dirick Roosa his father of Shawangunk, a freeholder, who consents to act as guardian of his son. It is ordered that Dirick Roosa be appointed guardian of the infant [i.e., underage] devisee.

RECEIPTS: A large number of receipts are in the file, including a receipt of Mrs. Christiana Roosa, administratrix of Derick Roosa deceased, dated 15 November 1831, and a receipt of Thomas P. Roosa who signs receipt 14 September 1839 against the estate of Derick Roosa deceased.

RECEIPTS: In addition to a large stack of loose receipts is a one page listing of receipts which appears to be of the heirs:

Receipt 8 Oct. 1839, proportionate share, signed by Derick D. Roosa.

Receipt same date, in full of my wife Nelly proportionate share, signed James Rea.

Receipt same date, signed by David Vernooy in full of wife Ann Eliza's proportionate share.

Receipt same date, in full of proportionate share of my children Aldert Roosa and Cornelius Roosa, minors, whose guardian I am. Signed by Christian Roosa.

Receipt same date, for proportionate share, signed John Roosa.

Receipt same date, for proportionate share, signed by Peter Roosa.

The value of the above original estate papers is readily observed. The estate packet is often the only place where receipts exist.[8]

TRANSCRIBING A WILL

We discussed transcribing in Chapter 1. Basically, all punctuation, capitalization, and spelling must appear exactly as they appear in the original.[9] You wouldn't take the time to make a transcription while at the courthouse, but it is necessary to read the will while still onsite. If the will seems pertinent to your search, have it photocopied and later make a full transcription at home. However, abstract it while still at the courthouse, even if you had it photocopied. That is important for it will enable you to quickly pick up clues to pursue while you are still at the courthouse.

The following is an example of a full transcript you'd make after you get home.

I James Rose of the Township of Newtown County of Bucks and State of Pennsylvania, Being Weake of Bod[a letter probably marked out here; a y written under it] But of sound Mind and Memmory Blesed be the Lord do this third Day of the Eighth month Anno domini one Thousand Seven hundred & ninety nine Make and [last word lined through] Constitu[ue?] & ordain this to be my Last Will and Testament in manner following

first my Will and mind is that all my just Debts & Funeral Expences be all paid and Discharged

Item I give and Bequeath unto my Brother Thomas Rose one Equal fourth part of all my Estate after my just Debts are paid

[Itmen?] [this word blurred, perhaps intended as erasure] Item I give and Bequeath unto my Brother John Rose one other Equal fourth part of all my Estate after my just Debts are paid

Item I give and Bequeath Unto my Sister Alse Hollingshead one other Equel fourth Part of all my Estate after my just Debts are paid

When you photocopy a will (or other record) examine the copy to be sure the whole document is there. It is easy to miss a line across the top, bottom, or words along the side. We've all done it!

[8] There are exceptions. Sometimes the clerk did copy receipts into the minute books, but that was not common.

[9] The exceptions, as discussed in Chapter 1: the thorn for "th," the "ff" for "F," and the "tailed s."

Item I Give and Bequeath Unto my Sister Presilla Reeder one other fourth part of all my Estate after all my Just Debts are paid And Lastly I do nominate and appoynt my friend [a possible short word blurred here] William Buckman to be my Executor of this my Last Will and Testament Rattefying this and no other to be My Last Will and Testament & Revokeing all Wills By me hertofore made Published and Declared to be his Last Will and Testament in Presents of us

James (his x mark) Rose   (Seal)[10]

Abner Buckman

Elizabeth Buckman

Bucks ss August 12th Anno, Domini 1799. personally appear'd Abner Buckman & Elizabeth Buckman two of the Subscribing witnesses to the within Instrument of writing and on their Solemn Affirmation, did say that they were present at the Execution thereof and saw and heard James Rose the Testator therein named Sign Seal publish and declare the same as and for his last Will & Testament and at the time of his so doing he was of Sound Mind & Memory & of a disposing understanding to the best of their Knowledge and Belief

Coram[11] me   James Hanna

Bucks ss Be It Remembered that on the 12th of August Anno Domini 1799. This the last Will and Testament of James Rose Decd was duly proved when Letters Testamentary were granted to William Buckman Executor therein Named he having just been Solemnly a[ff]irmed well & truly to Administer All & Singular the Goods & Chattles rights & Credits of the said Deceased & in one Month from This Date to Exhibit into the Registers Office for the County of Bucks a True Inventory and conscionable appraisement of the same and in one year or when thereto lawfully required to render a Just Account of their whole Administration. Witness my Hand & Seal of said office

James Hanna

Figure 7-1. *The above are three different seals. The top is a waxed seal, not too commonly used. The second is the most common—written after the name. The third is from a printed form of an original document. In this case, those signing it made marks over the seal to designate their use.*

ABSTRACTING A WILL
An abstract of a will should include all the essential details.

- Name of testator.

- Residency if shown.

- Name of spouse, and any references to "now" wife or "former" spouse with any devises and bequests. (The "now" wife, mentioned previously in this chapter, isn't an absolute guarantee that there was a former wife, but it is a clue to follow.)

---

[10] In early times the seal could have been a waxed seal, but the practice discontinued and the words were simply written in and circled.

[11] "Coram me" means "Before me."

- Names of children, together with specific devises and bequests.

- Name of executor(s).

- Any mention of minor children and directions for apprenticeships and guardianships.

- Date of will. (Just as it appeared; "8ber 1748" etc.

- Special clauses referring to inheritances, relatives, religious denomination, graveyard, etc.

- Signature (or mark) of testator.

- Witnesses, their marks if any, and residences if shown.

- The date the will was proved in court and by which witnesses.

- Name of executor appointed by court. (Not redundant, for the will may have named two or more executors, but perhaps only one was appointed.)

The following is an *abstract* of the will of James Rose (a transcription shown on pages 105-106), retaining its important elements.

[James Rose, Bucks Co., Pa. Original Estate Packet #2910.]

Will of James Rose of Twp. of Newtown, county of Bucks, Pennsylvania [no opening section "In the Name of God Amen"], am weak in body, make will on 3rd day of Eighth month 1799. Give to brother Thomas Rose one equal ¼ part of estate; to brother John Rose one equal ¼ part of estate; to sister Alse Hollingshead one equal ¼ part of estate; to sister Presilla Reeder one equal ¼ part of estate. Nominate friend William Buckman executor. Signed: James (his x mark) Rose. Witnesses: Abner Buckman, Elizabeth Buckman. Proved: August 12 1799 by Abner Buckman and Elizabeth Buckman who affirmed. Letters testamentary granted to William Buckman, executor, who affirmed.

In the name of God Amen

Some observations of the above will of James Rose:

1. Usually a will starts "In the Name of God Amen..." If it does not start in that manner, it usually (but not always) is an indication that the family was Quaker. In this case, that is particularly noteworthy, as there were many Quakers in Bucks County. That clue was noted in the remark added in square brackets.

2. Weak in body" is optional. I include it for it *could* be an indication of age though its always possible that the testator was weak because of illness, regardless of the age. It's only another clue, the kind we "keep stored in the back of our mind." It can also explain the use of a mark instead of signature in a man who did pen his name to earlier documents.

> **TRY IT AGAIN ...** take one of the wills in your possession which you abstracted in the past. Read it through and abstract it again. Did anything new come to light?

3. The date is taken exactly as it appeared since it specified the date by month. This is a common Quaker practice;[12] another clue to the religion of the family.

4. The witnesses affirmed—that terminology is retained for it indicates the witnesses were Quakers. (As explained elsewhere, they did not "swear" but affirmed their actions.)

By continually transcribing wills, your skill in picking out clues from within its contents will increase. So will your ability to abstract those wills quickly while working in the courthouse. You will know what is "boilerplate" (standard legal clauses). Words you do not understand should be noted so that you can check a law dictionary. It is permissible to abbreviate certain words in your abstract, such as "Let. Adm." for Letters of Administration. (However, retain names exactly as they appear.)

"Boiler plate," those repetitive clauses in documents, will become easier to spot as you read and transcribe documents.

WILLS ARE MARVELOUS IN MORE WAYS THAN ONE

Sometimes a person can be identified because of the devise or bequest received. In 1842 Maria Louise Rose received a bequest of a Negro slave named Monroe in Albemarle County, Virginia, under the will of her mother Mary Rose. When she moved to Shelby County, Tennessee, Mary Louise and her husband emancipated Monroe, thus proving through this document that Mary Louise of Tennessee was the same Mary Louise of Virginia.

At times identifications are possible by identifying the same devise or bequest. William Harris might inherit from his father John some slaves Lucy and her children, James and Joseph. Five years later William died and his intestate proceeding lists Lucy, James, and Joseph as part of the inventory. No disposition is shown of the slaves. A tax list several months later shows Aaron Harris owning Lucy, James, and Joseph. We now have strong evidence that Aaron is a son of William, in spite of the lack of a document specifically naming them as father and son. And since William had inherited them from his father John, you now have proof of three generations of this family.

Some of the wills are quite moving. The mother Mary, faced with a large family and not having enough for all, had to omit the older married children. She wrote that her children well understood and didn't need explanations, but for the benefit of those reading her will "it is not for less love I have for them, but because of the more helpless situation of the younger children …"

George Rose of Wethersfield, Connecticut, unmarried, gave his substantial estate to his siblings by his 1825 will filed in South Carolina. His beloved dog "Grouse," though, was entrusted to a friend.

---

[12] Taking the date just as it appears becomes essential in earlier records, before the change of the calendar to the Gregorian calendar. Before 1752 the year started with March 25th instead of January 1st, and thus the "Eighth month 1799" in an older record would represent October under the new Gregorian calendar.

Thomas Rose of Accomack County left no wife or children, but wanted to be remembered by his friends. He bequeathed his sloop "the *Rosanna*" to a friend, made several other bequests, and then gave a number of friends gold rings the value of five shillings. They were to be inscribed with the first letter of his Christian name and surname and his age engraved on each, "my age being at present better than thirty three." This custom of giving gold rings, prevalent particularly in the 17th and early 18th century, provided the age of this man.

Some wills are especially useful. The 1812 will of John Rose of Salem County, New Jersey, contains abundant clues on the family. It implies his previous marriage, for he gave daughter Mary the bed and chest of drawers "which were formerly her mothers." He states that his wife Jane is in a "state of pregnancy" and appointed her as guardian of the daughters and the posthumous child. Friend John Hall was named as guardian of the sons William, John, Samuel, and Reuben. Hall was to bind William and John as apprentices "to some good business" as soon as convenient, and to likewise bind said Samuel and Reuben as they arrived at the age of fifteen years. Now you not only know he had two marriages, the name of the second wife, and names of children, but you have some idea of the ages of the sons, all obviously minors.

IS A SEARCH AMONG ESTATES WORTH THE EFFORT?

Indeed, the search is worth the effort. It will take some time to understand all the paperwork in connection with estates and to mine all the clues you do find. But it is one of the most rewarding collections of documents for genealogists. By digging deeply into them, many of your unsolved problems will be unraveled.

Constantly, we must examine what we have accumulated, trying to keep an objective eye. We see at first what appears to be obvious. But, when there is a problem or conflict, look deeper.

In Berkeley County, West Virginia, in 1796, the will of Conrad Rose gives his estate to his wife Mary, and after her death, to my "Brother Henry, Christopher Rose and Henry Rose." This is the clerk's transcription in the will book; the original cannot now be located. What happened? Did the clerk simply err—should that third name have been something else? Surely Conrad did not have two brothers named Henry. I immediately thought that the clerk made a mistake—when he wrote the second Henry Rose, he had a momentary lapse. But, recognizing there was a problem here, I took the passage in quotes so later I would know I had not erred in my abstract. I could be assured that the transcript had indeed shown it in that manner.

109

When there is a conflict, we continually analyze what we have accumulated to see what else might bear on the problem. When I did this in the above case, I realized that another possibility *might* exist. The word brother is not plural. Could it be that Conrad was giving it to a brother Henry, and to two other Roses (relationship not specified) named Christopher Rose and Henry Rose? I won't know unless I examine the records further. But this demonstrates the importance of copying the passage exactly and enclosing clauses in quotes if there appears to be some problem.[13]

DON'T BE CONTENT WITH ONE RECORD

It is important that we not be satisfied with one record of an event. The additional records that were generated could have the answer we need to break through a brick wall. A case in point: the will book provided for the apprenticeship of the son of a widow. But, the court minute book was more specific, stating that he was the baseborn (illegitimate) son of the widow. What isn't specified in one record may be revealed in another.

CHAPTER POINTS TO PONDER

✓ We need to be aware of special clauses in wills and their meaning.

✓ The wording in wills can give us many clues not specifically written but implied.

✓ The wrong document may have been inserted in an original file packet.

✓ Transcribing documents needs to be precise for misinterpretation can otherwise result.

---

[13] In the given example, following the property after the death of Mary might provide the answers.

8 UNDERSTANDING THE COURT SYSTEM

Have you examined the vital records, estates, and land records, but hesitanted to venture into the other courthouse offices? Civil and criminal records can solve some of your lingering puzzles. My hope is that after you read this chapter and the next, you will want to revisit courthouses in which you researched in the past. There still may be valuable clues still there!

THE COURT SYSTEM

The records we'll discuss here pertain to state courts on the county level. There are other state courts operated beyond the county, and additionally, there are federal courts.

Once a case is heard, if one of the parties is dissatisfied and chooses to appeal the judgment, it then moves to a higher court. In the colonial court system, that usually meant the case would proceed to an appellate court held in the seat of the colony's government. Now there are one or more appellate courts scattered throughout each state (not just the state's capital) and the appeal will be heard by one of those. If the case is still not resolved in the appellate court, that is, one of the parties wants it pursued, it can then proceed to the supreme court of the state.[1] If the state supreme court decision hasn't resolved it, the appeal can continue to the nation's Supreme Court (if the latter agrees to hear the matter). Later in your search you'll no doubt want to seek some of these higher court records too. But begin with those in the local courthouse.

TYPES OF COURTS

Local courts carried a multiplicity of names and jurisdictions from state to state and in different time periods. On occasion,

---

[1] Except in New York where the Supreme Court is the lower trial court, and appeals go to the Court of Appeals, and in Texas where it is divided into the Supreme Court for civil matters, and the Court of Criminal Appeals for criminal matters.

the same court simply "put on a different hat," sitting one day as a probate court and perhaps the next as a criminal court. Each state set up (and monitored) its own system, but basically, there were many similarities but with local variances. A few of the more common court names:

APPELLATE COURT OR COURT OF APPEALS. A court whose duty is to review decisions of lower courts or agencies.

CHANCERY COURT. Has jurisdiction in equity cases.

CIRCUIT COURT. In some states the state civil courts were divided into "Circuit Courts," and served in the same trial court capacity as the Common Pleas Courts in other jurisdictions.

COMMON LAW COURT. Actions at common law.

COMMON PLEAS COURT. Usually a trial court of general jurisdiction hearing both civil and criminal cases.

COUNTY COURT. Civil and criminal jurisdiction.

COURT OF INQUEST. Inquiries into the cause of an unexpected or unexplained death.

COURT OF OYER AND TERMINER. Higher criminal court.

CRIMINAL COURT. Criminal matters.

FAMILY COURT. Family matters, adoptions, juveniles.

HUSTINGS COURT. Court in Virginia, in incorporated independent cities.

INFERIOR COURT. Lower court whose decisions can be appealed to a higher court.

JUSTICE OF THE PEACE COURT. Jurisdiction usually over civil cases of a lesser amount or criminal cases for certain misdemeanors.

JUVENILE COURT. A court having jurisdiction over dependent and juvenile children.

MAGISTRATE'S COURT. Usually lesser civil and criminal cases and some administrative functions.

MUNICIPAL COURT. Usually misdemeanor criminal and traffic cases, and civil cases when the amount in dispute is under a specified amount.

ORDINARY COURT, OR THE COURT OF ORDINARY. Renamed Court of Probate by states which had such a court.

ORPHAN'S COURT. Exists in a few states only; a court with probate jurisdiction and often maintains marriage records.

PROBATE COURT. Handles matters involving estates.

SMALL CLAIMS COURT. Civil claims for a lesser amount.

STATE SUPREME COURT. A court of last resort for the state; also supervisory jurisdiction over all other courts in the state.

SUPERIOR COURT. In some areas a court of general jurisdiction hearing both civil and criminal matters. In other areas a court of appeals.

There are courts with other names, but the above are among the most common that researchers will encounter.

OUR LEGAL SYSTEM

Some basics should be considered in order to better understand the records found in courthouses. The colonial legal system was based on the common law of England.[2] Common law is based on precedent—decisions in previous similar cases.[3] It can be superseded by statutory law, that is, laws that are enacted by governing bodies. Some points to consider follow:

Law vs. Equity. A court of law is based on the law (where a person seeks to recover monetarily for injuries sustained to himself, his property, his finances, or his reputation). It includes, for example, a breach of contract, or product liability, such as falling off a poorly designed ladder. In contrast, a court of equity is based on fairness to both parties. It can order parties to do, or not do, specific acts or revise the terms of written instruments in order to achieve fairness when money can't compensate for the possible harm.[4] Equity cases are heard by a judge (or chancellor in states with a chancery[5] court), rather than before a jury. Many states have abolished separate courts of equity and hear law and equity cases in the same court. Since equity cases often involve family disputes, they can be a bonanza for genealogists.

Trial vs. Appellate. Evidence is presented at the trial court, which is the court of original jurisdiction at the local level. To build a family history those records are first used as generally no new evidence is introduced in an appeal. The appeal however can assist, especially if the local file is now missing or has been destroyed. In many cases the whole trial court file was copied (by hand before typewriters) and sent to the appeal court when the latter heard the case. Thus, your efforts in locating that appeal may be amply rewarded by providing the missing papers.

Often the papers involving appeals have been transferred to the state archives. If they are not there, the archives staff may at least know where those documents are now housed.

One state supreme court case will demonstrate the value of appeals in understanding a family's life. In an 1838 case in the Supreme Court of Tennessee,[6] a man named William had become

---

[2] Except for Louisiana which was based on civil law.

[3] Written decisions are more recent. Early ones were usually recorded and published by private reporters or lawyers who took notes of the orally announced decision and reasons given for it.

[4] Divorces are not normally considered equitable actions, although many other types of family disputes are. Neglected wives could obtain separate maintenance orders from equity courts when they had no legal existence in the eyes of law courts, but while some states may have placed divorce jurisdiction in courts of equity, it wasn't common. In some states it was given to the Orphan's Court when the state's legislative body ceased to handle them.

[5] See chancery cases later in this chapter.

[6] The Supreme Court cases for Tennessee are housed at the Tennessee State Archives in Nashville, Tennessee. Their excellent card indexes facilitate the use of these informative cases. Other state archives may not only have the cases, but in some imstances have abstracts online.

Court cases can reveal details about a family's life.

intoxicated, returned home quarrelling, struck his wife Amanda in the back, and shoved her out the door. Amanda took refuge with a neighbor. William followed and insisted she return, but used no further violence. She took out a warrant and stated that he took spells of drinking and abused her. When sober, she stated, he was a "kind and affectionate man" and labored to support his family, consisting of his wife and several small children, the oldest being eleven. He was "very poor" and had no means of support "but by his daily labor." Amanda did not want him punished. He had told her that when she discovered him drinking she must leave him until he was sober, which was the reason she left home. William was ordered to spend one month in jail and pay $5 plus costs.

Why did this go to the State Supreme Court?

William, who could ill afford the fine or loss of work, appealed on the grounds that under Tennessee law a wife could not testify against her husband. Genealogically, the appeal not only furnished insight into this family's life, but also provided the name of the wife and some indication of the children.

Other supreme court actions can include family disputes over slaves (giving relationships and details on inheritance) and a trove of other cases with genealogical clues.

RECORD BOOKS

There are many types of record books used throughout the court system. Among those most commonly seen:

Bond Books. There are assorted bond books. One might be the General Bond Book for constables, justices of the peace, sheriffs,

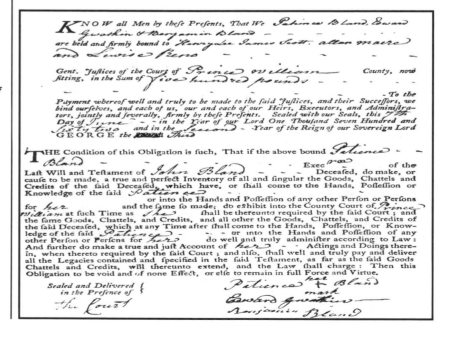

Figure 8-1. A bond from a bond book. Very often the "boilerplate" standard clauses of bonds are in a printed form, leaving the clerk only to fill in the particulars. This 1762 Virginia bond is for the executrix of the estate of John Bland and is typical of the bonds used in many areas. This is not the original—it is the clerk's copy written into the bond book which was comprised of printed forms. This bond was in the probate department; similar forms for bonds were used in the civil and criminal office for use as constable's bonds, and other matters.

etc. Others can be for specific purposes—perhaps only for bail bonds, or executor's bonds, or any of the other specific type of bonds. Often the books consisted of printed forms, which the clerk filled in.

Court Minute Books (in some states called Journals). The minute books are daily records of the court in session, and contain the court's diversified proceedings. One person came to the courthouse to acknowledge a conveyance, another to get reimbursement for the care of one of the county's poor. An unhappy farmer sued a neighbor for trespass. These were all duly recorded in the minute books.

Some courts kept their own minutes. Others combined the court proceedings of more than one court into the same minute book. In such instances, the minute book will specify that the court was "sitting as a Probate Court" or whichever court it was sitting as on that day or for those actions. If that information is not at the top of the page you are viewing, start turning the pages back until you get to the page with the notation indicating the date the court sat, and importantly, which court was hearing the matter.

Court Order Books. When the court issued an order, it was recorded (by law). It generally appears in a court order book, though that might not be the exact book title. Court order books should have indexes, though the indexes may be limited or may have been lost over time.

Court orders of more than one court may have been in the same book, or they may have been separate such as the Common Law Order Book, Chancery Order Book, Probate Order Book, Superior Court Order Book, etc. Sometimes court orders were mixed with court minutes. Typically the court orders were not as explanatory as the minutes. Succinct entries such as "the deed of Robert Rogers to John Jordan was ordered recorded," "the court ordered the matter continued," or simply "dismissed" may be the only notations.

One clerk's office (under various titles) may have kept the records of several courts (probate, civil, chancery, etc.).

Since early common law courts often heard a variety of actions, cases involving juveniles, criminals, and sundry civil matters may appear together in the same record book. In later times the county probably created separate order books for each type of action. Commonly seen on the courthouse shelves are records marked on the spine as "Juvenile," "Civil," "Adoptions," or "Criminal." Some (such as juvenile and adoption records) may be closed to the public.

COURT ORDER BOOK INDEX HINTS: While perusing the indexes in common law order books look also under "S" for State or "C" for Commonwealth (such as the Commonwealth of Virginia or

The record books of the Hustings Court from independent cities of Virginia (listed in Chapter 1 Page 3) include Hustings Law Order Books, Hustings Chancery Order Books, and others. Once a Circuit Court was established (and activities of the Hustings Court ceased) this independent city maintained Superior Court Chancery Books, Superior Court Law Order Books, Circuit Court Chancery Order Books, Circuit Court Law Order Books, and Corporation Court Chancery Orders. The unwary genealogist, not realizing this, would miss records if not examining them all. Some of the other independent cities have a similar situation. Try to ascertain a listing of their early microfilm from their website, or at the Family History Library website (see Chapter 11 Page 170).

the Commonwealth of Massachusetts).[7] Under those subjects you will find actions of the government against individuals which often involved juvenile or criminal matters.[8]

DOCKETS. The dockets (or in some states a Register of Actions) were normally calendars of causes prepared by clerks, to be tried in a specified term.[9] They usually listed cases in the order to be heard and often were accompanied by the assigned file numbers.

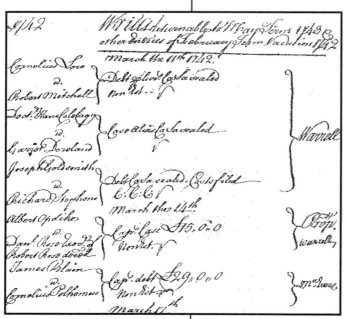

Figure 8-2. The above is a typical docket, listing a variety of cases in 1742. Listings in a docket are brief, usually showing the parties, the nature of the case, and perhaps the attorney. They often list a file number (though the above did not) which can lead to the original file packet. When the file number is lacking, the case has probably been filed by the term of court, in this case, May Term 1742.

Among the dockets in the civil department are appeal dockets, appearance dockets, common pleas, divorce, ejectment, execution, judgment, justice of the peace, judgment, liens, and others.

Dockets can help in locating the original file, either by file number or the court term shown in the docket. The docket is more cumbersome to use because it is not organized by names, but it still can be effectively used. You may have to check through many pages of entries of the pertinent time period, but finding a case involving your family can be worth the time involved.

Dockets can provide diverse clues when other records fail. For example, Bennet Rose did not appear in existing court indexes of Surry County, North Carolina. He was not a landowner, and thus absent from deed indexes, too. Further, it appears that he did not own sufficient property, either real or personal, to require that his estate be probated. He did appear on some tax lists in the early 1770s, which was the only proof that he had even been in the area. Finally, he was located by resorting to a page-by-page search of dockets at the State Archives in Raleigh.

> Surry County, North Carolina   #90
>   Trial Docket New Actions Aug. Term 1775
>   Benjamin Cleavland vs. Bennet Rose TAB[10]
> "Executed & broke Costody"
>
> Causes for Trial Nov. Term 1775 #90
> Benjamin Cleavland vs. #110
> Bennet Rose TAB Aug. 75 [case started], judgt for Deft

---

[7] In Virginia court records the abbreviation of C.W. or CW is commonly used for Commonwealth.

[8] Watch for the abbreviation of "NG" (Not Guilty) on these criminal or juvenile actions.

[9] In some areas the dockets have evolved into a brief summary or listing of the important actions in a case.

[10] TAB refers to *Trespass vi et armis*, that is, trespass with force and arms. This was a common law action for damages for any injury committed by the defendant with direct and immediate force or violence against the plaintiff or his property. In this case, the judgment was for the defendant. No explanation of the details was given, but the number 90 was probably a case number though that file has not been located.

Three years later in 1778[11] the Cleavland vs. Rose case appeared again—this time in the Execution Docket (described later on this page). A notation was included "in Wilkes County." These dockets supplied details not available elsewhere.

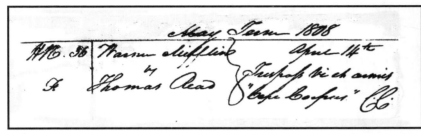

Figure 8-3. From an 1808 Appearance Docket in Delaware, another case of trespass vi et armis.

Another example demonstrating the value of dockets, in "The King vs. Sarah Barret."

> Criminal Action Papers Surry County, North Carolina [12]
> Surry County at Inferior Court August Term 1772, Sarah Barret late of the parish of St. Jude in the county aforesaid, spinster, on 7 August 1772, "one red pide [pied, i.e., patchy, splotched in color] cow the property of Oza Rose being found did milk and the said milk did take & carry away against the peace of said Lord the King his Crown & dignity."

Sarah's action created a record proving that Oza [known to be Hosea Rose] was in the Surry County area by August 1772, a number of years prior to the heretofore known date established for him in that area. (We also now know he owned at least one red color splotched cow!)

Execution Books. Contains information involved with the execution of a judgment. It lists property seized, property sold to cover the judgment, and other relevant details.

Fee Books. The clerk of the court noted the fees collected for the recording of various papers and other actions in these books.

Judgment Books. A book required to be kept by the clerk among the records of the court for the entry of judgments. (May be called a Judgment Docket.) For instance, in a suit for damages if the Judge ordered the defendant to pay $20 to the plaintiff, that information was entered in the Judgment Book. (In early times it may not have been a separate book; judgments may have been combined with other books, particularly the execution book when someone tried to recover the judgment.)

---

[11] It is presumed that Benjamin Cleavland's revolutionary war service was the cause of the intervening abatement.

[12] Loose criminal documents have often been transferred to the state archives. The Cleavland vs. Rose example given was located at the state archives in Raleigh, North Carolina.

Indictment Record. This is a record book which includes indictments returned by the grand jury in criminal offenses. The information varies but can include, besides the name of the defendant, the age, address, and more.

Jury Register. Comprised of the names of persons summoned for jury duty. It can include the name of the juror, the case for which he was summoned, and even the distance traveled. At times it is possible to get some idea of where the family lived by their distance from the courthouse. In earlier records jury lists were often among the court minutes.

TYPE OF DOCUMENTS

You will encounter many different types of records. A few of the most common are described briefly here.[13]

Affidavit. A voluntary written or printed statement of facts, confirmed by the oath or affirmation of the party making it. An affidavit is made before a person who has the authority to administer oaths.

Answer. The defendant's (or respondent's) written defense to a complaint (or to a bill).

Bastardy Bond. This type of bond was used in some states. It was a promise by the father of an illegitimate child to pay support. (These bonds were to protect the public from the expense of assisting an unmarried mother in raising her children. When the pregnancy was reported to the court, the expectant mother was questioned. When she named the father, he was summoned and posted bond to guarantee his support of the child. If she refused to name the father, a member of her family usually posted the bond guaranteeing the support. Lacking this, she could be confined.)

Bill. The first written pleading in an equity action, otherwise, the complaint in those actions.

Certified Copy. Copy of a document or record, signed and certified as a true copy by an officer in whose custody the original is entrusted.

Citation. A written order commanding the person named to appear on a specific day and take some action as specified in the order, or show why he should not take that action. Citations were published in at least one newspaper if the location of one or more of the parties were unknown.

Complaint. The original or initial pleading which starts an action, setting forth the facts of the claim.

For an example of a citation, in 1853 in Hunterdon County, New Jersey, a citation was issued to Catherine Swallow, Eliza Reading, Mary Ann Swallow, William Swallow, Martha Swallow, and Lucy Swallow, regarding the account to be heard in the estate of Bartlett Swallow, deceased. A wonderful listing of the heirs of the estate, or of the next of kin.

---

[13] As always, consult a law dictionary.

Decree. A declaration of the court announcing the court's judgment.

Deposition. The testimony of a witness taken in answer to either oral or written questions. The person who is deposed (otherwise, the person whose testimony is being taken) is called the deponent. (Often seen in records of will contests and other disputes.)

Exemplified Copy. Copy of a document which has been authenticated under the seal of a higher court or supervisory officer.

Injunction. A court order prohibiting a specified act or commanding someone to undo a wrong or injury.

Judgment. The official decision of a court in an action.

Memorial. A document presented to a legislative body or its executive containing a petition or a statement of the facts.

Show Cause Order. An order issued by the court requiring the appearance of a person to show why some action should not be confirmed or take effect. Also referred to as an "Order to Show Cause."

Summons. Notifies a defendant that an action has begun against him and that he is required to answer at a certain date and place within a certain time.

Writ. A written court order directed to the sheriff or other judicial officer to do what is commanded by the writ or see that it is done. See example of a writ in Figure 8-4 below.

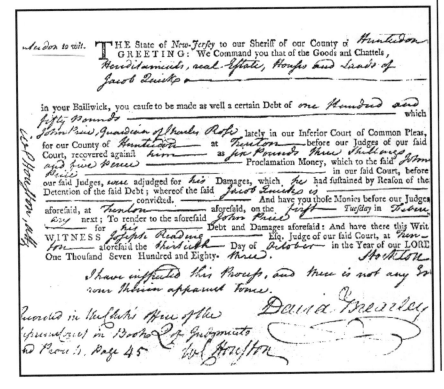

Figure 8-4. To the left is a writ, commanding the sheriff to seize some goods to cover a debt owing to John Price as the guardian of a minor to whom the debt was due.

CIVIL COURT INDEXES

The minute books and the court order books (discussed in this and earlier chapters) are among the earliest of court records. Unfortunately, the minute books were rarely indexed. The court order books are more likely to have an index, but usually only the plaintiff was indexed and not the defendant. And unfortunately, if there were multiple plaintiffs or defendants, usually only the first one was indexed. To further complicate matters, indexes that do exist were usually created for each individual minute book, necessitating a time-consuming search.

If an index is available, it should be either in the front or the back of the minute or order book or in a separate notebook which has been inserted into a slot on the inside of the front cover. (Look around the shelves. The present clerk may have removed all of the notebook style indexes and stacked them together in a pile. Researchers using them probably did not keep them in any order.)

To determine if the index is only for plaintiffs and omits defendants, examine a few indexed entries. Are any marked "ads." (*ad sectam*)[14] instead of "vs." (*versus*)?[15] If so, you know that the index does include defendants.[16]

If you note your ancestors' name in the index followed by several page numbers, follow through on every entry pertaining to the matter. Each may add details.

If there is no index you may still be in luck. Check at the local library to ascertain whether someone has abstracted and published the county's court minutes or court orders. The publication's index should prove to be more helpful than the original index. The published index will include all the names mentioned in the abstracts instead of just the principal names that appear in the original index. A caution—the published index is only as accurate as the abstractor's skill in reading the old writing and in abstracting. (And even if the abstractor is knowledgeable, the printer might err.) If the original index still exists, use both the published and the original to be sure you don't miss an important action.

By the mid-1800s many areas had instituted separate plaintiff index and defendant index books in their civil offices.[17] From that point forward you won't have to check each book individu-

---

[14] As an example, a case marked "John Smith ads. George Carson" indicates that John Smith was the defendant and Carson the plaintiff. An "ads" index would be indexed in this case under John Smith.

[15] In some areas the local custom was to use "adv" to indicate the opposite of versus, instead of "ads."

[16] When you copy the indexed entries be sure to note whether it is "ads." or "vs." for you may need that information to locate the papers relating to the case.

[17] "Civil side" is used in some places in referring to courts with both civil and criminal jurisdiction, just as "law side" is used for combined law and equity courts.

ally—the indexes will include a span of years, perhaps twenty, thirty, or more. Each entry will be comprised of the name of the parties, the type of action, date, and the reference to the book and page number where the clerk transcribed the document. If a file packet was created, a file number or designation is shown.

In an action without a defendant, the principal person was indexed in the plaintiff index only. As an example, if John Volvaire posted a bond to guarantee the performance of his official duties as a constable, the matter would be indexed under his name in the plaintiff index.

THE FILE PACKETS: Civil and Criminal

Loose clerk's documents for civil or criminal cases are an asset to the genealogist. You may find packets ranging from matters in debt, trespass, and countless others. Similar to the loose packets previously described in Chapter 4 for probate records, loose civil papers were folded and inserted into "jackets" bearing at least the names of the parties, type of action, and date.

Indexing and filing of loose packets. The packets were indexed and then filed in metal or wooden filing boxes. These may still line the walls of the office or may have been moved to attics, basements, or other storage rooms.[18]

Look for an index created specifically for the civil and criminal case files. Or, the file numbers may be part of a general index which includes book and page references, and also the file number. Another alternative is the docket. In using the docket look for numbers (usually at the top left or top right) on each docket entry. Those numbers should lead you to the original file packet.

Note all the information from the index to facilitate finding the loose papers.

We have discussed in other chapters how file boxes can be labeled by a box number, by file numbers, or by initial letter of surname. In the Civil office you will find yet another common label—by the term of court. One box might be labeled "Jan. Term 1846–May Term 1846." Within that box the packets might be arranged by file number, or surname, or just filed randomly by the term of court. If you have not noted the term of court from the index to the packets, you will need to go back and get that information from the index. Again, always note from the index all the details given. It is frustrating when you are in the attic or basement looking for the file to realize that you need to return to the main floor to get another piece from the index.

"The said Samuel ..."
Documents are full of the word "said." The body of a deed refers to the "said" John Gordon, a will states that the testator had a son named George, and later bequeaths a cow to the "said" George. Do we need to include all those "saids"? Are they ever important? Well, yes and no. If you read the document, and the "said" is only referring to someone earlier in the document and there is no problem in identifying to whom it refers, leave it out of the abstract. But, sometimes it *does* matter. Let us say that Joseph Shafer, Leonard Shafer, Mary Foster late Mary Shafer, and Jonathan Shafer petition the court for some purpose. They are shown as the petitioners. They state that Bernard Shafer died intestate leaving a widow Hannah and "eight children, including the said petitioners." Now the word "said" is important! Though the petitioners hadn't been identified as children previously in the document, the above quoted clause proves that they were children. Include it in your abstract when such situations arise, enclosing it in quotes so there is no misunderstanding.

From the case file index note:
- Name
- Date
- Box Number or designation
- File Number if any
- Term of Court

---

[18] A number of courthouses are now removing the files from the tin boxes, carefully unfolding each paper, and inserting them in manila folders.

Chancery Papers. Among the most useful of the loose papers are the chancery records. This court was a court of equity hearing diverse controversies, often involving your ancestors. All manner of complex family disputes, imbued with genealogical gems, are found among these papers. Spousal support, some partitions[19] of land—these and more will fund your store of bits to reconstruct your family's life. Was your ancestor a town merchant who often appeared in these records as a plaintiff? Was he constantly at odds with others as revealed by multiple equity cases? These actions should never be overlooked.

You will probably find separate indexes to the chancery cases. There may even be multiple chancery indexes—perhaps an index to chancery causes, another marked "Ended Causes" or "Ended Land Causes" for those cases which were concluded, and others.

In the indexes, look for book and page references for documents transcribed by the clerk, and look for file numbers for the original case papers. Chancery courts often encompassed more than one county. If the courthouse records burned in the county where your family lived, some chancery papers involving them may be in a court of another county in the area.

TERMINOLOGY

The following list is a few selected terms you will encounter as you peruse the suits and cases. There are many more.[20]

Abatement. An entire overthrow of a suit, so it is ended. (In Westmoreland County, Virginia, in a case of John Rose vs. John B. Steel for slander, the "cause abates by death of defendant." Thus, the suit is ended for one of the parties is deceased.)[21]

Action at Law. According to law, as opposed to an action in equity. `

Ads. Abbreviation for *ad sectam*, at the suit of. Often seen in early indexes to indicate the defendant. Thus, John Brown *ads.* William Loftin indicates that John Brown is the defendant and William Loftin is the plaintiff.

Assault and Battery. (AB) Assault places the victim in fear of harm, other than by words alone, while battery is an unlawful touching of another without justification or excuse. (This type of action was far more common in the early records than we might first suppose.)

The courthouse burned? Perhaps there was a chancery case involving the estate, property, or family. If the chancery court covered several counties, copies of those valuable documents may still be in existence.

---

[19] Though partitions of land can be a result of an equity action, those that arise out of inheritance are generally handled in probate rather than in equity.

[20] Consult a legal dictionary for those not in this list or for more detailed explanations.

[21] Under some circumstances abatement can also mean a suspension of the proceedings, rather than an overthrow of a decision based on an error. For example, if you sued someone in state court to recover damages for injuries sustained in an automobile accident, and while that lawsuit was pending the defendant filed for bankruptcy protection in federal court, one of the attorneys would file a motion in the state court to *abate* the proceedings pending resolution of the bankruptcy action. Once the bankruptcy proceedings were concluded, the Order of Abatement in the state court could be vacated (or lifted), and the case would be resurrected. All of this creates paperwork, which may name your ancestor.

Assumpsit. A promise by which one person undertakes to do some act or pay something to another person.

Bill. In an equity action, a complaint.

Certiorari. A written order issued by a higher court to a lower court to produce a certified record of a particular case.

Chattel. An article of personal property (as distinguished from real property.)

Civil law. Laws concerned with civil or private rights, as opposed to criminal laws. This is distinguished from common law.[22]

Common law. Based on usage and precedents, common law is distinguished from statutory law which is created by legislation.

Common law action. Action governed by common law, rather than statutory, equitable, or civil law.

Complainant. One who files a complaint (that is, the plaintiff).

Consanguinity. Kinship or blood relationship. The connection of persons descended from a common ancestor.

Contract. An agreement between two or more persons which creates a legally enforceable obligation to perform or not to perform a particular act. Certain criteria must be met to make it legal.

Coram. Before; in the presence of.

Co-respondent. Normally, in a divorce suit, a person charged with having committed adultery with the defendant.

Court of Record. A court whose proceedings are required by law to be kept on permanent record.

Demurrer. A defendant's allegation admitting to the facts in a complaint or bill, but claiming that those facts are not sufficient for the plaintiff to proceed or for the defendant to answer.

Detinue. This is an action to recover personal chattels from someone who had lawfully acquired possession but who then retained it without a right to do so.

Ear mark brand. A brand for one's livestock, registered so that its owner can be identified. For example, in Kershaw County, South Carolina, in 1832 Wiley Kelley appeared and made oath that his mark of stock for cattle, hogs, sheep, etc. was a crop and a hole in one ear, and a crop and half moon in the other ear.

Ejectment. An action to restore possession of a piece of property to the person entitled to it.

Emancipation. The act of freeing someone from bondage or restraint.

Endorsement, indorsement. When a holder of a negotiable instrument (a check, note, etc.) signs his name on it, thereby assigning or transferring it to someone else.

---

[22] The definitions given here for Civil law and Common law are very basic. The subject is far more complex and the terms can be used differently in states based on the common law of England, as opposed to, for instance, Louisiana, which is based on civil law. Those interested in a pursuit of this subject should consult a law dictionary, or law journals.

Equity. Justice administered according to fairness.

Estray. Usually defined as a wandering animal whose owner is unknown. (Seen c in early records especially.)

Ex parte. Done for or on the behalf of, one party only. An ex parte hearing is one in which the court hears only one side of the controversy.

Execution. Carrying out a court order until its completion. For example, execution of a money judgment is the legal process which enforces the judgment and can result in the seizure and sale of personal or real property, or both.

Feme covert. A married woman.

Feme sole. A single woman, including those who have been married, but whose marriage has been dissolved by death or divorce. (In some instances women who are judicially separated from their husbands.)

Fiduciary. A person or institution who manages money or property for another. Includes executor, administrator, trustee, and guardian.

Fieri facias (Fi. Fa.; sometimes FF). Literally, "you are to make it to be done." A writ directing the sheriff to satisfy a judgment from the property of the debtor. Originally used for the seizure and sale of personal property, but eventually enlarged to include real property.

Habeas corpus. An independent proceeding instituted to determine whether a defendant is being unlawfully deprived of his or her liberty. For example, in Montgomery County, Ohio, on the 1895 Civil Docket C. W. Eliff made application of habeas corpus for the production of the body of Henry Rose, declaring the "sheriff has same." Testimony was heard and Henry Rose was found unlawfully imprisoned and ordered discharged.

Imparlance. A continuance given to either of the parties to answer the pleadings of the other.

In room of; in the room of.. Instead of. For example, in Brunswick County, Virginia, in the Court Order Book of 1745 it was ordered that William Adam be appointed constable "in the room of" Thomas Rose. As soon as William was sworn, Thomas was to be discharged.

Indenture. In real property transactions, a deed in which two or more persons enter into obligations to each other.

Indictment. A formal written accusation originating with a prosecutor and issued by a grand jury against someone charged with a crime.

Instant (inst.). Indicates that the date referred to was in the same month as a previously mentioned date. In a newspaper notice of 25th April 1832, if the marriage took place on the 12 inst., it took place 12 April 1832.

Judgment. The official decision of a court in an action or suit.

Malfeasance. The commission of some act which is positively unlawful.

Manucaptor. In early records a person who assumed the responsibility for the appearance of a person under arrest.

Manumission. The act of liberating a person from slavery or bondage.

Orator. The plaintiff in a chancery action. (The term is generally no longer used and the orator is simply called the plaintiff.)

Ordinary. In some states, the judge of the probate court. Those states which used this term (such as Georgia) have generally now abandoned it.

Parcener. A joint heir; one who, with others, holds an estate before the inheritance has been divided.

Partition. The division of property between several co-owners. Usually starts with an action in a court of equity. The plaintiff(s) asks the court to sell the jointly-owned property and divide the proceeds, or to divide the property among those co-owners.

Redemption. Usually means the right of a person to repurchase his property which has been sold at a forced sale because of a judgment.

Release. A written or oral statement discharging another from a duty or a payment.

Replevin. An action by which the person is entitled to repossess goods from someone who has wrongfully taken or detained those goods.

Respondent. One who responds to a complaint or bill (otherwise, the defendant). Usually used in court of equity causes.

Scire facias. (Sci. fa.) Most commonly, a writ directing the debtor to appear in court and show why a judgment against him should not be revived. Alternately, a writ to have the judgment executed. (In most states this has been abolished.)

Security. That which is offered to guarantee the performance of a contract (written or oral); also, one who undertakes to fulfill or guarantee the obligation of another. Actions involving securities may contain family information. For example, in 1748 in Brunswick County, Virginia, the petition of John Ward and John Rose, who were securities for Mary Woods, state that as securities they are "now apprehensive." The court ordered William White who had married Mary, and Mary herself, to give the petitioners counter security. This action, instituted because the securities for Mary became worried about their financial responsibility after her remarriage, now provided proof of that remarriage in their action.

Statutory law. Created by legislature.

Surety. One who has contracted to be responsible for another person, especially one who assumes the responsibilities or debts of another person in case of default.

Tort. A civil wrong or injury.

Trespass. An unlawful interference with a person's property or rights. This was common among the early records but we are often left curious as to what happened. In Brunswick County, Virginia, in 1737 in an action of trespass between Sarah Daniel plaintiff and John Rose defendant, a jury found defendant Rose guilty of trespass and determined that the plaintiff had sustained damage in amount of *one shilling*. In a subsequent court Sarah Daniel was ordered to pay Lewis Parham for seven days of attendance for his evidence in the suit. A costly suit for Sarah considering the one shilling judgment!

Trespass vi et armis (TAB). Trespass with force and arms.

Ultimate; ultimo (ult.). In dates, refers to the previous month. A newspaper notice in May 1823 stating that a death took place on the 22nd ult. would indicate it took place 22 April.

Vacation of Judgment. The setting aside of a judgment entered in error.

Vagrant act. An act for the punishment of idle and disorderly persons. In King George County, Virginia, among the 1727 deed records is a statement that it was of the opinion of the court that John Rose and John Sacry "doth not come" under the Vagrant Act, but are drafted into "his Magesties

Service" to "make up the Number for this Countys Proportion [presumably for militia service]."

Verbi Dei Minister (V.D.M.). Preacher of God's Word.

Versus. Against. In the title of a cause, the plaintiff's name is put first, then "vs." and then the defendant's name.

In the next chapter we look more closely at the court process. This large body of records, often overlooked, is sure to assist in your quest for clues.

CHAPTER POINTS TO PONDER

✓ There are a number of local courts.

✓ There are a variety of record books in the civil and criminal department.

✓ There are numerous diverse court documents.

✓ Indexes may be nonexistent, but dockets can substitute as indexes.

✓ Criminal records can often be found among the civil records.

9 Civil and Criminal Court

Civil court records are often overlooked. Yet, their value is immense. Divorces, changes of name, naturalizations, adoptions, suits among family members—these and more provide insight into a family's life. Court actions may also explain why relatives are reluctant to share information about certain ancestors. When you encounter "secrecy," consider that perhaps either a criminal matter lies hidden, or there was perhaps a divorce or an illegitimate child[1] or something the family considered "shameful."

We need to use tact when trying to elicit details from family members. Our questions may be opening wounds which never healed.

CIVIL RECORDS

In civil actions those who are suing are "plaintiffs." Those being sued are "defendants." In courts of chancery (see previous chapter) the plaintiff is often referred to as the "Orator" or "Complainant." The defendant in equity cases is sometimes referred to as the "responder;" the judge as "Chancellor."

Not all court matters are adversarial; that is, many are not actions in which someone is being sued. Payments for wolves' scalps, the issuance of licenses to keep an "ordinary,"[2] appointments for Keeper of the Road and road hands to maintain the road were in their records, as were registrations for ear marks for stock and an array of others. Even the listing of names of the local militia could appear.

Nonadversarial actions can include:
- Adoptions
- Ear marks (for stock)
- Licenses
- Name changes
- Naturalizations
- Militia lists
- Payments such as wolves' scalps
- Road work appointments

The civil courts (in some states referred to as court of common pleas) handle such diverse activities as serving civil papers, bond validations, contract indebtedness, election returns, fictitious name applications for businesses, malpractice, mortgage foreclosures, indebtness, and others. Deputies serve subpoenas, writs, summonses, warrants in debt, show-cause orders, and can also

---

[1] Of course, there could be other reasons— the relative may really not know and be reticent to admit so little knowledge of the family, or there could be other motives for a reluctance to disclose details.

[2] A tavern or an inn providing meals.

execute evictions and levies on property. All of these actions and more create a dazzling array of records which family historians can use to illuminate the lives of their ancestors.

In some states and large counties there is a physical separation between the office handling civil cases and that which handles criminals. Other counties may house the records in the same office, or even hear them in the same court—for example, the Court of Common Pleas [civil] and Quarter Sessions [criminal]. Instead of naming a plaintiff and a defendant, as in civil cases, a criminal action normally names "The State vs. John Weiler" or, in colonial times, "The King vs. John Weiler."

To discover civil and criminal cases, examine the court minutes, summonses, judgments, executions, dockets, and anything else you can find on the shelves of the courthouse. In addition, look for file packets (described in Chapter 8). The original loose papers in those files should be the most illuminating. (See more on criminal actions later in this chapter.)

FINDING CIVIL COURT RECORDS IN THE COURTHOUSE

In some states the civil records are maintained by the County Clerk. In others it may be the Clerk of the Common Pleas Court, Circuit Court Clerk, or even Clerk of the Civil Office. If you are working in one of the few states with a Prothonotary (principal clerk of the common pleas court), that will be the office you seek.[3] If you still can't find it, ask, "Where is the office which handles the plaintiff and defendant cases?" Look for the early criminal cases in the same office; though sometimes they are maintained in a separate criminal office.

INDEBTNESS
Probably the most frequent court actions you will find as you examine the civil court records of your ancestors are those involving debt. The amounts sometimes are so small that we wonder how they could lose their land or their personal possessions for such sums. But they did.

Who was suing? Merchants, of course, instigated their share of court suits. But surprisingly, often the suits were among family members. Others were on notes given for loans, which were not repaid. Actions over debt created considerable paperwork. Court minutes, court orders, judgment dockets, execution dockets, writs of attachment, sale of the goods of the debtor—these and more fill the pages of the civil court records. Typical is the 1799

The records are full of instances where those who put up bond or gave security were forced to pay when a friend or relative in debt left the area.

[3] If the county has both a Prothonotary's Office and a Clerk of Courts office, the Prothonotary handles civil matters while the Clerk of Courts handles those of a criminal nature.

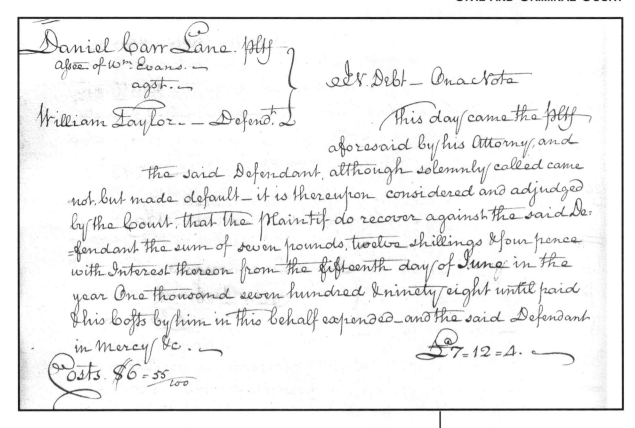

Figure 9-1. From a court order book, where three cases were listed on a typical page.

example in Figure 9-1, from an order book. On the same page were three actions: a Scire facias (to act on a judgment); the above illustrated suit involving a note; and the last on that page was again on a note. The record book was full of similar orders.

JUDGMENTS

When a judgment was ordered by the court, it could result in a number of different records. Any of these will, at the least, prove that your ancestor was indeed in the area or involved in some manner in the county.

In most cases the judgment was recorded in the court order book, or a separate judgment book. If the judgment was not paid (either by the plaintiff or the defendant, depending upon who won the case), the matter could proceed to a writ to execute upon the property of the debtor, and might even result in a public sale of the real property or personal property to the highest bidder. Or the debtor, if he felt the judgment was unfair, might appeal resulting in still more entries. The variety of "paper" that debts may generate varies depending upon the laws and procedures of the different jurisdictions. Look for them in the civil court office for, lacking any mention of your ancestor in other records, you might find him involved in those actions.

129

THE CIVIL COURT PROCESS

A simplistic outline of the court process will demonstrate the numerous opportunities for the case to have generated written records.

- A person filed a complaint (or a bill in an equity action).

- The court issued a summons to the defendant to answer in writing the complaint (or bill) within a certain time period.

- If the defendant did not answer as specified, judgment was entered in favor of the plaintiff by default.

- If the defendant did answer in writing in the time required, the case continued.

- If the case could not be settled between the plaintiff and the defendant, the case was heard in court. This could result in depositions of witnesses, and various other testimony, witness lists, etc.

- The court rendered a judgment. (Or, in the case of a jury trial, the jury rendered the verdict.) If money was awarded in the judgment, the party owing the money was required to pay.

- The execution: If a judgment for money was entered and not paid, the party to whom the funds were due could have the personal property of the debtor seized and sold to cover the debt. If that were insufficient, real property might be sold at a public sale to cover the debt. These actions generated paper including petitions to the court requesting the sale, newspaper notices, and postings at the courthouse and on the property.

Whenever there was a judgment against your ancestor, follow the paper trail to determine when the action started, when it ended, and every detail possible pertaining to the case.

Figure 9-2. The above is a summarized outline of the court process from beginning to judgment.

YOUR STRATEGY IN BECOMING ACQUAINTED WITH CIVIL COURT RECORDS

The list of record books could go on and on. Suffice it to say that your entry into the Civil Court Clerk's office will at first seem strange, if it is your first time in that section of the courthouse. Look around. See what books are on the shelves. Pick them up, see if they have an individual index in the book, or whether there is a consolidated index. Take time to look at any that are unfamiliar. That is how we all get our experience. You'll find that the clerks of that office are not used to having genealogists use their records. See what you can find on your own.

The best strategy is to work first with the earlier records in the Civil Court cases, feeling your way around. Get experience in those if you can, for it will then be easier to move forward to more recent records. The clerks will not be busy with the older records —you'll feel less intimidated doing your browsing. When you finish this chapter, reread the last one, and reread them both again when you plan that first trip into a Civil Clerk's office. It will be worth the effort to pursue their cases. Your "long lost" relatives might finally be found.

OTHER RECORDS WHICH MIGHT BE FOUND
CHANGES OF NAME
It is always surprising to find changes of name even among the early records. State statutes have many such notices. For example, Massachusetts' statutes passed in 1801 contained an act allowing Billy Hager of Marlborough, son of William Hager of Marlborough, to take the name of William Hager and also allowing Silvanus Coleman, the third one of that name, of Nantucket, son of Jonathan Coleman of Nantucket, to take the name of David Coleman. A number of others changed their names in the same act.

The place to look for the earliest of the name changes is in the House and Senate Journals of the states, or in the laws passed at each session ("session laws"). In later years you'll find them at the county level among civil court records.

TAX RECORDS
Tax records, especially the early ones, can boost significantly your efforts to place your ancestors in a certain location at a certain time. Records may include tax lists maintained for provincial taxes, county taxes, state taxes, and sometimes even for federal taxes.

Tax records can be useful in several ways. In addition to the above, the records can help us reconstruct the number of people in a family, proximity to others of the surname, and assist in tracking change of ownership among family members.

The records of county property taxes (real and personal) can consist of returns, assessments, and rates. This varies from state to state. Normally a warrant was directed to a constable or other appointed officer requiring him to draw up of a list of inhabitants. This list was to be returned to commissioners (or other designated body) by a given date. A list of taxables and the rates they were to pay was made in duplicate, one copy for the Tax Collector. Appeals were then heard. Then a second list of rates was prepared (again in duplicate), one going to the collector with a warrant to collect the taxes. Since this process created more than one tax list, if one is missing, you might find the duplicate.

At times the tax consisted only of a "poll." This poll tax was paid on free white males of a certain age, on non-whites of certain ages, and slaves.

Reasons for name changes can vary. In one 1800s case, several children changed their surnames because the father had been accused of murdering their mother.

When extracting information from a tax list, make a note whether the list was alphabetized. (I add just a brief notation "alphabetized" or "not alphabetized." as I copy the listings.) If it was alphabetized, some potential clues are lost. It's not possible to determine who the near neighbors were in such lists, though we do know they were in the same assessor's district. Wonder why the assessor took the trouble to go back through his list, alphabetizing the names? In some cases it was mandatory. Early laws in Virginia for instance required the tax commissioner to record "a fair alphabetical list."

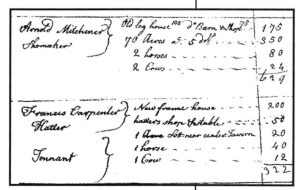

Figure 9-3. The above tax list from Chester County, Pennsylvania, is easy to read. Most lists are columnar, with descriptive headings at the top.

Ascertain from guidebooks or statutes who was subject to taxes. Otherwise the lists cannot be properly evaluated and interpreted. For example, in Pennsylvania early taxes were paid by: 1) householders (landowners and tenants); 2) inmates (a person residing within the household of another, either in the same house or in a building on the same property, and was married or widowed); 3) a freeman (single man over 21); and 4) a non-resident land owner. A typical tax list might include white male tithables over 21, white male tithables 16-21, and the number of slaves above 16 and under 16. Armed with the law's requirements, you can better understand the tax lists.

When your ancestor first appeared on the list of polls or tithables on a tax list, he probably had just achieved the age of sixteen. Be careful with this one though—the age varied from state to state and from time period to time period. Some of the tax records have specific columns for those 16-21, and those over the age of 21. It is also possible that his first appearance on the list is not because he just came of age, but because he just moved to the area.

How Tax Records Help You

The following is a demonstration of the usefulness of these records to calculate age, taken from Granville County, North Carolina, lists:

1749	Thomas Rose	3 (tithables)
1750	Thomas Rose Sr.	2 (poll)
	William Rose	1 (poll)
1752	Thomas Rose Senr. and Son Thomas Rose	1 (poll)
	William Rose	1 (poll)

With no other Rose in the same area we may infer that this is the family of Thomas Rose with two sons not yet sixteen in 1749. By 1750 the son William had turned sixteen and was therefore born about 1734. Two years later Thomas Sr. and his son Thomas Rose are listed and again William is listed. We can now conclude that the son Thomas (Jr.) had just turned sixteen and was therefore born about 1736.

This type of estimating is important. It's better to have some estimated range of dates than none at all.

In another example of the importance of tax records, the following was also located in Granville County showing Hosea Rose and John Rose in the same home. This type of coupling in the tax records is always an indication of a relationship between those of the same surname. The record proved important in placing this family in North Carolina in a heretofore unidentified location years earlier than their 1770s appearance in Wilkes County, North Carolina.

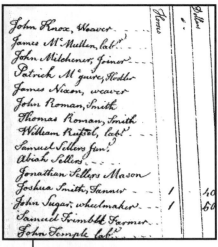

Figure 9-4. Tax records often list occupations, too, as demonstrated in the above.

> Tax, 1762-1763 – John Pope's list, St. Johns Parish
> John Rose   )
> Hosea Rose   ) 2 1762

WHAT WAS TAXED

It is fascinating to see what was taxed. As we might expect, in the early "poll" tax records white males were taxed (usually aged over 16), slaves, "colored," and also horses, cattle, mules, colts, and other livestock. Interestingly, for a time in Pennsylvania dogs were on the tax lists. (Though listed as "1 dog," "2 dogs," there was no tax actually assessed on them on the lists I personally examined.) Also, noted in the statutes was mention of a tax on squirrels and crows. At other times the luxury of windows and closets incurred taxes, as did whiskey, crops, watches, pianos, billiard tables, etc.[7]

LAND BOOKS

In Virginia you will find books labeled "Land Book" which are actually tax records. These will provide considerable information if studied closely and comparisons made from year to year.

The land books often showed the distance from the courthouse and the compass direction. In Sussex County, Virginia, in the 1840 land book Fielding Rose, listed as resident of Sussex, had 1051 ¾ acres on "Rackoon" Swamp, 9 miles south of the courthouse. Elizabeth Rose had 100 acres on Sappony Creek, 14 miles west of the courthouse. Shown as 1851 residents with land south of the courthouse were George Rose's 173 acres on Rackoon Swamp, Andrew Rose's 267 acres on Little Swamp, Virginia Rose's 173 acres on Rackoon Swamp. West of the courthouse was Elizabeth Rose's 100 acres on Stony Creek and Robert Rose's 100 acres

---

[7] Many of the state archives' websites include information on early taxes, who was taxed, and the ages.

on Stony Creek. These lists may provide the only clues to where in the county they lived. We can also make some inferences as to which were related.

In Fayette County, Kentucky, Mark L. Spotts district, the assessor included an explanation of "alterations" during the preceding year. In 1843 George W. Rose was listed with 90 ½ acres and 22 ½ acres on Howard's Creek, 13 miles east from the courthouse. Alterations in the preceding year, "Convd to Peter F. Rose ... one moiety[8] as an heir of Saml Rose dec'd." In 1844, also in Mark L. Spotts district, the Samuel Rose estate with Thos. Kirkpatrick executor appears on the tax list, with a notation that these taxes were "now charged" to George Rose.

TAX ASSESSOR

The tax assessor was normally responsible for ownership and location information, as well as tax maps for all properties.

Mapping provides listings of property owners. The information on which the maps and ownership are based was from recorded transfers of property and divisions of land. Tax maps show the boundaries of the parcel, the block and lot, the city or the town in which it is located, and various other information.

Some tax assessor maps are available for online viewing. Enter the name of the county in your web browser followed by the words "Tax Assessor." At the resultant website read the instructions on accessing these maps. Maps can consist of subdivision maps, surveyors' maps, and property ownership maps. When there is historic interest in the area, special maps might be available. For instance, in some of the Ohio counties within either the U.S. Military Tract or within the Virginia Military Tract,[9] special maps of those tracts are available in the those county courthouses.

In present times there is usually a separate Tax Assessor's office, and each parcel to be taxed is given a parcel number to facilitate identification. If you don't have a parcel number or if you are searching in a time period after addresses were assigned, try locating the map using that address.

Some states excluded persons who were aged, helpless, or those with limited income, from property taxes. This can still hold true. (For example, in California those with a very limited income can receive certain exemptions or reduced property taxes upon submitting proof of income.) In areas where exclusion was auto-

---

[8] One half or an equal part; sometimes an equal part of three parts.

[9] Bounty land was free federal land given for military service during various wars under acts passed between 1776 and 1855. (In the Revolutionary War, some states also allotted bounty land.)

matically allowed at a certain age, the notation in the minutes or orders to remove a resident from the tax list could be an indication that age had been attained. Treat this with caution, however, for as mentioned previously there could be other reasons the taxpayer was being dropped from the list. Even death.

When automobiles came into use, taxes on them brought in more revenues and created more records. In states that have a personal property tax specifically on motor vehicles, the tax assessor's office will have information on each vehicle registered. Usually, they obtain that information from the Department of Motor Vehicles of the state. Taxing of a motor vehicle is a relatively new tax and in many states this information is not open to the public.

TAX FORECLOSURES
Cases involving tax foreclosures were normally in the civil office, though the resulting deed of forced sale for delinquent taxes was recorded in the register of deeds office. Special indexes to tax sales may be maintained by the civil division. Those who did not pay their property taxes (or personal property taxes if the state imposed such a tax) would find their names on delinquent tax lists. Often these lists were published in the local newspaper and also available for public viewing in the civil office or in the tax assessor's office. Sometimes, the appearance of an ancestor on a non-payment list was the result of a move out of the area.

ROAD RECORDS
Road records consist of surveyor's maps, petitions of local residents either to build a road or to improve a road, and other related items. It is difficult to make a general statement as to where in the courthouse these records may be found. Usually, the early records which involve the appointment of a resident as "Keeper of the Road" to maintain a road and the appointment of "hands" to help him can be located in the court minutes and court orders. Sometimes separate books were later created for these records. Keep this in mind during your courthouse research. You may find record books on the shelves marked "Road Records," "Road Commissioner," or similar titles. If you don't, inquire as to which office houses these records.

ROAD COMMISSIONERS
The road commissioner oversaw construction and maintained the roads and bridges of the county. In the twentieth century these maintenance services were expanded to provide mowing along the roadsides, leaf pickup, removal of trees, and cleanup of ice and snow. Earlier records of road commissioners may be found among the records of the court of quarter sessions. Though that is a criminal court, it had responsibilities for some administrative duties. Later, this duty evolved to such a degree that in

many areas a separate division was required to handle road matters. Many of the county's men helped in this capacity—your ancestor perhaps was one of them.

CORONER'S RECORDS

The coroner handles deaths by suicide and those of a questionable nature. If it were determined that the death was suspicious or the cause undetermined, the case would be held for an inquest or for a jury decision. Some of the early coroner's records appear in the county's minute books.

Inquests into deaths were common. In 1654 John Rouse with Edward Bumpus and other inhabitants of Marshfield, Massachusetts, stated that they viewed a dead body (as part of an official enquiry). In 1788 jurors determined that a man named Ed who was "apparently drunk" (though the comment was marked through in the record) attempted to cross the "Monocasy" River and died by accidental drowning.

REGISTRAR OF VOTERS

In times past lists of registered voters and election returns were intermingled among court minutes and sometimes in court

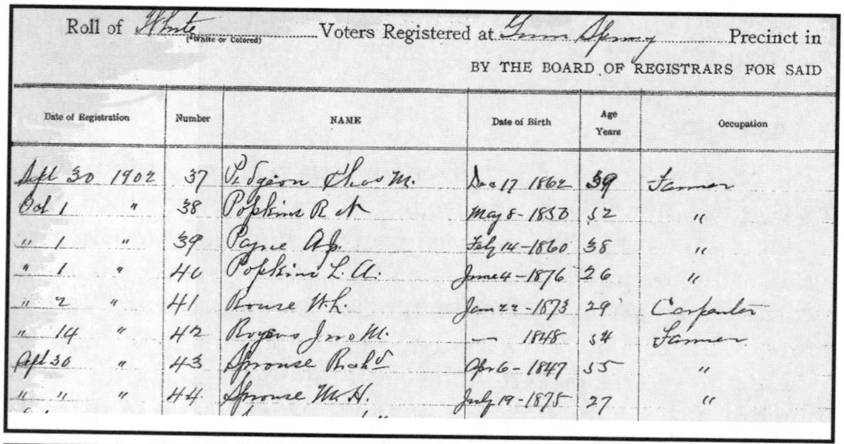

Roll of White (*White or Colored) Voters Registered at Green Spring Precinct in

BY THE BOARD OF REGISTRARS FOR SAID

Date of Registration	Number	NAME	Date of Birth	Age Years	Occupation
Sept 30 1902	37	Pidgeon Thos M.	Dec 17 1862	39	Farmer
Oct 1 "	38	Popkins R. A.	May 8-1850	52	"
" 1 "	39	Payne A. J.	Feby 14-1860	38	"
" 1 "	40	Popkins L. A.	June 4-1876	26	"
" 2 "	41	Rouse W. L.	Jan 22-1873	29	Carpenter
" 14 "	42	Rogers Jno M.	— 1848	54	Farmer
Sept 30 "	43	Sprouse Richd	Apr 6-1847	55	"
" " "	44	Sprouse W. H.	July 19-1875	27	"

Figure 9-5 (to the right) is the left-hand side of a voting register.

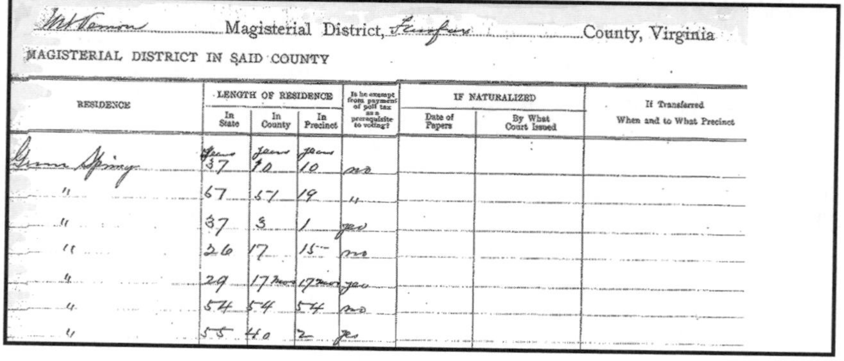

Mt Vernon Magisterial District, Fairfax County, Virginia

MAGISTERIAL DISTRICT IN SAID COUNTY

RESIDENCE	LENGTH OF RESIDENCE: In State	In County	In Precinct	Is he exempt from payment of poll tax as a prerequisite to voting?	IF NATURALIZED: Date of Papers	By What Court Issued	If Transferred When and to What Precinct
Green Spring	years 37	years 10	years 10	no			
"	67	57	19	"			
"	37	3	1	yes			
"	26	17	15	no			
"	29	17 mos	17 mos	yes			
"	54	54	54	no			
"	55	40	2	yes			

Figure 9-6 (to the right) is the right-hand side of the same voting register.

Figures 9-5 and 9-6 are the left-hand side and the right-hand side of the same document. This 1902 voting list in Fairfax County, Virginia, offers those looking for their families information on birth, age, occupation, residency in the county, and even a column for naturalization.

orders. Later, many counties established a separate Registrar of Voters office to create and maintain a list of registered voters. Additional information was added to the form required for registering to vote.

In the 20th century the expanded information included the voter's name, address, birthdate, and more. In some areas the lists are open to the public. If available, voters' records are among the most productive leads as you search for family members. Living descendants might be tracked through this source. Even when the contemporary records are now closed, you may find that the earlier lists are still available for viewing. Inquire at the Registrar's office in the county. This underused source is rich with potential value—see Figures 9-5 and 9-6 on the previous page, illustrationing that birthdate, age, and residency can all be on one convenient list. The lists may vary in content, but are sure to help if your family member is listed. Watch for these Voting Registers on the courthouse shelves and see for yourself the marvels they contain.

NATURALIZATIONS

Naturalization (or denizations[10] in colonial times) is the granting of full citizenship to those foreign born. Natives of English colonies did not have to establish citizenship. They were, though in America, living in a British colony. But others desiring naturalization (especially if they wanted to own land or to vote) had to take an oath of allegiance or otherwise establish citizenship. Some did so when entering the colonies while others made an affidavit or took an oath at a later time.

Before the Revolutionary War naturalizations usually were a mere notation in one of the court record books stating that the oath of allegiance was taken or that an order was issued granting citizenship.

After the Revolutionary War, when the new government was established in 1789, naturalization procedures were placed with the legislative branch. The first naturalization act by the federal government was passed 26 March 1790.[11] This act was limited to any alien who was a "free white person." That excluded slaves and indentured servants. The act also required that the person be of "good moral character," which was interpreted differently by different courts. The applicant had to be a resident of the United States for two years prior to the naturalization and be a one-year resident of the state in which he resided. Only then could he file a Petition for Naturalization with "any common law court of record."

---

[10]   To bestow citizenship upon an alien born.

[11]   1 Stat. 103, United States Statutes at Large.

Understanding the early procedure for naturalization will help us in locating records in the courthouse that pertain to our ancestor.

A subsequent act of 1795[12] changed the procedure and required five years United States residency and two years in the state of residence. Also, for the first time a Declaration of Intention (to become naturalized) was required.

Changes were continually instituted. A process developed[13] in which the Declaration of Intention became the "first paper," the Petition became known as the "second paper," and the third and "final paper" was the Certificate of Naturalization.

LOCATING THE NATURALIZATION PAPERS

Since the papers could be filed in any court of common law, there are a variety of courts in which you may find the record during your courthouse trip. Additionally, you may find that your ancestor's Declaration of Intention was filed in Iowa, while the final papers were granted five years later in another state. The scattering of the papers during the process and the uncertainty as to which court handled the papers, presents challenges in locating these treasures.

When you are in the courthouse, look particularly for books marked "Naturalization," "Citizenship," or "Declarations of Intention." Also examine the court minutes and court orders. Remember too, to look in all the offices of the courthouse; before 1906 any of the common law courts could have handled the process. (While you are at the courthouse look for clues to the existence of naturalization records in the voter's registers previously mentioned in this chapter and shown in Figures 9-5 and 9-6.)

How valuable are the papers?

In Santa Clara County, California, John Stark appeared on 18 July 1851 in the court of the 3rd Judicial District stating he was born 10 January 1790 in the county of Somersetshire, England, that he arrived in San Francisco 28 July 1850, and that he renounced allegiance to Victoria Queen of Great Britain and Ireland. "I have at different times resided in several different states within the last 40 years, when I left England." In another, Hugh Garside appeared in the Criminal Court of Sessions of Santa Clara County and declared that he was a native of England, aged about 44, arrived in the City of New Orleans, Louisiana, on 12 April 1849, then went to the City of Los Angeles, California, 25 December 1850. He renounced on 13 December 1852. Paul Vincent renounced his allegiance to the Republic of France on 28 September 1852; Jacob Levy renounced his allegiance to

---

[12] 3 Stat. 414, United States Statutes at Large.

[13] John J. Newman, *American Naturalization Records, 1790-1990, What they are and How to Use Them*, 2nd Edition (Bountiful, Utah: Heritage Quest, 1998). Another helpful booklet is John P. Colletta's *They Came in Ships: A Guide to Finding Your Immigrant's Ancestors Arrival Record*, Revised Edition (Salt Lake City: Ancestry, Inc., 2002.)

the King of Bavaria on 12 November 1852; Johnn Messerig native of Germany renounced his allegiance to the "Duke of Hass [Hesse] of Germany" in 1852; Ramon Abasalo emigrated from the Port of Valparaiso in 1849 and renounced the Republic of Chili; Antonio Parraga was born in Mexico in 1811, emigrated in 1849, and renounced allegiance to the Republic of Mexico. These few examples in Santa Clara County reflect the wealth of information that can be found. Though many of the Declarations show only the government being renounced and the date of the Declaration, there are many that supply additional details which add to the family's history.

NATURALIZATION OF WOMEN

In 1855[14] women who married a United States citizen, or whose husband became a citizen, acquired naturalization without going through a process required of others. A 1907 law added that a woman who was a U.S. citizen lost her citizenship if she married an alien. The act of 1922 separated her citizenship from that of her husband.

FORMATION OF BUREAU OF IMMIGRATION AND NATURALIZATION

In 1906 the Bureau of Immigration and Naturalization was formed and from that time forward the naturalization procedures have been under their direction.

The *Guide to Genealogical Research in the National Archives*[15] contains an excellent discussion of naturalization records and a state-by-state listing of records which have been transferred to NARA (National Archives and Records Administration) regional archives. These are in addition to the records that remain in the custody of courthouses.

Prior restrictions regarding photocopying, imposed by the federal government, have generally been removed, and now it is permissible to make copies. This is important to genealogists who may wish to have a full copy of the documents for their family memorabilia. Additionally, there are times when the photo attached to the papers as part of the naturalization process is the only photo now available.[16]

---

[14] Act of 10 February 1855. 10 (Stat.) 604. Provides that any woman "who might lawfully be naturalized under the existing laws, married, or who shall be married to a citizen of the United States, shall be deemed and taken to be a citizen."

[15] Anne Bruner Eales and Robert M. Kvasnicka, *Guide to Genealogical Research in the National Archives of the United States,* 3rd ed. (Washington, D.C.: National Archives and Records Administration, 2000), see Chapter 3.

[16] The inclusion of a photograph was a 20th century addition. In the author's family, the 1940 final paper of a family member holds the only photo in existence for him in his earlier years, for a fire destroyed all the family's belongings in 1952.

DIVORCES

For divorce actions before the mid-1800s,[17] try the state records. Look in the indexes of the senate and assembly journals for actions of "Dissolution of Marriage," "Divorce," or other similar title. Also check listings in the index listed as "Private Acts." You may find the parties to the divorces under that heading. And, check for the surname itself.

In addition, check the indexes of the statutes for the state, using the same technique as described above for the journals.

After the divorces came under the jurisdiction of county courts, locate them in the courthouse indexes of the civil office. Divorces can supply the marriage date, the location, names of children, possible relatives, and other helpful additions to your family search.

In some areas you may need the permission of the judge before accessing a divorce case. Be prepared, if necessary, to demonstrate how you are related to the individual you are seeking, and the purpose (genealogy of course!) of your search.[18]

A number of states also require that the final divorce decree to be filed with the state's Department of Vital Statistics. Check with that state department and ask whether they are filed there.[19] Michigan and New Hampshire started such divorce filings before 1900; others started later.

You should consider checking for a divorce proceeding when you know that the husband was living with one family in a federal census listing, and the wife living with another. (This doesn't prove they were separated, but is worth investigating.) Also, if you have a family in which the husband's will does not name a wife, but you find she is still living, the possibility of a divorce should be considered. Or you find the wife's tombstone showed she outlived her husband, but she wasn't listed in his home in the census. These and other situations could be a lead that there *might* have been a divorce, or a legal separation.

To obtain copies of the divorce proceeding or decree for divorce on the county level, get it while you are onsite or write to the county courthouse. Include as much of the following information as you have on the family, for it will make it easier for the courthouse personnel to identify your family.

Divorces in families were more common than we might suppose.

---

[17] The date varies from state to state. Some, such as Pennsylvania, were in county records much earlier.

[18] Several years ago a friend obtained a copy of the divorce of his ancestor, an attorney who had been divorced by his wife in the 1820s in New York City. He first had to obtain the judge's permission by presenting his family charts. When allowed to examine the divorce papers, he found that his ancestor had been guilty of adultery. He was impressed by the ruling—the court granted the divorce, but because it was adultery there was a provision that the wife could remarry as if the husband were dead, but he could not remarry until she *was* dead.

[19] Access the state's website information on vital records to ascertain when that state initiated its system of filing the Final Decree with the state.

- Full name of the husband and full name of the wife.
- Date of divorce or annulment.
- Place of the divorce—specifically the city/town, county and state.
- Type of decree if known.
- Your relationship to the parties.
- The purpose. (State this as genealogical).
- Your name, address, city, and state.
- Optional: Your telephone number and/or your email address.

Ask for a quotation for a copy of the decree. If you are seeking copies of all the papers in the file, the clerk may or may not assist. If not, hire a researcher to go into the courthouse if you cannot go there personally.

CAN'T FIND THE DIVORCE PROCEEDING?
You may be looking in the wrong place. Las Vegas, Nevada (among other locations) was a mecca for divorces because of shorter waiting times. Try the various counties in which the family lived, and if not located there, extend your search to other known havens for those seeking to end a marriage.

Some of the divorce meccas were small, nationally unknown cities, but well-known in the area for either relaxed laws, or unique locations for ceremonies. Inquiries might bring some of them to light.

CRIMINAL MATTERS
Actions in the criminal dockets can include bigamy, assault, murder, illegitimacy, and others. In a case filed in 1765 among criminal actions in Bucks County, Pennsylvania, Mary of Upper Makefield had delivered "two male Bastard Children." She came into court and named the father Jonathan, a brickmaker of Philadelphia, in order to obtain support for the children. Otherwise, she stated, their care was "Likely to Come Chargable To the said Township."

Not all matters which appear among criminal records pertain to a person accused of a crime. The witnesses summoned to testify in criminal actions created paper work starting with a summons or subpoena. They appeared on the witness docket or witness list and had their testimony recorded by the clerk.

A few examples—in Bucks County, Pennsylvania, a woman made the witness list for she was to give testimony in the case of the Commonwealth vs. Ulessus Kinsey and John Pettit. More records were created when witnesses received pay and were reimbursed their costs for "coming xx miles to court." Guards also appeared in the records.

In the Court Order Book of Montgomery County, Virginia, Israel Rose was paid "for Guarding a Criminal" for seven days at 50 cents. In another action in criminal papers, this one in 1785, a bond was issued to keep a "tippling house" (tavern). These are but a few of the proceedings that were non-criminal in nature.

THE "GAOLS"

It is unlikely that you will find early inmate records for jails (or "gaols") in separate books. The references will be scattered among the minute and court order books and the judgment dockets. You may also find among the minutes, payments to the "Keeper of the Gaol" for sundry expenses of the jail, and as previously mentioned, for the guarding of prisoners.

19th and 20th century records will be more easily available, and with some exceptions, are open to the public. Listings of prisoners, the nature of the charges, visitors, and much more are recorded.

BAIL BOND

Often found in the early records are bonds in which family or friends guaranteed the appearance of someone at court. Many times the accused person or a crucial witness left the area and his bondsmen (or securities) then had to pay the amount of the bond. These records might furnish your only proof that a person was even in the area. In Claiborne County, Tennessee, in 1814 Palmer Critchfield provided security for Samuel Rose's appearance to a case. Samuel Rose failed to appear and was ordered to appear in the next term. He still failed to appear. An order was issued in which Palmer Critchfield, (who had given security for Rose's appearance) was to show why the bond should not be forfeited. This created several entries in the minute books for a man who otherwise could not be proved to have been in the county.

DUTIES OF A CRIMINAL COURT CLERK

The system often evolved so that the clerk of the Criminal Division Office maintained all criminal related court actions including:

- Processing case files in adult and juvenile criminal matters.
- Processing appeals to higher courts.
- Collecting bail and maintaining records of bail.
- Processing and issuing bonds for the sheriff, deputy sheriff, constable, tax collector, and some others.
- Appointing court counsel.
- Issuing of private detective licenses.
- Considering petitions to seal or destroy records.
- Issuing bench warrants.[20]

---

[20] Most appearances in criminal court are mandatory. Failure to appear for a court appearance may result in a bench warrant (also called a capias) for arrest. A colleague reports his favorite: a "writ of body attachment," which requires the sheriff to attach and hold the body of the subject until he could be brought before the issuing judge—no other judge could grant bail.

JURIES

A jury consists of a certain number of men (and eventually women) selected and sworn to inquire into a certain civil or criminal matter.[21]

GRAND JURY. Receives complaints and accusations in criminal cases, hears the evidence, and returns bills of indictment if the jury is satisfied that a trial should be held. The number of jurors varies. A federal grand jury at the present is not less than sixteen nor more than twenty three persons.

INQUEST JURY. A body of persons summoned to inquire into particular facts.

PETIT JURY. The ordinary jury for the trial of a civil or criminal action; distinguished from a grand jury.

SPECIAL JURY. A jury ordered by the court to try questions of greater importance than those usually submitted to common juries.

TRIAL JURY. A jury summoned and impaneled for the trial of a case. In the courthouse many lists involving the naming of a jury will be scattered through the court minutes, court orders, and dockets. These are significant because they place the juror there at a specific time and indicate that he was of legal age. (In some cases it is also indicative that the juror was a property owner—check the state's statutes.)

CHAPTER POINTS TO PONDER

✓ Civil actions usually (but not always) include a plaintiff and a defendant.

✓ Not all civil actions are adversarial.

✓ The paper trail of a court case can lead to a number of varied record books and file packets.

✓ Naturalizations and divorces are an important part of civil records.

✓ Tax records can give clues on ages, inheritances, prosperity, occupation, and other tidbits of information.

✓ Criminal records can include a mention of your ancestor even if he did not commit a crime.

---

[21] There are no juries in equity cases— those are heard by a judge or chancellor.

10 BIRTH, MARRIAGE, AND DEATH

As genealogists we covet the discovery of those birth, marriage and death records which are the foundation of a sound family history. However, the paucity of early civil registrations often forces us to use substitutes. This chapter will help you find the records that exist in the courthouse, and will suggest alternatives when they don't.

REGISTRATIONS OF VITAL RECORDS

The scattered registration laws in the American colonies were largely ignored. New England states were the best in establishing a system, but even their colonial records are incomplete. As time passed, additional laws required civil registration, but met with mixed compliance.[1]

The level of registration did increase in the 1850s, and though discouragingly spotty, some listings are available. In some states laws for local registration were enacted and then rescinded, creating gaps until more stringent statutes were enacted.[2] About the 1870-1880 period compliance with continued new laws took an upward turn.

Some states, such as New York and Massachusetts, maintain their vital records in the town system, in spite of the fact that their land and probate records are maintained at the county level. Some others who maintain their land records by town (such as does Connecticut), maintain their vital records by town, also.

Also note during your research that some cities enacted procedures for vital record registrations before county (and later the state) registrations. Statewide registration was implemented mostly in the late 1800s and early 1900s.

Even though early vital record registrations were spotty, if your ancestor happens to be one of those whose record does exist, you will be thrilled!

---

[1] Massachusetts was the first to start town registrations in the year 1641, and the first to start statewide registrations in the year 1841.

[2] Pennsylvania required birth registrations in 1852, but rescinded the law in 1854 and didn't reenact it until many years later.

See Source References page 201 for *The Handy Book for Genealogists*, and the *Redbook*, previously mentioned. The latter has a helpful section on vital records in the individual state chapters which is particularly helpful.

WHICH COURTHOUSE OFFICE?

Local vital record registrations might have been handled through the county clerk's office, the civil office, a vital statistics office, or a local department of health. Records of marriages may or may not be kept in the same office as those of births and deaths. If you haven't ascertained the location of these records before you leave home, check the courthouse directory upon arrival.

When planning a research trip to a state where the vital records are under the jurisdiction of a town clerk, study your collected material to establish, if possible, the town or towns in which your family lived. If you can identify the towns, search on the Internet for the Town Clerk's website[3] to ascertain the address, hours, and other pertinent information. While at that Town Clerk's site look for the name of the Town Historian, too. In New York (and other areas which have them) the Town Historians are often local residents with a love of history or whose own families have lived in the town for generations.

Town Clerks may keep regular office hours, but Town Historians normally do not. Call for an appointment. Though you may not be allowed to view the record books in their entirety, the historian should be able to help you locate specific records on your family.

CITIES MAY KEEP THEIR OWN RECORDS

Many large cities (New York City, Baltimore, Philadelphia, and others) continue to maintain their own vital records, separate from the county records. The cities likely even started their registration years before the rest of the county.[4] If you're having difficulty finding the record you need, check *both* the city and the county. For example, if the family lived in Wayne County, Michigan, search both in Detroit records and those of Wayne County. If they lived in Hamilton County, Indiana, search both in Indianapolis and in Hamilton County records. Researchers are often surprised to find that their ancestors' records aren't missing. They are just in another jurisdiction in the county.

ARE THE RECORDS OPEN TO THE PUBLIC?

Accessibility laws vary. The trend now is to close the records, causing considerable dismay among genealogists as key documents are gradually removed from reach.

---

[3] Use http://www.usgenweb.org and follow links to the county. An alternate way to find the site is to enter into your browser's search feature the name of the town followed by the state and the words "Town Clerk." As an example, enter: Alfred New York Town Clerk. Note that Town Clerks' offices may not be open daily.

[4] Additionally, a few cities maintain their records apart from the state records. The booklet and website mentioned later in this chapter should be consulted.

Usually the early marriage records are available for examination even if births or deaths are not, although there are exceptions. Sometimes the marriage index is open, but not the marriage certificates. If the records are still open, usually the period of privacy is 75 years, If so, you'll be able to view those with earlier dates.

Policy differs from state to state and county to county. In some courthouses, when you find the indexed entry, the clerk will allow you to examine that particular record. The clerk may watch to be sure you don't turn pages to view others without their authorization. Conversely, in some areas, you won't be allowed to see the record before purchasing a copy from the clerk. And in some counties, certain data may be blocked out so that the public cannot access that specific information. This is especially true of birth records which note illegitimacy or adoption, and death records which include notations of insanity or social diseases.

The state may impose additional requirements. In at least one state you must you be a member of a genealogical society based in that state in order to view the records.[5]

If you have difficulty personally accessing records in the county, the early local vital records may also be available on microfilm through the Family History Library (see Chapter 10). Copies of that county's microfilm will probably also be in the local library or local genealogical society of the county you are visiting.

REGISTER BOOK INDEXES AND THEIR ORGANIZATION

Before statewide registrations were required, civil registration of vital records was recorded in local register books. Normally, the indexes to the register books were maintained in separate index books, though in some registers the index can be found in the front or back of that register.

Record books were maintained by dates of *registration* of the events, not the dates they occurred. Often the assessor or other court appointed official kept a list of births or deaths for his district, and every few weeks he delivered the list to the clerk for registration. Or perhaps a family member, weeks or months after the birth or death, reported the event to the clerk. With marriages, the minister or other official who performed marriages was required to bring the certificate (or a listing of those he married) to the clerk for recording within a certain time period. Compliance with the time period was poor and in some instances, not done at all.

---

[5] It is a good practice to take your membership cards with you so you'll be prepared. And read the guidebooks (see Source References page 201) to see if restrictions apply in the state you are to visit.

Births and deaths were indexed under the newborn, or the decedent. Marriages were indexed either by groom and again under the bride, or only under the groom. If there is no bride index,[6] check library catalogs to see if anyone has published the marriages of the county, for that publication's index will include the brides, too.

When using a marriage index it is possible that the grooms are in the front part of the index and the brides in a second index at the back of the book. Or, the grooms may be on the left hand page, while the brides are on the right hand page. They may both even be on the same page, entered chronologically and indexed by surname as the marriages were reported.

TRANSCRIBING AND ABSTRACTING VITAL RECORDS

Once you have located a record, a reminder. When you transcribe it, do not add punctuation. This becomes crucial with names. Two daughters with middle names may appear to be three or four daughters if commas are indiscriminately inserted.

Take care while abstracting as in transcribing, especially in records that could provide proof of the event if properly quoted. Note the following example which could be used as proof of birth. The executors of Charles Lewis deceased in 1847 in Loudoun County, Virginia, deeded to George Rose and Elizabeth his wife and their "four single daughters, Ann Douglas Maria Conner Harriet Francis and Jane Eliza Rose." If the word "single" had not been included in the abstract it would be easy for the reader to believe that Ann had married a Douglas, Maria had married a Conner, and Harriet had married a Francis. And, without the word "four" some problem could have arisen with the number of daughters. An addition of commas could also have distorted the figure. The best way to include clauses that might be misunderstood is to quote them exactly and enclose them in quotation marks.

BIRTH RECORDS

In the southern states civil birth registers were not prevalent until the latter half of the nineteenth century. Researchers with New England ancestors fare much better, for their registers of vital records started much earlier.

The earliest pre-state registration records of birth usually only provide the name of the child,[7] birthdate, name of parents, and perhaps the township or district of residence. Over time the

You'll fare better with records from heavily populated cities which generally antedated those of the county.

---

[6] Look through the index to spot whether there are any female names. If not, you have a groom index. Look around the courthouse shelves, there may be a separate bride index. If you don't find one, ask the clerk.

[7] Though even the name of the child may be omitted and the record could show "unnamed."

questions put to the informant were expanded and might include among others the maiden name of the mother, ages of the parents, the parents' residence, where the parents were born, and their occupations. If the child had not been named at birth, the entry will usually show "unnamed male" or "unnamed female."

In the mid-1800s the existence of birth registers increased, partly because of various laws enacted. Some of the birth registers (especially starting in the late 1880s) often show not only the birth, but information on the parents including the father's occupation. The following are captions from a Pennsylvania birth register but is typical of many others in the mid-west and western states in the same late 1800 time period.

- Date of Record
- Name of Child
- Sex
- Color
- Name of Father
- Name of Mother
- Residence
- Occupation of Father
- Date and Place of Birth

DELAYED OR CORRECTED BIRTH RECORDS

Delayed Birth Records are filed after the event, sometimes many years later. They may be filed to correct an error, to add information, or to file a certificate that was not filed at the time of birth. A dramatic increase in such filings occurred after the social security law was enacted in 1936, in anticipation of social security benefits. Security clearances for work connected with a war was also a contributory factor. To file such a certificate, affidavits were required to substantiate the additions or corrections, but once the clerk was satisfied, a delayed certificate was recorded. These certificates are usually kept separately and are easy to overlook if you're not watching for them.

OTHER COURTHOUSE DOCUMENTS CAN SUBSTITUTE FOR BIRTH RECORDS

You will find ways to circumvent the problem of no birth records. The family Bible, census, the gravestone, old letters, military files—these and others can help. Since we are concerned here with what might be found in the courthouse, let's consider possibilities among those records. Assuming that you were unable to find a birth register for the time period, or your ancestor was not entered in the register, the following might help.

Guardianship. The proceedings involving guardianships often include an age. And you have an added clue if a minor was choosing his or her own guardian, as that normally indicates that the minor was at least fourteen.

In Onondaga County, New York, the Index to Guardians in the Surrogate's Office was even more help than usual because it

> If a child was unnamed, you can often combine another record with it (e.g., a Bible, etc.) to provide the name.

included the *date the minor would come of age*. Thus, researchers can calculate the birthdate for anyone on the list.

The Onondaga County listing:

NAME	REF.	DATE OF [COMING OF] AGE
Howard E. Rose	F p 178	Jan. 2, 1881
Lilly M. Rose	F p 261	Aug. 3, 1880
Stella E. Rose	F p 633	Sept. 2, 1872
Edwin B. Rose	F p 635	Dec. 25, 1873
Malcolm R. Rose	G p 287	Oct. 5, 1873

Apprenticeship. Is your ancestor named in any apprenticeship record? If so, that should at least provide an age for him at the time of the apprenticeship enabling you to estimate a birthdate. Sometimes you will be even luckier. In Bute County, North Carolina, in 1769 the exact birthdate was established when Blackman Pardue, orphan, *14 years old next 14 October*, was apprenticed to William Reddock to learn the "business of a taylor."

Bastardy Bonds. These bonds were to protect the public from the expense of supporting an unmarried mother's child. The father of the illegitimate child gave bond for that child's support. If he did not follow-through, the securities on the bond were responsible for payment of the amount specified. For genealogists' purposes this provides the name of the father, and usually indicates an age for the child allowing for an estimated birthdate.

Deeds. In Bute County, North Carolina, a 1770 deed of 200 acres was recorded from Thomas Bell of Bute County to *Hugh Johnston orphan of Charles Johnston decd.* Although the age or date of birth are not given, this deed nonetheless can be used as proof of a birth for it names the father of this orphan. Additionally, we know the orphan was not of age in 1770 so, assuming 21 one was the legal age at the time, we can calculate he was born about 1750-1770.

In another use of deeds, they can establish a minimum age. Usually a male had to be 21 to convey land without a guardian. (He could, however, *own* land as a minor, as would happen with inheritances, entails, gifts, etc.) Assuming that when a man deeded land he was 21 you can then estimate a span of birth years, albeit a wide one.

There are sometimes exceptions under the law. Possibly the law allowed the grantor while a minor to make the deed, but the deed would have no effect or legality until the minor had attained the age of 21. Other exceptions could exist. If you have a perplexing case where the grantor appears to be underage, the statutes of the state may hold the answer.

Estates. Orphans named in an estate should at least establish which children were minors, and thus provide a range of dates. In Philadelphia, Pennsylvania, the matter of the orphans of David Rose was filed in 1808. Jacob Zigler was appointed guardian of Margaret and Benjamin Rose, minors above the age of fourteen, and of persons and property of Jonathan, David, Joseph and Ann Rose under fourteen, children of David Rose deceased. This means that the older children were born between about 1787 and 1794, and that the younger children were born about 1794-1808. Establishing at least some approximate dates will help in identifying these children in other records. If a Benjamin Rose appears in the 1850 census of the county as aged 47, we might consider that he could be the same Benjamin Rose of the court record and thus a son of David Rose[8] because we'd estimated the birthdate. Also, customarily the children were listed in the order of birth, but this cannot be relied upon. It is however another clue in reconstructing the above family.

LOCAL CUSTOMS HELP

Sometimes when a new family moved into a New England town, the births for the whole family were entered into the birth book upon their arrival. Errors may creep in when a record is not made at the time of the event, but nonetheless this listing is valuable. When encountering such a family recording, consider they *may* have just arrived in that town, though that is not necessarily the case. If so, then some of the family (if not all) were born elsewhere. In the Norwich, Connecticut, Birth Book for 1739-1824 we find recorded as a group:

Births of Thomas Rose of Norwich & Sarah Hariss of Plainfield
Margret dau. of Thoma[s] Rose & wife Sarah b. Feb. 4, 1742/3
Martha dau. of same b. July 25, 1744
Asa son of same b. May 25, 1746
Hannah dau. of same b. May 20, 1749
Thomas son of same b. Sept. 1, 1752
Sarah dau. of same b. Feb. 10, 1755
Elijah son of same b. July 26, 1757
Damaras dau. of same b. 29 July 1760
Bett*ge* [?] or Bettye [?] dau. of same b. Apr. 10, 1763

Research would be necessary to determine if they were all born in Norwich or had just arrived from another location. (Or even, whether the clerk had recopied entries.) The citation you include should indicate that the whole family was recorded together so that other researchers are alerted to the alternate possibilities on the location of the actual births.

---

[8] Further research would be needed to prove it, but the clues at least point in that direction.

The bride and groom can appear in a variety of marriage records, especially depending upon the time period.

MARRIAGES

Marriage records are not always in the same office in the courthouse as births and deaths. Check with the county recorder and the civil department.

In some states, marriage records considerably predate birth and death records. If it was the practice in the area to issue a license for the marriage, and the posting of a bond, you have several possibilities for records. The same couple could appear in at least three courthouse records: licenses, bonds, and the certificates. Though early records are incomplete, those that have survived have often been published in book form. However, your best records will be in the courthouse. The publications of abstracts often include only the names of the parties and dates, omitting such germane facts as the name of the person who performed (solemnized) the marriage, ages, number of previous marriages, and consents of a parent or guardian if one or both parties were underage.

THE PROCESS BY LICENSE OR BY BANNS

Those who chose to obtain a marriage license and post a bond followed a procedure:

- Application made and license issued.

- Bond posted.

- A minister, justice of the peace, or a judge performed (or "solemnized") the marriage.

- The person solemnizing the marriage completed the certificate with the date of the marriage, and by whom, and caused that certificate to be "returned" to the courthouse to be recorded.

- After the clerk entered the information from the marriage certificate into the marriage register, the original certificate could be claimed by the couple.

The other legal choice (in lieu of a marriage license) required the "publishing" (announcement) of the intended marriage in church weekly for three weeks[9] preceding the marriage. Called the banns of marriage, this process avoided the license and bond fees, making it a viable choice. This practice of publishing banns could explain why you have not located a marriage record. It also is one of the reasons it is important to establish the religious denomination of the family. If church records are still in existence, examine their church minutes and their church register. There may be a record in that source.

A justice of the peace, judge, or minister could perform the marriage after a license had been issued, or the banns published.

---

[9] The prescribed number of weeks differed from time to time.

MARRIAGE APPLICATION AND THE LICENSE

If a couple chose the process of marrying by license, an application for that license was made to the proper authority. A formal, written marriage application was normally a 19th century addition—before that time the application information was usually provided verbally to the clerk. The license was then issued permitting an authorized person to perform the marriage.

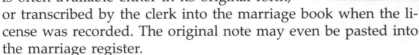

To obtain the license the parties declared they were of lawful age. Lacking that, the consent of a parent or guardian was necessary for minors. This could be done in person by a parent, or by a written consent. If written, it is often available either in its original form, or transcribed by the clerk into the marriage book when the license was recorded. The original note may even be pasted into the marriage register.

The license may have a clause in it that the bride and groom were not related closer than a specified relationship. The marriage of first cousins was permitted in most areas in earlier time periods, but is no longer allowed.

Be cautious about determining ages. The wording in licenses that the bride or groom "is of the age of 21" or "is of the age of 18" only means that he or she had attained the legal age for marriage in that area. The actual age could be much older.

In the mid to late 1800s information was expanded. We often find that the application or certificate will furnish such diverse data as the name of parents, where the bride and groom were born, where they resided, their ages, and their previous marital status (widowed, divorced, single). You won't find such complete applications for all marriages, but they are worth seeking.

An 1883 marriage in Montgomery County, Illinois, will demonstrate the value of the additional information provided as the requirements tightened during the progressing years. A license was granted for the marriage of William J. Sammons of Butler Grove, Montgomery County, Illinois, stating he was 21. This license permitted his marriage to Miss Alice M. Thalls of Litchfield, Montgomery County, aged 19. The return shows that Sammons was a farmer, white, American, that his father was Abner Sammons, and his mother's maiden name was Nancy C. Ketner. It was the groom's first marriage. The bride was identified as Alice M. Thalls, white, American, her father listed as James Thalls and her mother's maiden name as Hester D. Whitlock. It was the bride's first marriage, too. The return also stated that they were married at Litchfield on 15 August 1883, and that the witnesses were James Sammons and Nattie Axley. It was signed by C. [or E.] W. Souders, V.D.M.,[10] who performed the ceremony. When

---

[10] *Verbi Dei Minister*, Preacher of God's Word.

compilers abstract such records for publication they usually pick only selected information from the record, omitting many of the clues that would help you research this family. Searching for the record itself in the courthouse has many benefits.

MARRIAGE BONDS

Original marriage bonds, used primarily during the colonial period but in some areas through the 19th century, may now be housed at the state archives. However, the transcript of the county clerk should still be in the courthouse. As with any bond, the names of the bondsmen can lead to family relationships. The bondsmen usually included the groom, and one or two others, given to guarantee the groom's faithful performance of the bond.

The original bond had original signatures. Sometimes a consent for marriage was written on the bond, or attached to it.

Consents given for an underaged bride or groom can name fathers, mothers, and others. They are usually attached to one of the marriage documents or pasted in the register.

MARRIAGE CERTIFICATES

The person who performed the marriage had the marriage certificate recorded at the courthouse. As seen in Figure 10-1, this process was usually prescribed by law which specified how soon the event was to be recorded. (There were many exceptions and compliance was spotty.) This recording is sometimes referred to as the marriage "return." Besides the name of the parties and date, the certificate includes the name of the person who solemnized the marriage. If a minister married the couple he no doubt included the denomination with his signature. For example, "John Doe, M.G.,[11] Methodist-Episcopal Church." (or, as usually shown, M.E. Church). Now you can search for church records, too.

People with the same surname and married by the same minister (or justice of the peace) may be related—at least, it is a lead. Witnesses, if named on the certificate, should also be examined for they could be related. (In some certificates the relationship will be stated.)

The completed certificate was left with the clerk at the courthouse, usually by the person who performed the marriage. The couple could retrieve it after the recording though many original certificates were never claimed and are still in the courthouse to this day.

See the next page for Figure 10-1, a remarkable 1860 Virginia marriage certificate. Note that the naming of the groom's parents in that certificate gives proof of a birth which took place about 1795!!

MARRIAGE REGISTERS

The county should still retain the marriage registers in which a record of the return—the proof of the performance of the marriage—was entered. In some areas a consolidated register and

---

[11] Minister of the Gospel.

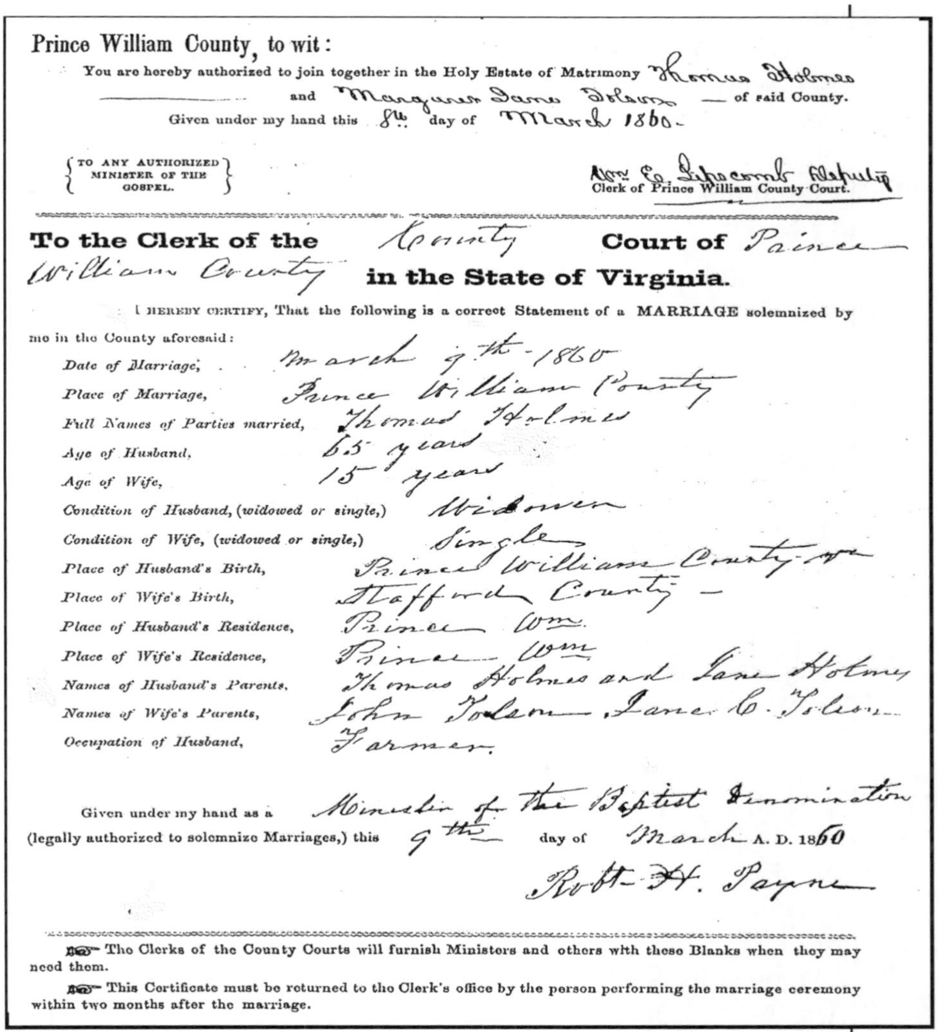

Prince William County, to wit:

You are hereby authorized to join together in the Holy Estate of Matrimony Thomas Holmes and Margaret Jane Tolson — of said County.

Given under my hand this 8th day of March 1860.

{TO ANY AUTHORIZED MINISTER OF THE GOSPEL.}

Wm. E. Lipscomb Deputy
Clerk of Prince William County Court.

To the Clerk of the County **Court of** Prince William County **in the State of Virginia.**

I HEREBY CERTIFY, That the following is a correct Statement of a MARRIAGE solemnized by me in the County aforesaid:

Date of Marriage, March 9th 1860
Place of Marriage, Prince William County
Full Names of Parties married, Thomas Holmes
Age of Husband, 65 years
Age of Wife, 15 years
Condition of Husband, (widowed or single,) Widower
Condition of Wife, (widowed or single,) Single
Place of Husband's Birth, Prince William County Va
Place of Wife's Birth, Stafford County —
Place of Husband's Residence, Prince Wm
Place of Wife's Residence, Prince Wm
Names of Husband's Parents, Thomas Holmes and Jane Holmes
Names of Wife's Parents, John Tolson, Jane C. Tolson
Occupation of Husband, Farmer

Given under my hand as a Minister of the Baptist Denomination (legally authorized to solemnize Marriages,) this 9th day of March A. D. 1860

Robt H. Payne

☞ The Clerks of the County Courts will furnish Ministers and others with these Blanks when they may need them.

☞ This Certificate must be returned to the Clerk's office by the person performing the marriage ceremony within two months after the marriage.

Figure 10-1. An 1860 "return" of a marriage certificate.

←The authorization.

←The return.

←The bride and groom. He is 65 and a widower, she is 15 and single.

←Parents of both.

←Religion. Now church records can be checked, too.

←In this county the person who performed the marriage was required to return the certificate to the clerk within two months after the marriage.

index was created at a later time, and included entries of bonds, licenses, and returns. As is always the case with any record created years after the event, the consolidation is subject to error in copying or transcribing.

MARRIAGE CONTRACT

Marriage contracts were discussed in Chapter 3, but note that the marriage contract itself is not proof that the marriage took place. Additional records need to be examined: marriage returns, deeds showing the relationship as husband and wife, his probate naming her as wife. These or others may provide proof.

WHERE DID THEY MARRY?

Marriage laws differed. While in one state the intended groom or bride could get married without consent at 21 and 18, the adjoining state may have given him or her that permission at a younger age. One state may have imposed a waiting period, while another did not.

Marriages traditionally took place in the bride's county of residence, or in the county in which her parents lived. An unmarried school teacher may have lived several counties away from her parents, met a man in that county who was to become her husband, but returned to her parents' home for the ceremony even though she lived the rest of her life where she and her husband met.

These and other reasons could influence the choice of locality, especially in those areas near a state line. If you haven't found the record in the courthouse where they resided, check a map and do some further investigating on possible locations.[12]

SUBSTITUTE MARRIAGE RECORDS

As with births and deaths, deeds can be useful in proving marriages. In Washington County, Pennsylvania, an 1800 deed of Ezekiel Rose to Ignatius Barnet conveyed property subject to "the claim of Dower of a certain Mary Rose formerly Mary Higkins ..." That in itself was not enough to prove that Ezekiel's wife was formerly Mary Higkins. It could have been an earlier dower claim on the property before it came into the possession of Ezekiel Rose. When the deed was recorded it was immediately followed by a recorded receipt in which Mary Rose stated that she received twenty seven pounds "being in full for my Dower ..." That too did not furnish the needed proof that she was the wife of Ezekiel Rose. Continuing further, the clerk had appended the personal acknowledgment which Mary made of her signature. In that acknowledgment it states that she was "Mary Rose Wife to the above Ezekiel Rose." Finally, the proof! This demonstrates the necessity of not only examining the document, but all the clauses that have been attached before and after.

A marriage can also be confirmed by the estate of the bride's father. In 1853 Morgan County, Illinois, the estate of Francis Ketner indicated that he died intestate and left sons and daughters including "Nancy Sammons wife of Abner Sammons."

BREACH OF PROMISE

Genealogy does provide some interesting sidelights. In Cadiz, Harrison County, Ohio, one couple was married in 1875 in the sheriff's office. Why? According to the newspaper, she had him arrested for breach of promise.

In another instance in Pickaway County, Ohio, the intended bride sued the intended groom to recover damages for a breach of

---

[12] The couple could even have gone elsewhere to be married in a relative's home, or to a popular marriage mecca.

promise stating he had promised to marry her. He claimed he did not, but asserted that she agreed to receive $20.00 as full satisfaction. It went to a jury. They ruled that the defendant did promise to marry and awarded to her a judgment for nonperformance in the amount of $169.50 with costs. All creating records for those seeking this family's history.

COMMON-LAW MARRIAGES

Your ancestor's marriage may never have been solemnized in the ordinary way. Under certain conditions, a couple who had an agreement to marry followed by a certain period of cohabitation could have had a common-law marriage. It may be impossible to prove (though at least one state has a procedure to register such marriages), but could explain the absence of records.

SPECIAL NOTES ON MARRIAGES

Also note the prefixes to the name, and copy them exactly. In Centre County, Pennsylvania the 1844 marriage of George Boal was to "Mrs. Elizabeth (William) Johnston." The "Mrs." is a tip-off that she had a previous marriage. She was likely a widow, though she could have been divorced. The insertion of "(William)" could indicate that it was her maiden name, or that her previous Johnston husband was named William. These potential clues should be followed, but would have been lost if the "Mrs." had not been copied. But, as always, some occasional exception can occur. A colleague reports that one marriage register he examined showed *all* the brides as Mrs.!

Watch too for a male of a surname marrying a female with the same surname. She may have been the widow of his brother,[13] or he could have been marrying a relative with the same surname. Occasionally, two of the same surname married but were of no known relationship at all.

DEATHS

Early death registers, when they exist, may report nothing more than the name of the person, date of death, and perhaps the district in which the deceased lived. Slowly the records evolved to include the name of the deceased, the date of death, age, marital status, "color," the township or community where the death took place, and the birthplace of the deceased. The addition of the names of parents wasn't widespread until the mid to late 1800s though. Exceptions occurred if the deceased were a child — in that event it was commonly shown that the child was "the son of" or "the daughter of" a named father and/or a named

---

[13] In some areas this was not considered proper, and may even have been prohibited. In other states it was a common event.

The death certificate for Charles Rose to the right also provides a window into much earlier records. By providing the name of his parents, and his own age, it tells us that parents Charles and Priscilla Rose were in North Carolina about 1781. We can look for their records there.

mother. Even after a column was provided to enter the parents, the clerks were slow to implement it and many registers are frustratingly blank in that column.

Death registers often had another important column—the name of the informant. The event may have been reported by the assessor or other public official. Or, that informant column may furnish the name of the father, mother, son, daughter, or other family member. (Unfortunately, it also might only say the informant was "the father" or "the mother" with no name!)

Some examples will demonstrate the value of vital records. In Tazewell County, Virginia, the 1859 death record of Aaron Rose indicates he died at Clinch River of fever at aged 17 and was a son of Charles and Priscilla Rose. The informant was "his brother Solomon Rose." In the same county the death record of Charles Rose states he died aged 75 on 6 November 1856, was born in North Carolina, died near Cedar Bluff of a liver complaint, and that he was a son of Samuel and Lydia Rose. It tops it all off by adding that the informant was "wife Priscilla Rose."

WHERE IS THE DEATH REGISTER AND WHAT'S IN IT?

The early death register may be on the shelves of the courthouse, or, it may be in the city or county health department. If you do not find the registers, ask the clerk where they are housed.

After statewide registrations went into effect, copies of the state's

Figure 10-2 to the left is the left-side of a Death Register. Figure 10-3 below is the right side of that page. Note the important information available in this 1892 register of Fairfax County, Virginia. It shows color, sex, date and place of death, name of disease or cause of death, age, parents, where born, occupation, consort of, or unmarried, and source of information. Similar late 1800 registers exist in many areas all throughout the United States.

Figure 10-3 to the right; the right-side to the Register of Deaths in Figure 10-2 .

original certificates should be in the local health department. If the copies are available locally, that can speed up the process of procuring a copy for your records. Often the local office will provide them the same day of your visit and perhaps even for less cost than the same service from the state. Or the local office will take your order and mail the certificate in a week or two.[14] The local department, however, may not make a practice of providing copies and may refer you to the state.

Additional clues in death records are contained in the location of the death. Even when the cemetery is not given, the community where the death occurred is a starting point. Look for cemetery surveys of the county or maps of the area which may show cemeteries near that location of death.

WHEN YOU CANNOT FIND THE DEATH RECORD

Sometimes your onsite search is not successful even after local or state registrations started. You may have to write, requesting a search and copy of the record if found.

When you complete a form requesting a search or copy of the record, use care. Provide alternate spellings of the surname and the full first and middle names. (Lee Roy Schneider might turn out to be filed under Roy Schneider, which wouldn't surface if the middle name had not been provided.) If you think you know the exact death date, still take the precaution of inserting "about" or "around" to give the date some leeway. When providing the name of the community where the death occurred, give it as "perhaps at — —." You may think they lived in a particular area of the county, but they could have actually resided in another town or in an unincorporated area.

There is a charge for a copy of the death record. Most states (and some counties) have a set charge for searching, whether or not a record is found. Some entities will search a specified time period, say ten years, so you may be requested to provide a date range. Specify uncertified copies; they usually cost less and are acceptable for genealogy.

SUBSTITUTE RECORDS CAN PROVE A DEATH

While you are in the courthouse there are other avenues of pursuit which may provide information on a death when a death register entry cannot be found.

Probates. An estate proceeding may give the exact date of death. (Many 20th century probate files even include a certified copy of the death certificate.) If it doesn't, you can estimate when the death occurred. A testator died between the date of his will and the date the will was proved. A widow died between the date of her husband's death, and the date her estate was probated.[15]

---

[14] If you have to wait for them to copy and mail it, ask if you can at least see it while there so you can note the information. The certificate might provide the name of the cemetery which you can visit while are in the area.

[15] In your compilation specify this by a clause such as "Aaron Smith died between 1 April 1831 (date of his will) and 25 May 1831 (date his will was proved) ...": Add the citations for the will and the proving as footnotes.

159

Some areas kept a special book of death dates. For example, an "Oath of Death" register in Bedford County, Pennsylvania, includes the oath of George H. Rose who stated that William Rose, late of Colerain township, died on 22 October 1898.

Probates can also establish that a person at least was deceased by a certain date. The 27 February 1812 will of John Holland in Montgomery County, Maryland, bequeathed to children of son Stephen Holland deceased. This effectively proves the death of Stephen before the date of his father's will. You'll find other records which can help to estimate the dates, too. In the Orphan's Docket of Bedford County, Pennsylvania, when the will of Joseph Rose came up for probate, the petition stated that he died 19 February 1906.

And in some areas, it was customary to include the actual date of death in the probate petition.

Guardianship. In looking for a way to prove the death dates of parents, it's possible the guardianship proceeding of minors may give that date. This surprisingly was not too common, but it is a possibility.

Court record. Sometimes a court case can at least narrow the time frame for the death by a certain date. This is demonstrated in a Lunenburg County, Virginia, action of 2 November 1747 in the suit of John Coles & Co. vs. Christopher Bingham, stating that the plaintiff John Coles "departed this life since last continuance" and thus "this suit abates." He therefore died before 2 November 1747. Determine the date of the last continuance mentioned and his death date can be narrowed even further.

Deeds to prove death. Sometimes the deed is explicit as in Washington County, Maryland, when Walter Boyd and others deeded their portion of a tract and set forth that John Bond late of Washington County died on or about 13 September 1808 and left nine children (all named). This deed serves not only as proof of death, but also as proof of birth. Additionally, many deeds mention a former owner as "deceased." Though it doesn't give the date of death, it at least indicates that the person mentioned died before the date of the deed.

VITAL RECORD ASSISTANCE

A helpful publication for nationwide information is *Where to Write for Vital Records* by the Department of Health and Human Service.[16] Additionally, a useful Internet site at <http://www.vitalrec.com> can facilitate the search for records. Included at that website, state by state, is background information on

If you are obtaining the record for a client, be prepared with a written authorization. It should state that you are obtaining copies for genealogical purposes on behalf of the client. Have the client sign and date it.

---

[16] The current cost should be posted at the website. Send your check to Superintendent of Documents, P.O. Box 371954, Pittsburgh, PA 15250-7954.

the commencement of statewide registration, cost, forms, restrictions, etc. Importantly, it includes the names, addresses, and phone numbers of the pertinent departments in all the states. If there is a question on the form as to your purpose in requesting the copy, insert "genealogical study." Otherwise, they may not search without further communication to ascertain your reason, thus delaying your request.

Another website which can help is that of the National Center of Health Statistics at <http://www.cdc.gov/nchs/howto/w2w/ w2welcom.htm>. From there click on the state of your interest.

ONE ACTION CAN PROVE BIRTH, MARRIAGE, AND DEATH

Persistent courthouse research may be especially rewarding. Note the following treasure that demonstrates the multitude of clues which can be found in one record:

> In the Orphans Court held in Philadelphia 19 April 1816, upon petition of Joseph Rose, Leonard Frailey and Mary his wife late Mary Rose, Benjamin F. Rose, Jacob Hoffman and Hannah his wife late Hannah Rose, William Rose, John Rose, Eliza Rose a minor by her guardian Samuel Gibson and Peter Rose a minor by his guardian Nathan Jones, setting forth that William Rose the father died intestate about the year 1810, leaving a widow Hannah Rose and eight children, the petitioners. Said Hannah Rose is since deceased. William Rose died intestate seized of a tract in Blockley township. Petitioners pray that the court will partition the tracts. (Plats of the tracts are also included in the record book.)

This petition established that William Rose married Hannah, and provided a death record for William Rose as about 1810. It proved the marriage of two daughters and the names of their husbands. Additionally, it provided proof of birth for six children who were born before about 1795 (they were not minors at the time of the 19 April 1816 document above. We can calculate the approximate date of birth of the two minors as about 1795 to 1810 (minors in 1816, but born in or before 1810, the year of their father's death). William's wife's death can be placed between about 1810 (she was living when William died) and 19 April 1816 (the date of the court hearing which declares that she was deceased).

This petition proved births of eight children, an estimated span of their birth years, marriages of two children, death of the father about 1810, and the mother by 19 April 1816. Great info!

Another word about vital records. They tend to be one of the records that genealogists generally use in the first stages of their search. But, the researcher should regularly return to them as additional information is gathered, often from other records. A probate, land, or court record that gives a married name for a daughter allows for search for a marriage record under another name, or perhaps for her death record, or even the births of the couple's children.

CHAPTER POINTS TO PONDER

✓ Early registration of vital records was spotty.

✓ Many cities maintained vital records which predate county registrations.

✓ Many cities continue to maintain their own separate records, aside from the county records.

✓ When a birth, marriage, or death was not recorded, other records in the courthouse can supply proof of the events.

In the next chapter we will take a look at some other ways we might locate courthouse records when we can't make the trip, and effective preparatory work when we *can*.

11 The Internet, Microfilm, and Libraries

Perhaps you are unable to undertake the trip to the county yourself. Health problems in the family, jobs with little vacation time, expenses, these and more might prohibit that personal exploration. Can you conduct courthouse research on the Internet or through libraries and microfilm? Yes, if you understand the limitations and use some of the resources in this chapter. Even if you can go personally, the preparation discussed here can smooth your trip.

THE INTERNET AND COURTHOUSE RECORDS

The Internet now offers many excellent websites. Indexes to county records such as deeds, deaths, and taxes, descriptions of the breadth of documents in their possession, explanation of the laws of earlier times—these and more might appear. Additionally, they often have historical background of the county. And, to facilitate your visit to the county, they generally post courthouse hours, suggest parking facilities, and may even list other repositories in the area.

CYNDI'S LIST IS ALWAYS A PLACE TO START

Start your Internet search at <http://www. cyndislist.com.> This site offers more than 200,000 links to a pool of websites of value to genealogists. The thousands of links are categorized for easy access. One of the best ways to become familiar with this massive undertaking is to allow a bit of time each day for exploring. Reach beyond the websites offering indexes and records to discover those featuring terminology, interpretation of records, instructions such as calculating the value of old currency, and more.

The main categories in Cyndi's List lead you to scores of specific courthouse records. Try links to many different subjects—you may be surprised how useful they can be. But start first with those particularly relevant to courthouse research:

- Births and Baptisms
- Death Records
- Land Records, Deeds, Homesteads etc.
- Marriages
- United States Index, then go to U.S. - Vital Records
- Wills and Probates

Many of the links under the listed subjects will transport you to locality sites— a town, city, or county. Contents of those sites vary. Some include indexes for a specific span of time (e.g., deeds 1820-1840). Others include abstracts, or historical background. All can be of value.[1]

OTHER CYNDI'S LIST RESOURCE ITEMS

Check the following categories for help of a different ilk.

Calendar and Dates. Those unfamiliar with the old style calendar and dates will benefit from Internet articles listed in this category. They will clarify the often misunderstood calendar change from Julian to Gregorian in 1752.

Handwriting and Script. Included in this Cyndi's List category are a number of sites with examples of old handwriting and transcribing techniques. Also in Cyndi's List, found under "Societies," is Board for Certification of Genealogists at <http://www.bcg certification.org>. Once at their site go to the "Skillbuilding," link shown. Click on it and from there, to "Test Your Skills."[2] You'll find samples of documents and their transcriptions. Practicing with these will familiarize you with the old script and the boilerplate clauses within the documents.

Dictionaries and Glossaries. This category is useful for finding explanations of words and terms in old inventories, Latin phrases, and translations. For example, within these pages you can find obsolete medical terms defined in today's language.

USGENWEB

The best starting place on the Internet for courthouse research is the volunteer USGenWeb Project. This network of county sites

---

[1] If you plan to compile anything for publication in book form or on the Web, remember that books and websites of other compilers are copyrighted. Do your own abstracting to avoid potential problems.

[2] Currently this link to "Test Your Skills" is at the bottom of the "Skillbuilding" page, but websites change.

throughout the United States, maintained by volunteers, is impressive. Go to its home page at: <http://www.usgenweb.com>.

Once there click on the county of your interest by using either the map of states or the table of states.

The information provided at each of the county websites differs. The dedicated volunteers who donate their time as webmasters and assistants have varying skills, and often have limited time to devote to the project, but all the sites will help you to some degree. Their combined efforts have enabled researchers to plan their trips and advance their genealogical endeavors in the counties.

The sites may contain some, if not all, of the following:

- Courthouse address and hours.
- Public libraries, genealogical libraries, and archives in the area.
- Listing of published books of the county's court records.
- Indexes of courthouse records.
- Listing of county residents who were war veterans.
- Historical background of the county—when formed, parent county, etc.
- Availability of records—destruction by fire, or other losses.
- A forum for posting queries on county residents.
- Offers of help, either for a fee or by volunteers.

Some local websites are so outstanding you will be amazed!

COUNTY FORUMS
The USGenWeb Project mentioned above usually has a forum at each county site. You can post your messages and respond to others. You may locate someone researching the same family; perhaps you can even plan the needed county research together. To access a forum go to: <http://www.rootsweb.com/~jfuller/gen_mail.html#USA>. From there, choose the state of your interest and then the county.

COUNTY SITES OTHER THAN USGENWEB
Many counties have their own "official" website, generally sponsored by the county's government. Simply enter the county and state in your browser and see what surfaces. For example, try "Surry County North Carolina." Once there, you will discover links to both the official Surry County government website and to the USGenWeb Project site for that county.

Entering the name of the county in your search engine is also a quick way to access other sites related to your search. "Hamilton County Ohio" brought up the excellent Public Library of Cincinnati and Hamilton County. The Hamilton County Chapter of the Ohio Genealogical Society, the USGenWeb project for Hamilton County, the Hamilton County Recorder's office which provides land searches for the past few years online, and others.

STATE ARCHIVES ON THE INTERNET

The most important websites for each state are usually those of its state archives, state library, or state historical society.[3] These websites provide historical information which will facilitate your search for the records, and your understanding of what you collect. For example, the Connecticut State Library's website explains that probate districts (not counties and towns) have jurisdiction over probate matters in that state. The 130 current probate districts evolved from four original districts. A town, therefore, may have been in three or four different probate districts during a span of years. It becomes important to determine the correct district for a particular date. This information, available at their state website, will help you locate the records.

Another example is that of the Maryland State Archives website. Among their informational pieces is a description of each category of Maryland's estate papers. You'll learn that before 1777 there should be three copies of each will—one in the Prerogative Court records, one in the county record books, and the original will (now in the custody of State Archives). Certainly essential knowledge for those searching in this state.

These are just a few examples of what may be found at the state sites. Their efforts contribute to our understanding and interpretation of their records.

And, there's even more. Often the websites include listings of published books on state and county records—abstracted records, maps, indexes, digitized images. And, importantly, state libraries and archives may post a catalog of their manuscripts.

FEDERAL-LAND RECORDS ONLINE

As was discussed in Chapter 3, some states are "Federal-Land States." In those states, the first patent to the land came from the federal government to an individual or group of individuals. Though these are not "county" records, nonetheless, you can use them to better understand the county land records you discover. Your ancestor may not be listed in the grantee index as a purchaser because his land was obtained by patent from the federal government. If that is a possibility, check the General Land Office (GLO) website for the Bureau of Land Management records at: <http://www.glorecords.blm.gov>.

In some states (such as California), it was customary after the federal patent was issued to record a copy of that patent in the county courthouse. In many areas, however, it will only be among the federal records.

Bureau of Land Management
General Land Office Records

Search Land Patents | Visitors Center | FAQ

The Official Federal Land Patent Records Site

Welcome to the new Bureau of Land Management (BLM), General Land Office (C web site. We provide live access to Federal land conveyance records for the Pul provide image access to more than two million Federal land title records for Fac

---

[3] The state library and the state archives may each have their own websites, or they may be combined.

LOCAL LAND RECORDS ONLINE

Some counties have posted limited listings from their deeds indexes online. Normally the images are not included on their online postings, though there are exceptions. Try accessing the county's site at the USGenWeb project previously mentioned in this chapter, to determine availability.

Also try <http://www.cyndislist.com> and then "Land Records, Deeds, Homestead, Etc." A number of general sites are listed which can take you to related websites such as software to plat the land, land descriptions, and others.[4] Or, try the "locality specific locations" in this Cyndi's list category. Many engrossing links will surface. Clicking on one, I quickly found Clay County, Minnesota 1909 township maps[5] taken from the Alden Publishing Company of Chicago *Standard Atlas of Clay County, Minnesota*. A few seconds later I had the 1909 township map for Elkton township on my screen, with the names of all the property owners. Other townships of Clay County were as easily accessible. Check these "locality specific" listings and you'll see the many possibilities for assistance.

Another helpful website is the NETR online Public Records website at: <http://www.netronline.com/public_records.htm>. Here you will first link to the state. Once there, click on the county. Names and phone numbers are displayed for the Revenue Commissioner, the Probate Judge, and others. If any of these offices have records online, that too will be noted.

Another website, this one with links specifically to the Tax Assessors' county website, is at: <http://www.pulawski.com>. Many of the county sites allow you to enter the property parcel number to access further information on that parcel.

Also available is a useful listing, state by state, of the county (or town) recorder, including the address and phone number. This website can be viewed at <http://www.zanatec.com/home.html>. It does not include links to the websites of these offices, but nonetheless is helpful.

PROBATE RECORDS ONLINE

Scattered wills and estates are available online, but nothing that would approach complete listings for an area. Nonetheless, start with the standard <http://www.USGenWeb.com> website previously described and go to state, and then the local link. Also, go to <http://www.cyndislist.com>, then to "Wills & Probates." You'll find sites for interpreting and understanding estates, and

---

[4] When platting the land you recreate a map of the actual tract. By platting the surrounding tracts you fit together the pieces of land each neighbor owned.

[5] The Elkton township map was located at: http://www.info.co.clay.mn.us/History/ElktonTownship.pdf.

a few websites leading you to specific localities. For example, one listed website offers the transcriptions of early 1800 inventories of Franklin County, Indiana. Even if you don't have ancestors in that county, these postings can give you a glimpse of these fascinating records. View them at their website at <http://departments.mwc.edu/hipr/www/inventories/franklin/19cinfra.htm>.

VITAL RECORDS ONLINE

In Chapter 10 the site at <http://www.vitalrec.com> was discussed. This site leads to individual pages for all states and includes information on the starting dates of statewide registration. Costs, forms, and other data are included, as are addresses

where the records can be ordered. Another similar site is at <http://www.cdc.gov/nchs> which is the National Center of Health Statistics. Then go to the Top 10 Links and click on "Fastats A to Z" link. Or, go directly to <http://www.cdc.gov/nchs/fastats/Default.htm> for the state listings.

These aren't the only useful sites on vital records. A number of indexes are online, as well as general information and locality-specific websites. Check at: <http://www.cyndislist.com>, then go to "United States Index," and then "U.S. Vital Records." The USGenWeb site (previously mentioned in this chapter) may offer scattered listings. State sites may offer even more. As an example, the Ohio Historical Society posted an index to their death records for 1913-1937.[6] See: <http://www.ohiohistory.org/dindex/index.cfm>. Michigan posts actual abstracts of death records from 1867 to 1897 at: <http://www.mdch.state.mi.us/pha/osr/gendisx/search.htm>.

Try also the website at <http://home.att.net/~wee-monster/deathrecords.html>. This one is categorized by state and then by counties, listing what is online in each. Included are selected obituaries, cemetery records, and death indexes.

A number of states are doing a magnificent job of posting some of their state vital records on line, at least in index form.

---

[6] Always read the instructions when using the search engines at these websites. For instance, on the site for the Ohio death index, you need to select a span of years. If you don't know the year of death, start with the first listed group; if not there, go to the next span of dates until you find It. If the name still does not appear, check alternate spellings. Check also for delayed registrations (see Chapter 10) which have not been posted to the website. Ultimately, you may need to accept the possibility, especially in early years of state registration, that the event was not recorded with the state. Try the county office on the chance it was recorded there but not with the state.

In other instances a local resident or a researcher of the county may abstract vital records and post them on their own website of an area. Or a local library may include them on their website. Try entering into your browser's search engine "vital records Nashville Tennessee" or "Hardin County Illinois Births" or areas of your interest and see what emerges.

CIVIL RECORDS ONLINE

At this time there are only scattered civil records online (aside from vital records). Some of the best places to find the civil records are at the state archives' sites and at the county archives' sites as previously mentioned. Also, check the USGenWeb county sites, for they often have links to any compiled indexes or abstracts.

ONLINE SUBSCRIPTION SERVICES

There are a number of online subscription services. For a fee, you can access their various databases. They won't have all the records available in the courthouse. Nonetheless their databases can assist if you are not able to go onsite personally, or to supplement what you have. You can locate these fee-based sites by going to <http://www.cyndislist.com>. Then go down to "Databases-Searchable Online." Once at the latter link, click on "Commercial Fee/Subscription Databases." Several are listed.

MICROFILM FOR COURTHOUSE RECORDS

Microfilm records can be of immense assistance to researchers. In some cases they may be a gateway for those who cannot go personally to the courthouses; in other instances they can fill a void when to the originals is restricted.

FAMILY HISTORY LIBRARY (LDS) AND THEIR MICROFILM

The Church of Jesus Christ of Latter-day Saints (LDS)[7] maintains enormous collections of microfilmed genealogical data, based on records throughout the United States (and, in fact, the world). These records are not complete but can help immeasurably. Besides the main Family History Library in Salt Lake City, LDS has over 3,700 centers throughout the United States. Patrons do not have to be a member of the church to use their holdings.[8] Their extensive collections of microfilm are available for use in their main library in Salt Lake City, and their centers nationwide.

Microfilm can assist those who cannot go personally to the courthouses.

---

[7] Church of Jesus Christ of Latter-day Saints (Mormon) headquartered in Salt Lake City, Utah.

[8] Patrons, church members or not, often donate a copy of their research to assist in expanding the FHL collection.

FINDING FAMILY HISTORY LIBRARY AND CENTERS

To get basic information about the main Family History Library so that you can order and view their microfilm, go to: <http://www.familysearch.org/Eng/Library/FHL/frameset_library.asp>.

To find a center near you, either check your telephone book, or phone the main library in Salt Lake City for the location. But better yet, go to their online website at: <http://www.familysearch.org/Eng/Library/FHC/frameset_fhc.asp>.

Use the FHL handy search engine to locate a center near you. You'll be able to order microfilm through them for viewing at their facility.

FHL CATALOG

You need to ascertain the roll numbers of the microfilm you will need. You can access the FHL catalog from the computers at the FHL centers or from your own computer. From their home page at <http://www.familysearch.org> select "Library" and then click on "Family History Library Catalog." You should then be at the following screen: "Search the Family History Library Catalog." You will be presented with several choices:

- Place Search
- Surname Search
- Keyword Search
- Title Search
- Film/Fiche Search
- Author Search
- Subject Search
- Call Number Search

Try first the "Place Search." A screen will be displayed asking for 1) *Place,* and 2) *Part of* (optional) (see Figure 11-1). If you are searching for records of Solano County, California, enter Solano (minus the word county) as "Place," and California as "Part of." Over thirty entries pop up as links—diverse records

Search for matching places.

Place |

Part of (optional) |

Search

Figure 11-1. In the Family History Library search engine, when you get to the above screen enter the county in "Place" and the state in "Part of (optional)."

such as history, maps, cemeteries, land records, and others. Click on the one of your interest, and further lists will be revealed. Each item has the option to see and print a descriptive list with all the rolls and roll numbers for that particular item.

Use the form provided on the website to borrow the films through their main library for a nominal charge. The rolls will be sent to your local center where you can view them. They will be held for a prescribed period of time—check with the library to see how long. Also ask them about their policy of holding them indefinitely for a small additional charge.

The FHL library catalog is also available for purchase on CD for a minimal fee. The CD version of the catalog is particularly convenient for those who use laptop computers in their research, and want to check the FHL Library's holdings from a remote location. To order, go to the FHL homepage at <http://www.familysearch.org>. Click on "Order/Download Products;" then, click on "Family History Research Products." Then go to "Software and Databases," followed by "Miscellaneous Databases," where you will find the catalog for purchase.

ORDERING FHL MICROFILM

The numbers of films pertaining to your place of interest will likely overwhelm you. The temptation is to start ordering films indiscriminately. Formulating a strategy can save you time and rental money.

First, place an order for the index for whatever series interests you. If, for example, you want to examine deeds, start with the grantor and grantee *indexes* for the appropriate time period.

Once the index arrives, view it and note *all of the entries for the surname* in the pertinent time period of your search. (If you don't list them, later you'll probably have to reorder film and reexamine it as new clues surface.)

Using the research tips provided in the various chapters of this book (Chapters 3 and 4 if you are working with land records), pick the indexed entries most likely to help and place an order for those rolls. If the indexed entry shows Deed Book B p. 85, you then order the microfilm which contains Deed Book B. Be aware that at times, an original record book has so many pages that it has been broken into two parts for filming. The microfilm catalog may show "Book B pp. 1-357" on one roll, and Book B pp. 358-801" on the following. To avoid disappointment, be sure to order the right roll.

On the next page (Figure 11-2) you will find a sample search among the records in the Family History Library catalog.

SAMPLE SEARCH: FAMILY HISTORY LIBRARY CATALOG

This strategy is specifically for a place search so you can find county records. There are other ways to search as you will see when accessing the following links.

Start by going to: <http://www.familysearch.org>
That will take you to the homepage of the Family History Library.

Then click on the link: Library
Then click on: Family History Library Catalog

On the catalog screen pick: Place Search
A screen will come up with two choices: Place, and Part of "optional."

If searching for Surry County, North Carolina, enter:
　　Place: Surry
　　Part of: North Carolina

The results show: North Carolina, Surry. Click on it and a long listing appears of various books and other resources on military, genealogy, and other topics. A few which were included:
North Carolina, Surry – Biography
North Carolina, Surry – Business records and commerce
North Carolina, Surry – Center
North Carolina, Surry – Census [listed 1790, 1830, 1840, 1850, 1860, 1870, 1880 and 1900 in separate listings]
North Carolina, Surry – Church history
North Carolina, Surry – Court Records
etc.

Each of the above listings is a link (shown in blue, and under lined). Clicking on the link will bring up a second listing of the items represented by that link; for example, Court Records would bring up a listing of books and microfilm on that subject. Each of those items are also links. A few for Surry included:

　　County Court minutes, 1779-1867, with suits
　　Lunacy inquisition records, 1899-1963
　　Orders, decrees and special proceedings docket of various court
　　　　actions and judgments, 1868-1958
　　Schedule of debts, 1897-1901
　　Special proceedings, 1915-1963
　　Superior Court minutes, 1807-1940; equity minute dockets, 1820-
　　　　1825, 1855-1867, 1807-1940
　　Surry County, North Carolina court minute abstracts, 1768-1789
　　Surry County, North Carolina, overseers of roads 1807-1833

All of the items immediately above are also links which will bring up the author, title, and catalog number of books, and the roll numbers of microfilm.

At each step along the way you can choose to "print" so you can take the information with you on your visit to the library.

Figure 11-2. Sample search from the Family History Library catalog. Any microfilm you locate through the search can be ordered through one of their centers. You may find at least some of the books in your own area libraries.

MICROFILM OTHER THAN FHL

Often a county (or a state entity) has its own microfilm of selected records independently microfilmed, apart from those filmed by the Family History Library. You may find films of deeds, court records, tax records, or others. In fact, the courthouse clerk may require that you use their microfilm of early records to preserve the original records. If they have only one microfilm reader, be prepared to relinquish that reader after a few minutes if someone on the staff needs it. In that case you may want to see if the local library has the same microfilm and more microfilm readers available.[9]

When the records were microfilmed by a state or county entity, the rolls are usually not available for loan. There sometimes are exceptions. Check with your own library's interlibrary loan department to inquire about availability.

MICROFILM PROBLEMS

The quality of microfilmed reproductions varies. Some films are excellent; you will have no problems using them. Others are of such poor quality that it is utterly impossible to use them effectively. When that happens, ask the courthouse clerk whether the original record books are accessible. They may be at an offsite location or even in a storage room of the courthouse. (Your hope is that the county did not discard the ones you need, and that the clerk will allow you to use them.)

LIBRARY GENEALOGICAL COLLECTIONS

FAMILY HISTORY LIBRARY BOOKS

Earlier in this chapter the microfilm of the Family History Library was discussed. The FHL also has extensive holdings of books. You will use the same search—that is, enter the "Place" and "Part of" in the proper boxes. When the listing of items is displayed, as you click on those of your interest you will be able to ascertain if it is microfilm, or a book.

OTHER MAJOR LIBRARY COLLECTIONS

To find books published on the county you are researching, find a major library and use their online catalog to locate the titles of books published for that area. Submit your search parameters (such as county and state) and print the search results. It is always best to use two or three library websites as one library may have some books another does not. Don't depend only upon known genealogical libraries—probe the sites of university libraries, too. Often the latter have significant holdings which

Library books can help us prepare for our onsite trip. Books of abstracted court records can help by providing an all-name index.

---

[9] The local library is also a good place to go when the courthouse closes down for the lunch hour!

can assist family historians. The purpose is to determine the titles of all the books which have been published on the county courthouse records, and to locate libraries holding copies of those titles. You may find yourself in that locality sometime and can personally visit the library and examine the books. Or, you may find that your local library can obtain the books on interlibrary loan. Even if you can't examine those books before your leave on your trip, once you are onsite, your printed lists will facilitate locating those books at that local library or genealogical society.

The ability to connect to major holdings of genealogical collections is a tool under-utilized by genealogists.

There are many excellent libraries. A few have major collections devoted to genealogical pursuits. Among them:

Allen County Public Library (Fort Wayne, Indiana) at <http://www.acpl.lib.in.us>
This immense collection contains over 38,000 volumes of family history, nearly 105,000 printed volumes on local history, and many volumes in other categories. Their genealogy and local history periodical collection is the largest in the world. While you are working up a list of published books of the county records, use this library's catalog to add titles to your list.

Wisconsin Historical Society Library (Madison, Wisconsin) at <http://www.wisconsinhistory.org/libraryarchives>
This library possesses one of the largest genealogical collections in the country. The collection is not limited to Wisconsin history and genealogy, but includes family and local history material pertaining to all regions of North America. Their online genealogical research service offers assistance for searching pre-1907 Wisconsin births, deaths and marriages. Though this site does not have county courthouse records online, their ArCat does identify the records (including many county courthouse records) and indicates their location, format, availability, etc.

Daughters of the American Revolution Library (Washington, D.C. at <http://dar.library.net>
The Daughters of the American Revolution Library in Washington, D.C. has an extensive genealogical collection. It's easy-to-use library catalog can be accessed from their website. Use it to search for published material on the county of your interest by entering the name of the county and state.[10] If you go personally, you can also use their helpful analytical card catalog, view DAR applications on microfilm or microfiche, and make use of other assistance they offer.

---

[10] Also try the county name alone. Though it will bring up all states with a county by that name, sometimes it turns up some which did not display when I entered both county and state.

St. Louis County Library at <http://www.slcl.lib.mo.us>
The National Genealogical Society's[11] collection of more than 20,000 volumes is now part of the circulating collection at the St. Louis County Library in St. Louis, Missouri. Use the St. Louis County Library catalog not only to locate information on books containing county records, but to find books you may borrow through your own library inter-library loan service.

Library of Congress at <http://www.loc.gov>
The Library of Congress, as stated in their mission statement, is the nation's oldest federal cultural institution and serves as the research arm of Congress. It is also the largest library in the world, with nearly 128 million items on approximately 530 miles of book-shelves. The collections include more than 29 million books and other printed materials, 2.7 million recordings, 12 million photographs, 4.8 million maps, and 57 million manuscripts. This massive collection is available either personally, when you visit the nation's capitol, and some of it online. You can browse the catalog at your leisure at their website. You won't want to stop at their genealogy collection—they have much more to offer including images, maps, and others.

The libraries listed above are not the only ones with significant collections of interest to genealogists. Every state has at least one, and usually more, libraries with major collections.

ADVANTAGES OF LIBRARY PREPARATION

Why do you want to take the time to find every published book on your county of interest? Well-done compilations of transcribed and abstracted records can be a tremendous help.[12] They can be a shortcut to the original records you want to see or order from the courthouse.

Although every available published record should be examined, there is a caveat. Do not rely solely on the published records. Their accuracy depends upon the skill of the abstractors and individuals involved in the production of the book. An error made in published abstracts can mislead you for years. Some of the problems:

- An abstractor unskilled in reading the old handwriting.

- An abstractor omitting important points and clues from the document.

- An abstractor unfamiliar with legalese and its application in a particular time period.

- Proof reading or publishing errors.

---

[11] National Genealogical Society, 4527 17th Street North, Arlington, VA 22207, at <http://ngsgenealogy.org>.

[12] When using published abstracts, it is best to follow-up with an examination of the original document (or microfilm copy).

If it is an especially important document, you can order a copy from the courthouse by writing to the proper department and citing the book and page number. Be sure to ask for a price quote—in some areas the cost is very high for copies. And in some (such as some New York counties) an extremely high fee can be imposed just to access their record books. In those cases it may be better to hire a researcher to obtain the document for you for the costs of obtaining the documents in person is usually much less.

However, in spite of possible shortcomings of publications, they can be a tremendous help. The compiler may well have become an "expert" on the records, and provided insights on the records' arrangement, their completeness, etc. that would otherwise not be apparent. Additionally, if the compilation is well done, they can:

- Offer in a nutshell all the transactions of the area and time period, not just those of your family.

- Provide an easy way to check other family names connected with your family.

- Give you an all-name index enabling you to spot records where your ancestor was not a party, but was a witness, or a neighbor, or a bondsman, etc.

The last point is the most important use for published abstracts. Your ancestor may never have made it into an index which included only the names of the main parties. Without the index from published abstracts you might never find other records pertinent to your search without resorting to a page-by-page search. Why are those others important? The following list indicates the records which would not have revealed your ancestor's name in the county's index:

1. If you ancestor witnessed a document, he may have been related to or a neighbor of one of the principals.

2. If one of the principals was of the same surname as your witnessing ancestor, they are likely related.

3. If your ancestor was listed as a neighbor of one of the principals in a deed, it will help place where in the county your ancestor lived.

4. If your ancestor was a bondsman for someone, they may have been related.

5. If your ancestor acted as administrator, guardian or executor, he may have been related.

6. If your ancestor gave testimony in a court action, he may have been related to one of the parties.

USE WORLDCAT OCLC

If you don't have a computer, try to get to a library which allows online access. Particularly, find a library with WorldCat online even if you do have your own computer. WorldCat allows access to Online Computer Library Center (known as OCLC). Through this you can find publications for the county or town, and importantly, can also study their catalog to locate libraries near you who have those books in their holdings. You cannot access WorldCat through your personal computer; it is only available through the computers of member subscribers.

If you don't know how to use a computer, the librarian may look up one or two items for you on WorldCat. For a more extensive search the librarian will probably show you how to use the computer. (And don't forget to get a printout of the entries.)

LAW LIBRARIES FOR STATUTES

There are times when it becomes necessary to consult a state's statutes in order to properly interpret a record. How do you find, for instance, information on who were the heirs at law in the state of Pennsylvania in 1835, or in Ohio in 1842? Start with that year in the statutes of that state, available at its state library or in a law library. (Law libraries throughout the U.S. normally have microfiche of the laws of all states.) In the above instance of Pennsylvania, once you have located a set of Pennsylvania statutes, begin with 1835, looking in the index under subjects such as "intestacy," "heirs," "estates." If there were no laws passed in 1835, keep working *backwards* until you find the last law that went into effect before your target date of 1835. If, for instance, the law on the subject were amended in 1827, that 1827 amendment should be annotated with information on previous laws on the matter. You can keep following those, too, until you are satisfied your question has been answered.

If you live near a university with a law degree program, they will also have a law library. Most university libraries allow the public to use their books. Also check your own area—you may be surprised to find that your county has a law library open to the public.

UNITED STATES STATUTES AT LARGE

In addition to state statutes, the United States Statutes at Large can be useful in your search for statutes passed by our federal government, especially their private acts.[13] Though these statutes can be found in book form in many libraries, the images of

To learn more about OCLC go to <http://www.oclc.org/worldcat>. You don't have to be a subscriber to access the site and learn about this service. To use their search capabilities, however, you'll need to access the search feature through a library or other eligible subscriber.

---

[13] Private acts are those passed for the benefit of an individual or a group of individuals, as opposed to a public act for the benefit of the public. You can also access the statutes through "session laws," i.e., those laws passed each session of Congress. Check the law library for these, too.

the first 18 volumes covering the period 1789 to 1875 are also on the Internet at <http://www.loc.gov>. Click next on "Law Researchers," then on "A Century of Lawmaking," and then on "Statutes at Large." This is a wonderful resource, allowing the viewer to access many of the page images from early records. You'll find it handy as you ponder over some of your research problems.

In the indexes, check not only for your family names, but also check listings under "Private Acts," or listings by subject such as "Pension," "Divorce," etc.

NEWSPAPERS

The local newspapers are full of items involving court records, but unfortunately, when compilers index these newspapers they usually include only vital records. Among the pages are additional items—the "legal" notices required by law to be published when the heirs cannot be located, or notices to creditors which adds to our estate information, and a host of others involving courthouse records. Without an index it is time consuming to investigate this source, but someone may have indexed those newspapers of the area and may have included court-related items. (It does happen, just not often enough!)

There are also newspapers which specialize in court notices, publishing only legal notices, the calendars of upcoming cases, and other related court information. These can usually be found in large cities and vary as to their date of establishment. Current telephone directories and online databases should locate them under the heading of "court newspaper" or "legal newspaper." Check with them as to see if their establishment date meshes with your time of interest.

OTHER FINDING AIDS

There are finding aids that will greatly assist in locating special collections and manuscripts.

Welcome to the National Union Catalog of Manuscript Collections (NUCMC)

USING **NUCMC**

The National Union Catalog of Manuscript Collections (known as NUCMC) is a reference series which will help you locate special collections in many libraries and repositories. If a title company (insurers of title on property) went defunct, their records may have been donated to a repository. If there are deeds in private collec-

178

tions, they might be found. Not all NUCMC cataloging records are in an online data base. NUCMC began cataloging in 1959 and published printed volumes of the collection from 1959 until NUCMC ceased its catalog in 1993. From 1986 until 1993 the NUCMC listings were included in the RLG[14] database. Since 1993 *some* NUCMC entries may also be found in the OCLC (Online Computer Library Center) database.

Since the NUCMC program began in 1959 and did not begin cataloging in the RLG data base until 1986, the RLG database generally does not include the pre-1986 NUCMC listings. To access this magnificent collection, go to <http://lcweb.loc.gov/coll/nucmc/anucmc/nucmc.html>.

Once there, clicking on "Searching FAQs" will give you essential background information on the collection. After that, there are two links of particular value in your search. One is "Searching the NUCMC RLG catalog" and the other is "Searching the OCLC catalog." Try them both. After clicking on the RLG link, enter the county you are searching and the term "land record" or "wills" or "marriages" or other specifying term and see what comes up. Try this also with the OCLC link. You are bound to find some unexpected and exciting surprises! There are records from land companies, surveyors, attorneys, family collections, and many more.

PERSI INDEX TO PUBLISHED ARTICLES

The PERiodical Source Index, known as PERSI, is a comprehensive subject index to many periodicals of genealogy and local history. Originated by the Allen County Public Library (see page 174), there are now close to 2 million entries. Articles from close to 6,000 different periodicals are included. Some are indexes or abstracts of county records. PERSI is available on CD-ROM, at genealogical libraries, and on the Internet at: <http://www.ancestry.com>. (Ancestry is a subscription-based service.)

Find out what's been printed from PERSI. Easy-to-use, it will lead you to many articles and abstracts of county records.

From Ancestry's homepage click on "all databases." The next screen will include the letters of the alphabet, A through Z. Click on P, and when that listing comes up, choose PERiodical Source Index. Once into that webpage, the search feature will guide you through selections by surnames or localities. For instance, entering the keywords "Probate Records" I turned up 3011 entries. Each included the title of the article, the name of the periodical, and the citation giving the volume number and other pertinent citation data. Entering "Baldwin Probate" I turned up 11 articles involving probate records of Baldwin County, Alabama.

---

[14] RLG (Research Library Group) included over 160 universities, national libraries, archives, historical libraries, and others. Their own present website is at <http://www.rlg.org>.

Once you locate an article of interest, you can check a library near you for the periodical, or order a copy of the article from the Allen County Public Library at <http://www.acpl.lib.in.us>.

COUNTY INVENTORIES AND COUNTY GUIDES

Also very useful (and little used) are other privately published guides to a county's records, or guides published under the auspices of the county's government. Look for these while you are doing your library search. Such guides can reveal some of the county records no longer in the courthouse, but available in other repositories. An example is Donna Valley Russell's *Frederick County, Maryland, Genealogical Research Guide.*[15] Similar guides will turn up when you access library websites, as described elsewhere in this chapter. And, look also for state produced archival guides—a wonderful help when they are available.

WORK PROJECT ADMINISTRATION (WPA)

Another source for courthouse material comes from the products of the Work Project Administration (known at times as the Works Progress Administration). This project to transcribe court material, which started in 1936 as part of the Federal Writers Project of the WPA,[16] was to inventory the records of each of the county governments. The purpose was to decrease unemployment during the depression by providing job opportunities.

The first goal of the project was to produce a reference volume listing manuscripts, church records, and public records in county offices for the use of county officials and the general public. The second was to locate, classify, and catalog all extant county and city records to make them more easily accessible to county officials, historians, and research workers.

WPA also undertook to transcribe a variety of county records. When funding ended, many of the transcriptions were not complete. Those that were compiled or were partially finished still exist in most instances. The WPA records are transcribed records and, although subject to error, are tremendously useful.

The best place to locate the WPA transcripts, (as they are called), is at the state library of the state, and in the public or genealogical library of the county. Since the work was interrupted, not all

---

[15] Donna Valley Russell, *Frederick County, Maryland, Genealogical Research Guide* (New Market, Md.: Catoctin, 1987).

[16] The following two compilations will prove helpful for WPA records. They cover both the published and unpublished records of that massive undertaking:

Sargent B. Child and Dorothy P. Holmes, *Check List of Historical Records Survey Publications* (Washington, 1943, reprint, Baltimore: Clearfield, 1969).

Loretta L. Hefner, *The WPA Historical Records Survey: A Guide to the Unpublished Inventories, Indexes and Transcripts* (Chicago: Society of American Archivists, 1980).

volumes have indexes, but when they do, they are tremendously useful every-name indexes for the records transcribed. Many court minutes were a part of the WPA project so it's worth the effort to locate them. Then, using the references given on each of the transcriptions you can follow-up by examining the original record in the courthouse.

ORIGINAL COURTHOUSE RECORDS FOUND ELSEWHERE

Though we think of the county records as being in the courthouse, that is not always so. In many instances the colonial records have been transferred to a state repository. Some county records are now in the custody of the local genealogical society, library, or historical society, usually necessitated by a lack of space in the courthouse. Some states are rigorously supporting a system of county archives, and yearly we see more of these in existence. Pennsylvania has some wonderful county archives and historical societies housing county records, as does Tennessee and many other localities. The archivists of the county archives are usually very knowledgeable about the early records in their custody. Also use the published guides to the records of the state or county you are researching to help locate local records. (Sometimes you can readily find them by asking a longtime employee of the county.)

Special note on regional archives. Illinois has a system called Illinois Regional Archives Depository (or IRAD). These regional facilities maintain a number of records for the several counties of that region. The IRAD homepage can be accessed at: <http://www.cyberdriveillinois.com/departments/archives/irad/iradhome.html>.

Among their holdings (as listed on their website) are:

- county board proceedings files and meeting minutes
- records of births, deaths, and marriages
- land deeds, mortgage, and tax sale records
- assessors' and collectors' tax books
- poll books and voter registers
- naturalization records, including declarations of intent
- probate records, including wills and will records, case files, administrators' and executors' records, guardianship records, and inventory and appraisement records
- civil and criminal court case files, chancery court case files, divorces, docket books and court proceedings, and insanity proceedings and records
- coroner's inquest records and inquest files
- miscellaneous county records, including almshouse/county home records and jail registers.

A listing of the depositories with their addresses, phone numbers, and jurisdiction is at the above mentioned website. Some of the other states (particularly in the midwest) also have a regional system. Check the guide books or the state's website for information.

UNUSUAL WEBSITES

It's always fun to discover sites on the Internet that can answer questions we've wondered about. One such site is at Yale University's Avalon Project website which includes the full text (searchable) for Sir William Blackstone's *Commentaries on the Laws of England (1765-1769)*. This was the first effort to consolidate English common law. Those with an interest in learning about the early laws (many of which were the basis of the common law in the colonies) can access the full text at <http://www.yale.edu/lawweb/avalon/avalon.htm>.

Then use their search engine and read the full text of these interesting and informative laws.

CHAPTER POINTS TO PONDER

✓ The Internet is a good adjunct to genealogical research, but there is much more that is not available on their websites.

✓ The Internet now offers assistance far beyond family message boards.

✓ Microfilm can help when a personal trip to the courthouse is not possible, or when access to the originals is restricted.

✓ Library research should be broadened to include university libraries, law libraries, and others.

✓ Though the Internet, microfilm, and libraries, are immensely useful, they don't substitute for personal onsite research if you can make the trip.

Enter keywords in your browser's search engine, and find not only specific county-related material, but aids that will help you understand and interpret what you find. Such is the case with Blackstone's *Commentaries on the Laws of England*.

12 Strategies That Work

Gathering a mass of records is not enough. We need to understand how they intertwine and how to use them to unscramble our puzzles. We need to perceive what the records imply about our ancestors. We need special knowledge for unusual circumstances. When we are discouraged, we need reminders of why we do this and what keeps us going.

Let's start with some problem-solving techniques.

EXAMPLE 1: ALLOW ONE RECORD TO LEAD TO ANOTHER

Descendants of Lorenzo Dow Rose were trying to prove that he was a son of Elisha Rose. The following deed surfaced in Knox County, Tennessee:

> E. W. D. Wrinkle, John Rose, Samuel Rose, Starling Rose, Lindsay Rose, Jesse Rose, L. D. Rose, Margaret Willhite, Louisa Dunlap and Sarah Kennedy to Phebe Brown, all of Knox County, for $500 convey all undivided interest in a tract known as the Elisha Rose tract, now held under a mortgage given by Elisha Rose to E. W. D. Wrinkle. The land is just below a gully, beginning French Broad River, H— [?] lower corner, W. B. A. Ramsey's line, Isaac Hinds line, John Reagan, conditional line on E. Fords line. The tract contains 25 acres. Signed by: E. W. D. Wrinkle; Starling (his X mark) Rose; John Rose; Jessee F. Rose; Margaret (by her X mark) Willhite; Louisa Dunlap; Lindsay Rose. Witnesses: James Kennedy, Amos Pickle. Acknowledged: 7 or 17 July 1868; registered 6 October 1868.

Could L. D. Rose named in the deed as a grantor be the Lorenzo Dow Rose who was sought? Other records had indicated that Lorenzo Dow Rose was probably of Knox County, and there was reason to consider that he was a son of Elisha Rose. But, Lorenzo Dow Rose had died in Iowa before 1868. How could he then be a grantor on the above 1868 deed? The deed had to be rejected as involving the Lorenzo Dow Rose of the search.

Or, did it?

Many puzzles are solved by scrutinizing the document for alternate interpretations. When the deed was reexamined, it was noted that the signatures did not match the names of the grantors in the body of the document. Signatures for Samuel Rose, L. D. Rose and Sarah Kennedy were lacking. As a result, the deed could not be a legal conveyance of the interest of those three in the land. There had to be further records.

A trip was made to the Knox County Courthouse in search of chancery records, as that court was the most likely to handle property disputes in that state. After consulting the clerk as to the present location of those records, I was told that they were still in the old courthouse. The clerk, key in hand, took me and my husband to the old courthouse. Very quickly the Elisha Rose case was located in the chancery indexes. Soon I was holding in my hands the original papers which recounted the saga of the family property.

The action started in 1864 when E. W. D. Wrinkle sued defendants Jno. Rose, Sterling Rose, Lindsey Rose, Samuel Dunlap and Lucy his wife, Jno. Wilhite and his wife Peggy, Jno. Brown and his wife Phoebe, James Kennedy, and Elisha Kennedy, all of Knox County, and Samuel Rose, Jesse Rose, and children, if any of Lorenzo D. Rose. The complaint recited that on 29 September 1860 "one Elisha Rose, late of said County" executed and delivered to the complainant a deed of mortgage on a debt. To prevent a sale of the mortgaged property for the taxes due, the Complainant (Wrinkle) paid the taxes at different times, amounting to $9.27. Elisha Rose died in the spring of 1862, and left surviving him John Rose, Sterling Rose, Lindsey Rose, Lucy Dunlop wife of Samuel Dunlop, Peggy Wilhite, wife of John Wilhite, Phebe Brown wife of John Brown, and [an erasure here], James Kennedy and Elisha Kennedy, children of Emily Kennedy who was a daughter of Elisha Rose deceased, all of Knox County, Samuel Rose of Texas, and Jesse Rose of Iowa, his only heirs at law known to the Complainant. Elisha had a son, Lorenzo D. Rose, who domiciled himself in Iowa "several years since," and died before his father. The Complainant stated he was not informed whether Lorenzo D. left surviving him any children or not. No administration was granted on the estate of Elisha Rose; in fact, the Complainant charged, Elisha left no personal property to be administrated and consequently the Complainant had no means of collecting the balance of the mortgage debt due him, except through a decree of the court foreclosing the mortgage.

> "To this end, may it please your Honor to cause process to issue to all the aforesaid heirs at law of the said Elisha Rose, residing in Knox County, and advertisement to be made in pursuance of law, for the non resident heirs, including the children of [evidently an erasure here] Rose, deceased, in the event any such are living, to appear and answer the same ..."

[Other papers in the file included a copy of the mortgage; also the citation to those who were living in Knox County; a summons, and other miscellaneous papers.]

Now the matter was clear. L. D. Rose of the deed was indeed Lorenzo Dow Rose, the subject of the search, who had died in Iowa. Lorenzo's death accounted for the omission of his signature, and that of Sarah Kennedy (whose children represented her portion). Lorenzo's brother Samuel Rose was in Texas, the probable reason for the omission of his signature.[1] Not only was the lack of the grantor L. D. Rose's signature on the 1868 deed now explained, but though the deed itself had only implied that the grantors, as heirs, were children of Elisha Rose,[2] the chancery case confirmed it.

This example demonstrates that: 1) it is important to include the signatures when making an abstract of any document and study them with the text of the document; and 2) we must study documents for possible irregularities or alternate interpretations. When problems surface, we need to pursue the records in other offices of the courthouse which might shed light on the matter.

Following this deed into the chancery record case pinpoints another important search strategy. Records are usually not isolated. Consider the process to see if there are records that could have been filed before or after the document you found. A will entered in the courthouse records was usually preceded by a petition for letters testamentary and followed by the judge's order to grant the letters, as well as the inventory, accounts, sales, and related documents. A partition deed was preceded by an action in a court of equity asking for division of the land or the proceeds from the sale of land. It was followed by a public auction and ended with recording of the partition deed. A marriage record was preceded by the license, and perhaps a bond, and ended with the return of the marriage certificate to the courthouse. The list goes on.

> "Records are usually not isolated."

EXAMPLE 2. LOCATING THE CHILDREN

Courthouse records abound with clues to finding the names of children. Every office in which you search–land, estates, vital records, and civil, and criminal, can have records to help in identification of children.

---

[1] The portion of Samuel Rose was not the focus of this particular search but no doubt there was a later deed transferring his interest in the property.

[2] Being heirs does not confirm that the relationship was father and children. Those heirs could have been, for instance, heirs of a deceased brother who died married and without children. The clarification in the subsequent papers was important for it clearly established the relationship.

Some suggestions:

- birth record
- death record if a child were the informant
- consent on a marriage record
- guardianships
- apprenticeships
- estates
- deeds to children from parents

An excellent source for relationships is the estate, especially in states where the petition for probate required the inclusion of all the next of kin and their residences. An example:

> Estate of Susan M. Rose who died intestate. Petition 17 May 1892 for Letters of Administration, Charles R. Gould of the Town of Batavia, county of Genesee, New York, states he is general guardian of Eta E. Rose, minor daughter of Susan M. Rose, late of Town of Batavia, deceased. He states that the deceased died 2 April 1892 in Batavia aged 56 years; the estate is valued at $500. Heirs and next of kin:

Families move west but they leave clues behind.

Adoniram J. Rose, husband, residence unknown
Freeman Rose, son, res. Kansas City, Mo.
Fred W. Rose, son, res. Perry, Wyoming Co., NY
Eta E. Rose, dau., res. Batavia, Genesee Co., aged 19
Gilbert W. Rose, res. Batavia, Genesee Co., aged 12

With a goal of finding the children of Adoniram J. Rose and his wife Susan, this estate is excellent since the petition names them. But, our study has only started. Now we need to glean all we can from clues in this record.

First, it provides the residences of both the older sons; now there are places to search for further records.

We learn additionally that the two older sons were of age. How did we deduce that, since it wasn't stated? The last two kin listed included their ages, implying that those whose ages were included were minors, and the others were not. Examining the record further, the husband's residence was unknown, inferring a possible separation. And, an important lead—the exact date of death of Susan is furnished. Now a search for her obituary can be conducted in the local newspaper. If found, it could supply more family details.

For further research on the family, the estate of Susan Rose would suggest a number of additional possibilities. Some of these follow:

- Check civil records for a formal separation between her and her husband. (It might also be worthwhile to check the criminal records with respect to the husband. He may have been a fugitive, or there may have been some type of warrant outstanding against him for not supporting his family.)

- Because the husband was not local, the statutes would require that notice of the probate hearing be published in a newspaper, usually both locally, and at the location of his last known residence. A copy of that newspaper notice might be in the original probate packet, and may provide his last known residence if it were other than the county in which she died. The original packet could also reveal whether the husband was finally found, with subsequent documents giving the residence.

- Check the 1880 federal census to see if Susan's husband was living with her at that time. If he was not, look for him in other areas.

- Check for a guardianship proceeding at the courthouse for the youngest child Gilbert W. After his mother's death, he would have needed an appointed guardian to handle his portion of the estate.

- Check records of Kansas City, Missouri, and Perry, Wyoming County, New York, for the two oldest sons.

- Check the 1900 U.S. federal census for Adoniram Judson Rose.

- Try to determine if the administrator Charles E. Gould is related.

As an aside, the husband's name of Adoniram J. demonstrates that some knowledge of early ministers is always helpful. For example, many are named Humphrey Posey after the minister of that name, many are named after Lorenzo Dow, Martin Luther, and other well known clergymen. In our present example at the left, a knowledge of clergymen would reveal that Adoniram Judson was a pioneer missionary highly admired. When a search of the 1880 census for Adoniram J. Rose failed, Susan's husband was readily located in the 1880 census under the name of Judson A. Rose.

EXAMPLE 3: LOCATING PARENTS

When trying to locate the names of parents, there are a number of possibilities. Since we are specifically discussing courthouses, we'll omit obituaries, tombstones, and others. Some examples of the data in courthouse records:

BIRTH RECORD OF A CHILD. In Franklin County, Illinois, is recorded the birth of Louise C. Rose on 15 June 1874 stating that she was born in Franklin twp., female, white, *father* John Rose, *mother* Mary J. Garner. Further, that the parents resided in Harrison County, and the birth was reported by the Assessor of Franklin twp.

DEATH RECORD OF A CHILD. In 1921 in Knoxville, Tennessee, Bessie Rose, aged 5, died. Her father Mr. Ben Rose, born in Tennessee, and her mother Hattie Perkins, born in Tennessee, were named in the record. Parents are generally listed after statewide registration went into effect. They may or may not be listed in earlier death records. But we shouldn't assume they won't be named. In 1884 in Lee County, Virginia, when Edward Kirk, aged 22 died; his *parents* were identified as Presley and Amanda Kirk, and additionally, the informant was identified as his *"father in law"* Samuel Rose.

DEED OF PARENT TO CHILD, CHILD TO PARENT, OR OTHERWISE MENTIONED IN A DEED. In the 1796 deed of John Oxley of Loudoun County, Virginia, Oxley deeded land to John Rose. The land was described as adjoining Henry Oxley *"father of said John Oxley."* In another example, John N. Rose found himself considerably in debt from business ventures and because of this William M. Rose in 1829 came to his assistance by delivering some listed personal property on loan to his *"father* John N. Rose." Continuing the examples, in 1837 Albemarle County, Virginia, John N. Rose Jr. of the City of Mobile, Alabama, conveyed for use of his *"mother"* Mary Rose, as her separate property from any claim of "her husband" John N. Rose Sr. a lot.[3] And, in Bute County, North Carolina, in an 1830 deed, William P. Rose and Delilah his wife conveyed a tract to Edmund White, *which is the land devised to Delilah in will of her father John Langford decd.* Deeds are full of such clauses proving relationships.

APPRENTICESHIPS. Though apprenticeship papers may name the parents, it is not common. Nonetheless, they are worth examining for your ancestor's papers may be the exception and name one or both parents.

GUARDIANSHIPS. In Bute County, North Carolin, in 1795, it was ordered that William Coppage be appointed guardian to Lucy Coppage, *orphan of James Coppage deceased.* Guardianships often named at least one parent.

MARRIAGE LICENSE AND RETURN. In Franklin County, Illinois, Hiram Benjamin Marshall, age 34, white, resident of Ewing twp., farmer, *father* William Marshall, *mother* Judah Minor. Bride Susan Elizabeth Williams, resident of Ewing twp., age 25, white, born Franklin County, father William S. Williams, mother Mary Matthews, married at home of Mrs. Mary Williams in Franklin County on 18 September 1881. Witnesses were John M. Darr and Mary J. Dunbar. The marriage solemnized by John Washburn, J.P.

MARRIAGE RECORD GIVING CONSENT OF A PARENT OR GIVING THE LOCATION. In Boone County, Kentucky. In 1812 consent was given by Hugh Stewart Senr. for the clerk to grant a license between Mr. Lewis Rose and *"my Daughter Mary Stewart."*

ESTATE OF A GROWN CHILD NAMING A PARENT, ESPECIALLY IF THE TESTATOR WERE UNMARRIED OR MARRIED BUT CHILDLESS. For example, in Onondaga County, New York, Almina Rose made her will in 1884 and specifically gave to *her father* Lyman Wilcox of Dryden, Tompkins County, a life lease on the place where he was living. We can now identify her maiden name. (As a bonus she named her brother Elias Wilcox and her niece Mary Wilcox, helping to further identify the family.) And, in Amherst County, Virginia, the 1831 will of Patrick J. R. Rose left five slaves in trust to his sister Susan A. F. Price for support of his *mother* Jane Rose during her lifetime.

EXAMPLE 4: FOLLOWING THE SEPARATIONS AND DIVORCES

Ezekiel Rose's wife Mary Rose, proved to be formerly a Higkins through a deed, was discussed in Chapter 10 Page 156. But married bliss did not follow this couple. The 14 April 1794 issue of the *Potowmac Guardian, and Berkeley Advertiser*, Martinsburg, Virginia [now West Virginia] reported that:

---

[3] These deeds do not necessarily indicate an estrangement among members of the family. They were an effort to assist the parents while protecting the property from creditors.

WHEREAS Mary Rose, the wife of me the subscriber, has left my bed and board, without any just cause, I therefore caution all persons trusting or in any manner dealing with her on my account, as I will not be answerable for any debt she may contract, or any dealing she may make, after this date. [Signed] EZEKIEL ROSE Hampshire County [Virginia], March 15, 1794.

The couple lived in Washington County, Pennsylvania, previously but evidently moved to Hampshire County, Virginia (where members of Ezekiel's family had lived earlier). Sometime after the marital separation Ezekiel Rose moved to Muskingum County, Ohio, and left his will there dated in 1818. He bequeathed to his daughter Rachel Prior 84 cents, to his daughter Sarah Williams 84 cents, to his son Ezekiel Rose 84 cents, to his daughter Nancy Smith 84 cents, to his son William Rose 84 cents. The remainder he left to his daughter Hannah Rose and made her the sole executrix.

Besides our curiosity at the odd amount of 84 cents (!), we notice that his wife Mary is not mentioned. If we were unaware of the newspaper notice, we might assume that she predeceased him. But assumptions can trip us up. Further investigation of Muskingum County records disclosed the estate filed there of a Mary Rose in August Term 1827. A man named William Rose was appointed administrator. Since Ezekiel had a son named William in his 1818 will, the naming of a William Rose as administrator of Mary Rose was significant. With that similarity the possibility arose that this Mary Rose could be Ezekiel's wife or former wife. If so, the omission in Ezekiel's 1818 estate of any mention of a wife Mary would appear to be further evidence that they had a legal separation. Subsequent searches did not reveal the divorce record in any of his known locations.

What to do?

The original estate packet for Mary Rose was sought. This revealed that the sale bill in her 1827 estate file included buyers Hannah Rose, William Rose, Jeremiah Lowry, and others. We have evidence that Ezekiel Rose had a son William and a daughter Hannah from his will, and other records prove that the wife of William was a Lowry. Mary's estate not only indicates a connection to a William Rose and a Hannah Rose, but additionally a Lowry was a buyer at the estate sale. A good case can be made that she was indeed the former wife of Ezekiel Rose. An assumption that Ezekiel's wife predeceased him based solely on the omission of her name from his will would have been erroneous.

EXAMPLE 5: THE WILL IS MISSING

When the will is missing because of lost records, other sources may uncover it. Some examples:

If a will is missing in one location, scrutinize for leads that might indicate a *copy* was filed elsewhere.

189

Chancery or Equity Records: In one case, the will of Zachariah Rose no longer survives in the records of Bradley County, Tennessee. However, a suit was filed in McMinn County where the Chancery Court was sitting. Complainants James H. Walling, Isaac L. Walling and Sarah E. Singletary, citizens of Illinois, sued John M. Miller, citizen of McMinn County, Tennessee; Nancy Atkinson and husband; Campbell B. Atkinson; Mary Elliott and husband John Elliott, citizens of Bradley County, Tennessee; Emma Clark and husband William Clark, citizens of Dade County, Georgia; and John K. Atkinson of Bradley County, Tennessee. The Complainants stated that Zachariah Rose died in 1855 in Bradley County, Tennessee. Further, that in the terms of his will, his property was to be divided upon the death of his widow, who died in 1858. It was the belief of the complainants that the sale of assets brought $4000.00, of which their 1/4 amounted to about $1000.00, but they received only $400.00. This was the basis of the suit. In filing the action, they included a copy of Zachariah Rose's will, which is now the only extant copy since the will is not in the Bradley County records.

Property Owned Elsewhere. Duncan Rose's 1785 will of Dinwiddie County, Virginia, would have been completely lost to us because those records are missing. Luckily, it was also filed in Shelby County, Kentucky, since he owned land there. This important document not only names his heirs, it also proves that he had a brother Thomas Rose of "Inverness North Britain." This emphasizes the importance of checking in each of the counties in which property was owned, especially when local records have been destroyed.

EXAMPLE 6: WIDENING THE SEARCH

What appears at first to be a simple record, when properly analyzed can serve as a springboard to other documents.

We've already seen in Chapter 6 that Ann Rose, widow of Jonathan, renounced his will even though he had left her a third dower. Let's examine this family and its records in more detail.

The will of Jonathan Rose, a wealthy inhabitant of Berkeley County, Virginia (now West Virginia),[4] as filed in that county in Will Book 1 p. 392. A summary:

> 13 May 1779, Jonathan Rose of Berkeley County, Colony of Virginia, yeoman, to wife, [called both Anne and Nancy Rose[5] in the will], the home and whole plantation whereon I now live in Berkeley County, 614 acres. Also her choice of two horses, also choice of two cows, all the household goods

Broaden the search by evaluating every record.

---

[4] Pre-West Virginia records are in the courthouses or archives of West Virginia, for they remained in the courthouses when West Virginia was formed.

[5] Nancy was a common nickname for Anne; the testator included both names.

and furniture and the negro woman Jin together with all the plows, harrow, wagon and their tacking during life, if she remains a widow, but if she alters her condition by marriage, she to receive 1500 pounds Pennsylvania currency. To Elizabeth Harmison during her life, land above the run that divides John *Miers* and his son Francis *Meyers*, whereon Francis *Myers* lived, also negro girl Cate, until Elizabeth Harmison's daughter Sarah is of age or married. To John *Coulter*, for life, tract belonging to me called Poor Mans Habitation together with the resurvey I took upon it as far as the run. Sarah the daughter of Elizabeth Harmison shall have all my lands and tenements in Maryland and Virginia after death of "my wife Elizabeth Harmison and John *Colter*." Stocks and moveables after wife's choice are to be sold, and debts and funeral charges paid. He named as executor his "brother in law James Robinson." Jonathan Rose signed the will and it was witnessed by Thomas Mains and Paul Hulse Jr. and proved 16 August 1785.

The first key item to notice is that though Sarah is referred to as "daughter of" Elizabeth Harmison more than once, Sarah's own surname is not given in his will, but later records call her Sarah Rose. This omission of her surname will become important.

Notice, too, that Jonathan named his "brother in law James Robinson" as his executor. It would be easy to assume that Jonathan's wife Anne was a Robinson. In genealogy though we look beyond what seems obvious, and from the above can only state that she *might* be a Robinson. As it turned out, additional courthouse records proved she wasn't a Robinson at all, but a Campbell. In Harrison County, Virginia, Anne Rose, widow of Jonathan Rose, in 1800 for $1 deeded to "my brother Thomas Campbell" her interest in the estate of "deceased brother" William Campbell who had died intestate.

The will of Jonathan Rose was not clear. Did he intend for Sarah, daughter of Elizabeth Harmison, to obtain her interest as each of the three devisees died? Or not until all three were dead? In the latter case, who then was to have possession as each died, until all three were deceased? This ambiguity was the basis for a subsequent deed in which James Robinson and his wife Hannah (whose maiden name was Rose, as she was a sister of Jonathan Rose) were paid 30 pounds to relinquish any interest they might have in Jonathan's lands because of this confusion.

The Robinson's 1794 deed sets forth that because "Doubts have arisen" whether Sarah [who had married Lancelot Jacques] and her husband can take any part of the landed estate until after the death of Ann Rose, Elizabeth Harmison, and John Coulter, or whether "in the meantime except so much as is devised to the person last named" should descend to the "Heirs at Law of the said Jonathan Rose as being undisposed of by his will to wit Sarah Cox widow Hannah the wife of James Robinson aforesaid and Abigail the wife of Thomas Hinds Sisters and co-heiresses of the said Jonathan Rose." The deed further states that Sarah is in possession of the land except for portions devised for the life of Ann Rose and Elizabeth Harmison, which implies that John Coulter (who had been devised the other third) was now deceased.

What did we learn from the Robinsons' deed?

- That Hannah (Rose) Robinson, one of the three sisters and coheiresses of Jonathan Rose, gave up any possible interest because of the ambiguity, for a 30 pound payment.

- That Jonathan Rose left no brothers since only the sisters were the coheiresses.

- That Jonathan had no legitimate children, as they would have had a claim to any undisposed part.

- That John Coulter had died, since Sarah (daughter of Elizabeth Harmison [called Sarah Rose when she married to Lancelot Jacques] was in possession of Coulter's part of the land. .

The Robinsons' deed presented another puzzle. Sarah's last name was not mentioned in the will of Jonathan Rose—she is only referred to as Sarah, the daughter of Elizabeth Harmison. Other research located the estate of Daniel Rose of Frederick County, Virginia, father of Jonathan Rose, and proved that Jonathan also had two brothers. Those brothers appear from the records to have died unmarried. So, how was Sarah, given no surname in Jonathan's will but only referred to as daughter of Elizabeth Harmison, related to Jonathan Rose? She would seem to be since her marriage was under the name of Sarah Rose. She evidently was not a niece. To this day, no explanation has been uncovered. Elizabeth Harmison's daughter Sarah Rose was special to Jonathan to have been treated so generously in his will. Could Sarah, daughter of Elizabeth, have been an illegitimate daughter of Jonathan? Or, could Elizabeth Harmison have been a Rose either by birth or marriage, had a daughter named Sarah Rose, and then remarried to a Harmison accounting for the different surnames of Elizabeth and her daughter Sarah? All possible interpretations need to be researched.

The term "in-law" can lead to misidentifications!

Returning to the will of Jonathan Rose, and his appointment of his brother-in-law James Robinson as his executor. Combining that with the above Robinson deed, we can now see that James had married Hannah, the sister of Jonathan Rose. James, however, for unknown reasons did not serve as executor, and Ann Rose, the widow, was appointed administratrix cum testamento annexo (with the will annexed).[6] (See Chapter 6).

---

[6] The fact that James Robinson who was named as executor chose not to assume that duty, and Ann Rose (who had not been named by her husband as executor) was subsequently appointed as administratrix cta, may imply that there was some dissension in this family.

This example[7] demonstrates how easy it would be to be led astray with clauses such as "brother-in-law."[8] It also shows the importance of examining additional records—in this case the deed was vitally important.

We might also look beyond the actual records and speculate that there was some dissension in this family. The widow renounced her dower so she would get one-half instead of one-third, the brother-in-law did not serve as executor, and the sisters were not content with the will.

STRATEGIES FOR LETTER WRITING

Writing to courthouses can elicit some good results. Or, the letter may be ignored. Why? What could have made the letter more effective? Some pointers to help avoid your letter languishing on a clerk's desk, unanswered.

GENERAL RULES WHEN WRITING

Keep letters brief; never over one page. Two or three short paragraphs is best. Put your name and address on both the letter and the envelope. Additionally:

- Be specific in stating your request.

- Write a separate letter for each *kind* of record you are requesting if those records are maintained in different courthouse offices. For example, if you need deeds you can write to the Register of Deeds. If you also need an estate record, write a separate letter to the probate office; don't combine it with your request for deeds. If you request them in the same letter, the chances are not favorable that one office will fulfill your order and then send your letter on to the other office.

- If you need several documents, even if they are from the same department, split the request over a period of time. It would be permissible to request 2-4 deeds in one letter, but if you need eight of them, you will have better success by ordering a few, and after they arrive, ordering the remainder. Otherwise, it is too easy for busy clerks to set aside your request until they have time to gather everything you need.

- Ask for a price quotation. Some areas (such as some New York counties) charge large fees on mail requests just to look at indexes, and impose high fees for photocopying. In some cases the lookup charge alone can be $75.00. If you know the page numbers of the whole document, phone them (or write) for the amount before you send the order. If getting your quote by telephone, be sure to contact the correct office. The fee for a marriage record copy, for instance, is usually more than the per-page copying fee of a deed.

Letter writing is becoming a "lost art" but its importance to genealogical pursuits does not diminish.

---

[7] The other two sisters also settled their claims in related court actions.

[8] Mentioned in Chapter 5 is the possibility that "brother-in-law" is a stepbrother, too.

Improving writing skills can not only assist in getting information by mail, it will enhance our compilation when we write our family's history.

- Be explicit. Are you requesting the will only? Or, the will *and* the petition for probate? Do you really want the will, or do you want the *original* will? Or, do you want *all* the papers in the original probate packet? It may be best to request only one or two of the documents at first, to be sure you have the right estate. If the complete packet is voluminous, your chance of getting photocopies of the contents diminishes. You may need to contact a local researcher in the area to obtain them for you.

- Always include a long (called No. 10) self-addressed, stamped envelope. (Referred to as a LSASE.)

STATING THE REQUEST CLEARLY

We've all had situations in which we've written letters asking for information or documents, and to our surprise, the request was misunderstood. What went wrong? The following few examples demonstrate how we need to hone our requests

Facts: Your records indicate that your ancestor arrived with his family in the county in 1810 and they left in 1820. You want their land records while they lived there.

Poor: I request photocopies for any deeds for Elias Cunningham recorded between 1810 and 1820.

Better: I request photocopies for any deeds for Elias Cunningham, either as grantor or grantee, recorded between 1805 and 1825.

Note the addition of "grantor and grantee"—otherwise the clerk will not understand what you are requesting. If you want just one or the other, specify which. And, why did I change the dates? Elias may have bought land before his arrival in that county and then moved there with his family. Or, he may have still owned land after he left the county and sold it later. Give the dates some leeway.

You might also consider, before ordering any deeds at all, to first ask for a photocopy or listing of all of the surname from the deed index as there may be many more deeds than you anticipated. Then you can choose which to order. This is not always effective, however, for some deed indexes (as previously discussed in Chapter 2) do not group the names together. Or the courthouse may not allow photocopying of the index books. (You could also first order microfilm of the deed indexes from the Family History Library, and use that listing to order the copies from the courthouse.)

Facts: You know your ancestor Joseph Jordan was in the 1840 census, but you don't find him in 1850. You suspect he died before the latter year. Now you are seeking his estate from the courthouse.

Poor: I am seeking the estate of Joseph Jordan who I believe died before 1850.

Better: I am seeking the estate of Joseph Jordan who I believe died 1840-1850.

Note that you added a beginning date too, so that the clerk needs only to do a ten-year search instead of a more extensive search.

Facts: You know from the tombstone that George Matthews died June 1855, and you have record of an executor which indicates that he left a will. You want a copy of that will.

Poor: I request a photocopy of the will of George Matthews who died 1855.

Better: I request a photocopy of the original will of George Matthews who died in 1855. If the original will is no longer in existence, I request a photocopy of the copied will in the will book.

If you haven't specified in the above that you want the original, you will surely get the copied will instead which is subject to a clerk's error in transcribing. You may have to settle for that copy, though, if the policy of the courthouse is not to photocopy the original.

Facts: Your ancestors William Smith and Mary Holden were married in the county, probably shortly before the 1880 census.

Poor: I request a copy of the marriage record of William Smith and Mary Holden who married by 1880.

Better: I request a photocopy of the marriage license or application, and a photocopy of the marriage certificate, of William Smith and Mary Holden. They married probably 1875-1880.

In the above marriage example you have broadened your request to include other important papers, and assisted the clerk by narrowing the years.

Facts: You know Abraham Jessup died in the county. He was aged 84 in the 1880 census.

Poor: I would like to know if you have a death record of Abraham Jessup.

Better: I would like to obtain a photocopy of the death record for Abraham Jessup who was aged 84 in 1880, and died within a few years after that time.

STRATEGIES FOR FINDING AFRICAN-AMERICAN RECORDS

Documents involving African-Americans are scattered throughout court records. The following few observations should help researchers overcome some of the difficulties in tracing their lineage.

> Clerks appreciate letters that don't leave them guessing as to what's requested.

In the vital records, there were often separate books for the records of births, marriages, and deaths marked as "colored." If the records for all races are combined, be sure to check the column designating "race" or "color." If you don't see any marked as "black," "colored," or "mulatto," there may be separate registers. In some areas, the deaths of slaves were reported by their masters. In one register of deaths in Fredericksburg, Virginia, "Rose," a slave, died in August of 1862 at Fredericksburg, Virginia, of typhoid fever, aged 29 years. The death was reported by the master, W. H. Fitzhugh. In another, Rose, a slave girl, died in April of 1854 at Fredericksburg of dropsy, aged 4 years, born in Stafford County, Virginia. She was the "daughter of Hannah." The death was reported by R. D. Thorburn, owner.

When using deed indexes, look in the column captioned "kind of instrument" for the words "manumissions," "free negro," or other designations to indicate that an African-American was involved in the record. The information contained can add interest to your compilation of the family's history. In Fauquier County, Virginia, in 1861, Elizabeth Sands alias Douglas was emancipated by deed from Joseph Conard, administrator of Mary Conard deceased. At that time Elizabeth was described as being of dark brown color with a large scar, a mark on the inside of the left arm above the "rist," was about fifty-two years of age, and five feet four inches in height.

In estates, look at all of the estate papers of those you believe might have been owners of the slaves in your family. It's impossible to predict which paper in the estate might prove to be useful. The will can, of course, name slaves, but the inventory of the estate can be even more useful. If you find a record of which family member inherited the slaves, follow that family member through deeds and estate papers to see if you can reconstruct what happened to those who were inherited. Did that family member sell those inherited slaves? Do they appear on his tax lists? Do they appear in his own will or inventory later?

The designation of "FN" by a name indicates "free negro." Free negroes were sometimes apprehended as if they were slaves, and had to prove they had their freedom. In some cases they were kidnapped and then sold as if they were slaves. In a Free Negro Register in Fauquier County, Virginia, in 1844, Charles G. Eskridge, Clerk of Court, certified that William Winters, the son of Sarah Winters, was free born as proved by the oath of Miriam Aole, "said boy about [?] years old and a dark mulatto." Also, free negroes can often be located through the tax lists.

WPA Interviews. The WPA records (see Chapter 11) from 1936 to 1938 contain interviews of over 2300 former slaves. Most were born in the last years of slavery, and were therefore young children at the time. Samples of these transcriptions of the interviews are fascinating and can be accessed at: <http://xroads.virginia.edu/~hyper/wpa/wpahome.html>. This is how the Internet excels; its ability to furnish us with glimpses into the lives of our family not easily available to us elsewhere. Our family comes "alive" with such `firsthand accounts.

Fugitive Slaves. States had various laws regarding fugitive or runaway slaves. In Pennsylvania, for example, an act was passed on 27 March 1820 to prevent kidnapping. Judges were required to record the name, age, sex, and general description of such fugitives or runaways. Evidence in the case was to be recorded and a certified copy of the information sent to the county where the fugitive or runaway resided. These records are not easy to locate since you may not know that your ancestor was involved in such an action. However, when doing your overall research, keep an eye open for records in the criminal court of each county in which your ancestor was known to live. Your ancestor may have been the center of such an action, and if so, valuable details might be added to your family's history.

STRATEGIES FOR "KNOWING" OUR ANCESTORS

Can you use courthouse records to help understand the family's life? Yes. Perhaps it isn't readily obvious, but let's look at some of the hidden clues.

Family Unity

- Did the children contest the father's will?
- Did the father find it necessary to specify which rooms in the home were to be occupied by each child after he was deceased, and to provide that they all had a right to use the kitchen?
- Did the husband give his wife property for her outright use with no restrictions?
- Did the family make a concerted effort to purchase contiguous property? Sometimes a number of family members ended up living on the same street or road, inferring a closely knit group.
- Was there an unusual number of witnesses to the will, implying some possible concern over the terms of the will?

Judgment

- Did your ancestor buy property and constantly sell at a loss?
- Did he buy and constantly sell at a profit?
- Did his estate show that he held a number of notes against others?
- Did others hold a number of notes against him?
- Did he own land in several counties, indicating perhaps that he was a speculator? (Or, that he had "itchy" feet?)

Love of Animals

- Did your ancestor make provision in his will for the pets? Specify who was to care for them, and leave a bequest to cover that care?

Reading "between the lines" can give us a sense of the family.

197

Measure of Prosperity

- Did your ancestor heavily mortgage his land?
- Were there numerous liens against him?
- Did he have to borrow money yearly to plant a crop?
- Did he lose his property at a sheriff's sale because of debt or judgments?

Occupation

- Did deeds and other records in large cities mention his occupation?
- Did the inventories in their estates mention tools of the trade such as shoemaker's tools? Unusual amounts of fabric? A large number of bee hives?

Temperament and "Respectability"

- Did you ancestor serve frequently on juries? Did he act as bondsman for others? Was he the guardian of family members or others?
- Was your ancestor being sued on numerous occasions by others for slander? Assault and battery? In criminal records?

Religion

- Did the will mention the church bench, the churchyard cemetery, or other indication of religion?
- Did the testator "affirm" and thus give a clue that he was probably Quaker?

Spirit of Adventure or Restlessness

- Was he always moving on to the "new" frontier?
- Did he live away from settled communities?

Abraham Roose's will of "Mamaeocotton " twp., Ulster County, New York, mentions his "banch" in Shawangunk Church. Though such dispositions are not too commonly found in wills, they furnish another snippet of our ancestors' lives when they do.

KEEPING US GOING

While you search you will find numerous records that will bring a smile, tug with poignancy, or make you aware of individuals' efforts at fairness. I am always impressed with the provision that two sons are to share property—one is to divide it, and the other to have first choice after the division. Or the father who was determined to prevent friction in his family by specifying which room of the house each was to occupy. Or, the husband who specified that the son was to daily bring his mother a sufficient amount of firewood, and see that she was mounted on the best horse to go to church every Sunday. In one will, the father left minor sons their normal portion of his estate, which they were to receive when 21, if they had not committed an offense costing more than 10 shillings during those years.

My thoughts wander into sadness when I read the wills such as that of W. P. Rose who left his daughter nothing, "not having heard from her in more than fifty years, I do not know if alive or dead."

THE SAGA OF A REVOLUTIONARY SOLDIER

You have read this book, and you may be thinking, "What is wrong that I haven't been able to solve my problems?" Let me assure you, we all have at least one problem (and probably many!) that defy our efforts to solve them. Such is the case with James Rose. Let me tell you about him.

James Rose was in the Revolutionary War. His very extensive Revolutionary War pension papers gave me the first real glimpse of this man. They show that he was born 10 March 1751. He married first to a woman named Mary Ann who was aged "about 100" (close to 30 years his senior) when James appeared in the Wilkes County, North Carolina, court in 1824 to make his declaration for pension. While doing so, he mentioned a grandson John, and declared himself a resident of King George County, Virginia. But that wasn't the last I would hear of this man.

James' wife finally died and he married again in 1828 in Grayson County, Virginia, to Rebecca (Phipps) Durham, the widow of Isaac Durham. A separation soon followed, though if there was a legal divorce, the record has eluded all researchers.

A will of James Rose is dated in 1831. He declared himself a resident of Hawkins County, Tennessee. That will was taken to the courthouse in Tennessee and there it remains to this day. In it he mentioned his Revolutionary War pension, gave a friend Benjamin Bunch a tract of land in Grayson County, Virginia, and added an enigmatic "N.B." that "the pension ... I reserve for my own use free from this will ..." It's unclear what use he would have for that pension since he would be presumably deceased when the will was probated! No mention is made of the wife he married only three years earlier, but we'd better not jump to the conclusion that she is deceased. Nor is there mention in his 1831 will of any children by his first wife.

In any event, James Rose lived for many years, and why the will was even taken to the Hawkins County courthouse is a mystery. He didn't die until 1842, and a newer will dated that year was probated in the King George County, Virginia, courthouse. In this one he gave to "my relation Wm Rowley all my land in Russel County," a tract containing 185 acres, and also gave to Wm Rowley three horses "now in his possession," but in case "my Son" Wm Rose and his heirs or the heirs of "my sister Frankey Rose whose residence is unknown, should come and make application for any part ... they shall have an equal part of the three horses." He further specified that the relation William Rowley "shall take care of his mother Mary Rowley." No executor was named. James Rose made no mention of other children nor of the grandson John mentioned in his 1824 pension declaration. He again neglected to mention his second wife Rebecca, who it turns out was still living. No explanation as to whether he was divorced or separated, appears in any of the papers, and dower interest of a wife in the land is not mentioned.

But, the saga has not ended. The second wife ended up in the poor house, old, and in pitiful circumstances. Pleas on her behalf by a townsman related the tragedy that befell her. Rebecca had been defrauded by others of her pension for which (it was stated) she was eligible through the Revolutionary War services of her husband James Rose.

In spite of the number of records obtained on this family, at each juncture only questions appear instead of answers. Why did he make his 1824 declaration in Wilkes County, North Carolina, though he was a resident of King George County, Virginia? How did his 1831 will end up in the Hawkins County courthouse, when James didn't die until over ten years later in Virginia? Why didn't James in either of the two wills mention his second wife, even if only to satisfy possible legal questions about his marital status? If they were still legally married, why didn't she have a dower claim to his Russell County property or to his King George County property? Someone must have been aware that she was still living subsequent to his death, evidenced by the fact that she was defrauded of her pension. And, why was she still eligible for the pension if they were divorced? What happened to James' son William and to James' sister Frankey? Why wasn't the son William named in the 1831 will? Did James have other children?

Every document collected on this family has only expanded the list of questions and intensified the desire to answer them. Do you have a similar situation? I can only say, persevere. And keep your good humor. One day the problem *will,* we hope, be solved. It is, after all, the challenges that keep us going. And through these challenges and our efforts to resolve them, we are forced into deeper research, learning all the way.

SOURCE REFERENCES

This includes the titles mentioned in the various chapters, and also some additional suggestions.

BOOKS AND ARTICLES

Black, Henry Campbell. *Black's Law Dictionary.* St. Paul, Minn.: West Publishing Co. The later editions include the current usage of terms, but look in the older editions for many of the outdated terms and definitions genealogists will need.

Bentley, Elizabeth Petty. *County Courthouse Book.* 2nd edition. Baltimore, Maryland: Genealogical Publishing Company, 1995. Use the 2nd or latest edition for listings of courthouses, phone number, dates of organization, and other pertinent information.

Bockstruck, Lloyd. *Revolutionary War Bounty Grants Awarded by State Governments.* Baltimore: Genealogical Publishing Company, 1996. An important guide explaining state bounty land and the state laws, and also including lists of those who received state bounty land.

Bouvier, John. *A Law Dictionary.* Revised Sixth Edition. Philadelphia: Childs & Peterson, 1856. A useful online law dictionary almost 150 years old.

Colletta, John Philip. *They Came in Ships: Guide to Finding Your Immigrant Ancestor's Arrival Record.* Revised Edition. Salt Lake City: Ancestry Inc., 2002. Anyone seeking their ancestor who immigrated will want to read this important guide.

Child, Sargent B. and Dorothy P. Holmes. *Check List of Historical Records Survey Publications.* Washington, 1943. Reprint. Baltimore: Clearfield, 1969.

Eales, Anne Bruner and Robert M. Kvasnicka. *Guide to Genealogical Research in the National Archives of the United States.* Washington, D.C.: National Archives and Records Administration, 2000. Though not written for courthouse research, nonetheless many of its records can help reconstruct land records, vital records, and others.

Eichholz, Alice ed. *Redbook.* Salt Lake City: Ancestry Inc., 1992. In spite of the years which have elapsed since its publication, this book remains an essential source for the family historian. Not only does it include courthouse addresses, formation dates of counties, etc., but each state also has a summary written by an expert on that state's records and their organization. Extremely useful.

Greenwood, Val D. *The Researcher's Guide to American Genealogy.* 3rd edition. Baltimore, Md.: Genealogical Publishing Company, 1999. This is an excellent guide to multi aspects of genealogical research including court documents.

Handy Book for Genealogists, Tenth Edition Logan, Utah: Everton Publishers, 2002. Includes essential information for the courthouse researcher; addresses, formation date of county, parent county, records available, maps, and other pertinent information.

Hatcher, Patricia Law. *Locating Your Roots: Discover Your Ancestors Using Land Records.* Cincinnati, Ohio: Betterway Books, 2003. Important land information is in this book.

Hawkins, Kenneth. *Research in the Land Entry Files of the General Land Office. Record Group 49.* Revised. Washington, D.C.: National Archives and Records Administration, 1998. This free publication may be obtained from the National Archives. It is also available online at <http://www.archives.gov/publications/general_information_leaflets/67.html>.or at <http://www.rootsweb.com/~mnbecker/land_entry.htm>.

Hone, Wade E. *Land and Property Research in the United States.* Salt Lake City Ancestry Inc., 1997.

Hefner, Loretta L. *The WPA Historical Records Survey: A Guide to the Unpublished Inventories, Indexes and Transcripts.* Chicago: Society of American Archivists, 1980.

Keim, C. Ray. "Primogeniture and Entail in Colinial Virginia." *The William and Mary Quarterly* Third Series. XXV (1968): 545-586. This helpful article can assist in understanding the use of primogeniture in the colonial period.

Knepper, George W. *The Official Ohio Lands Book.* Columbus, Ohio: The Auditor of State, 2002. A magnificent booklet on the various surveys of Ohio. The latest edition is available by contacting the State Auditor's Office, Ohio. An earlier edition is online at <http://freepages.history.rootsweb.com/~maggie/ohio-lands/ohlands.html>.

Kirkham, E. Kay. *Handwriting of American Records for a Period of 300 Years.* Logan, Utah: Everton Publishers, 1973. In spite of the age of this book, the examples and explanations are still useful.

Melnyk, Marcia D. *Genealogist's Handbook for New England Research,* Fourth Edition. Boston: New England Historic Genealogical Society, 1999. New England has states on the county courthouse system, and states whose records are in town halls and probate districts. This guide will help you plan your research trip by providing that information and more.

Mills, Elizabeth Shown, ed. *Professional Genealogy: A Manual for Researchers, Writers, Editors, Lecturers, and Librarians.* Baltimore: Genealogical Publishing Company, 2001. This book is an important contribution to various aspects of genealogy by a number of authors who are experts in their fields. Some of the chapters are directly pertinent to the skills required for courthouse research, such as abstracting, analyzing evidence, etc.

Mills, Elizabeth Shown. *Evidence! Citation and Analysis for the Family Historian. Baltimore, Md.: Genealogical Publishing Company, 1997.* This book is an absolute must for anyone doing any kind of genealogical research. In courthouse researching it isimportant to take full citations of the abstracted items, so later the same record can be easily retrieved by others conducting research on the family.

Myrick, Kory L., ed. *Printed Sources: A Guide to Published Genealogical Records.* Salt Lake City: Ancestry Inc., 1996. This compilation will point you to many of the sources to assist with the courthouse search.

Newman, John J. *American Naturalization Records, 1790-1990, What they are and How to Use Them,* 2nd edition. Bountiful, Utah: Heritage Quest, 1998. A great deal of knowledge essential to understanding our immigration laws lies in this book.

Rose, Christine. *Genealogical Proof Standard: Building a Solid Case.* San Jose, Calif.: Rose Family Association, 2001. This is a concise guide and explanation of this standard.

———. *Nicknames: Past and Present.* 4th edition. San Jose, Calif.: Rose Family Association, 2001. Though knowledge of nicknames is important in any index, in some, such as the Campbell index described in Chapter 2, it is especially important since the entries are indexed by given names (and sometimes nicknames).

Rose, Christine and Kay Germain Ingalls. *The Complete Idiot's Guide to Genealogy.* New York: Alpha Books, 1997. See particularly Chapter 12, "A Little Traveling Music, Please," relating to courthouse research.

Russell, Donna Valley. *Frederick County, Maryland, Genealogical Research Guide.* New Market, Md.: Catoctin, 1987. This will demonstrate how a good county guide can help.

Salmon, Marylynn Salmon. *Women and the Law of Property in Early America*. Chapel Hill, N.C.: University of North Carolina Press, 1986. A fascinating book that includes valuable observations about women's rights. It will help in understanding some of the records you'll find.

Schaeffer, Christina K. *Guide to Naturalization Records of the United States*. Baltimore, Md.: Genealogical Publishing Co., 1997. This lists many sources to assist in locating your ancestor's naturalization records, many of which are available in courthouses.

Shammas, Carole. "English Inheritance Law and Its Transfer to the Colonies." *American Journal of Legal History*. 31 (1989): 145-163.

Smith, Juliana Szucs. *The Ancestry Family Historian's Address Book*. Salt Lake City,: Ancestry Inc., 1997. This is useful in providing addresses of many of the agencies or repositories you'll want to visit on your trip.

Sperry, Kip. *Reading Early American Handwriting*. Baltimore, Md.: Genealogical Publishing Company, 1998. Many illustrations and an excellent bibliography exhance the good advice in this book.

Szucs, Loretto Dennis and Sandra Hargreaves Luebking. *The Source*. Salt Lake City: Ancestry Inc., 1996. In particular, Chapters 3, 4, 7 and 8 will assist those working with courthouse records.

Thode, Ernest. *German-English Genealogical Dictionary*. Baltimore, Md.: Genealogical Publishing Company, 1992. If you need help with German handwriting, this book will be useful.

Torrence, Clayton. *Virginia Wills and Administration, 1632-1800*. Baltimore, Md.: Genealogical Publishing Company, 1930, 1990, 2000. This is one of the earliest of the state-wide published indexes to probates. Studying it together with census and other records will help demonstrate the value of using a printed index with other available records to pinpoint where a family may have originated.

Warren, James W. and Paula Stuart Warren. *Your Guide to the Family History Library*. Cincinnati, Ohio: Betterway, 2001.

TAPES
Also check <http://www.audiotapes.com> for listings of lectures on courthouse research given at various national conferences.

Glossary

A consolidated listing of the terms in the chapters.

Abatement. An entire overthrow of a suit, so it is ended.

Abutting owner (or abutter). The owner of land which adjoins where no land, road or street intervenes. Thus, the abutting owners' property touches the specified land.

Acknowldgment. A statement that either the person signed an instrument personally or that he witnessed the signing.

Action at Law. According to law, as opposed to an action in equity.

Administrator (-trix). A person appointed by the court to handle an intestate proceeding, that is, an estate without a will.

Administrator cum testamento annexo (administrator *cta*). This indicates that there is a will. Either an executor was not named in the will and the court was appointing an administrator to handle it, or the executor died, refused to qualify, couldn't qualify, moved from the area, etc. In many areas this term has fallen into disuse and instead the administrator cta is referred to as "administrator with the will annexed" and abbreviated as "w/w/a."

Administrator de bonis non (administrat or *dbn*). A person appointed by the court to handle the remainder of the estate. This situation might arise if the administrator died before the estate was settled, moved from the area, was judged incompetent to continue to administer, or various other causes. More modern usage in many areas is "successor administrator."

Ads. Abbreviation for *ad sectam*, at the suit of. Often seen in early indexes to indicate the defendant. Thus, John Brown *ads.* William Loftin indicates that John Brown is the defendant and William Loftin is the plaintiff.

Affidavit. A written or printed statement of facts, confirmed by oath (or affirmation) of the party making it.

Affirm. To make a solemn and formal declaration that an affidavit is true, that the witness will tell the truth, etc. Substituted at times for an oath, especially by by Quakers.

Agreement. A meeting of two or more minds; a coming together of opinion or determination. Not exactly synonymous with a contract; an agreement might lack one of the essential elements of a contract.

Alienate. To convey, to transfer the title to property.

Anno domini, A.D. In the year of our Lord.

Answer. The defendant's (or respondent's) written defense to a complaint (or a bill).

Appertaining. Belonging to or relating to.

Appurtenance. That which belongs to something else; an appendage. Something annexed. This would include a right of way, an outhouse, barn, garden, easement.

Assault and Battery. (AB) Assault places the victim in fear of harm, other than by words alone, while battery is an unlawful touching of another without justification or excuse. (This type of action was far more common in the early records than we might first suppose.)

Assign. To transfer, make over or set over to another.

Assigns. Those to whom property is, will be, or may be assigned.

Assumpsit. A promise by which one person undertakes to do some act or pay something to another person.

Beneficiary. One who will benefit through the will.

Bequeath. To give personal property by will.

Bastardy bond. A promise by the father of an illegitimate child to pay support.

Bill. The first written pleading in an equity case; a complaint.

Bill of Sale. Written evidence of sale, usually of personal property.

Bond. The court required two or more bondsmen (or "securities") to guarantee the performance of the executor, administrator or guardian. The bond is the written evidence of that obligation.

Bondsmen. See Bond.

Brother-in-law. The husband of a married sister, sometimes the husband of a married sister-in-law. In early times could be a stepbrother, or occasionally an adopted brother. (See also Sister-in-law.)

Caveat. Let him beware. Warning to be careful.

Cemetery Deed. Sometimes a deed to a cemetery lot, and sometimes a deed to the cemetery land.

c.t.a. See administrator cum testamento annexo.

Certified copy. Copy of a document or record, signed and certified as a true copy by an officer in whose custody the original is entrusted.

Certiorari. A written order issued by a higher court to a lower court to produce a certified record of a particular case.

Chain carriers or chain bearers. Those people who carried the measuring chains used by surveyors. (Two were usually required. They were often related; their names appear on the survey.)

Chattel. An article of personal property (as distinguished from real property.)

Chattel Mortgage. See Mortgage.

Citation. A written order commanding the person named to appear on a specific day and take some action specified in the order.

Civil law. Laws concerned with civil or private rights, as opposed to criminal laws. This is distinguished from common law.

Committee. Usually a group of people, some of whom may be related, delegated to a particular duty such as advisors or managers of an estate of an incompetent person.

Common law. Based on usage and precedents, common law is distinguished from statutory law which is created by legislation.

Common law action. Action governed by common law, rather than statutory, equitable, or civil law.

Complaint. The original or initial pleading which starts an action setting forth the facts of the claim.

Complainant. One who files a complaint (that is, the plaintiff).

Congressional township. See township.

Consanguinity. Kinship or blood relationship. The connection of persons descended from a common ancestor.

Consideration. The cause, motive, price or compelling influence which induces the parties to enter into a contract. In a deed, this is usually monetary; however, it can be for "love and affection," the exchange of property, or for other considerations.

Contest (will). To oppose, resist or dispute a will.

Contract. An agreement between two or more persons to do or not to do a particular thing. Certain criteria must be met to make it valid.

Convey. To transfer or deliver to another.

Coram. Before; in the presence of.

Co-respondent. Normally, in a divorce suit, a person charged with having committed adultery with the defendant.

Court of Record. A court whose proceedings are required by law to be kept on permanent record.

Coverture. The status of a married woman under common law.

cum testamento annexo. See Administrator cum testamento annexo.

Curtesy. An estate by which a man was entitled, on the death of his wife, of the lands and tenements which she owned. For the husband to be entitled to curtesy, they had to have had lawful issue born alive (even if the child subsequently died). It is an estate for the term of the husband's natural life only.

Curtilage. Originally, a place enclosed around a yard, such as the land and outbuildings around a case, or a courtyard. Now, any land or building immediately adjacent to a dwelling, usually enclosed by shrubs or a fence.

de bonis non; dbn. See Administrator de bonis non.

Decree. A declaration of the court announcing the court's decision.

Deed of Heirs. Usually a deed made by those who inherited land through an intestate proceeding.

Deed of Lease and Release. See Lease and Release.

Deed of Trust. See Trust Deed.

206

Demurrer. A defendant's allegation admitting to the facts in a complaint or bill, but claiming that those facts are not sufficient for the plaintiff to proceed or for the defendant to answer.

Deposition. The testimony of a witness taken in answer to either oral or written questions. The person who is deposed (otherwise the person whose testimony is being taken) is called the deponent.

Detinue. This is an action to recover personal chattels from someone who had lawfully acquired possession but who then retained it without a right to do so.

Devise. To give real property by will. A devisor is the giver (the testator) while the devisee is the recipient.

Discharge. This can be a military discharge. In other usage, can mean that a debt has been discharged, that is, paid. It can also mean that a person appointed has been relieved of duties, for example, an executor upon completing his duties in the estate can be discharged upon the closing of the estate.

Dower. The provision for alloting a portion of the land the law makes to a widow. Usually one-third, but can be one-half in some circumstances.

Dower Release. A widow may choose to release her dower in land, either for a price, or as a gift.

Ear mark brand. A brand for one's livestock, registered so that its owner can be identified.

Ejectment. An action to restore possession of a piece of property to the person entitled to it.

Emancipation. The act of freeing someone from bondage or restraint.

Endorsement, indorsement. When a holder of a negotiable instrument (a check, note, etc.) signs his name on it, thereby assigning or transferring it to someone else.

Entail. This limits the succession of real property. It alters the rules of inheritance to heirs of the donee's body (his lawful issue), going in a specified line of descent as prescribed by the entail. It commonly is limited to males, and commonly to the eldest son of each succeeding generation. Though entails were most often established by a will, many were established by a deed.

Equity. Justice administered according to fairness.

Escheat. The reversion of property to the state when there is no individual entitled to inherit.

Estray. Usually defined as a wandering animal whose owner is unknown.

Exemplified copy. Copy of a document which has been authenticated under the seal of a higher court or supervisory officer.

et al. Latin; *et alii*, and other persons.

et ux. Latin; *et uxor*, and wife.

et vir. Latin; and husband.

Ex parte. Done for or on the behalf of, one party only. An ex parte hearing is one in which the court hears only one side of the controversy.

Execution. Carrying out a court order until its completion. For example, execution of a money judgment is the legal process which enforces the judgment and can result in the seizure and sale of personal or real property, or both.

Executor (-trix). A person named by the testator in a will to handle the estate.

Fee simple. These words, when used alone, convey an absolute estate with no limitations or conditions. The owner is entitled to the entire property unconditionally.

Fee tail. See entail.

Feme covert. A married woman.

Feme sole. A single woman, including those who have been married, but whose marriage has been dissolved by death or divorce. (In some instances women who are judicially separated from their husbands.)

Feoffment. The grant of lands as a fee, commonly accompanied by livery of seizin (*q.v.*).

Fiduciary. A person or institution who manages money or property for another. Includes executor, administrator, trustee, and guardian.

Fieri facias (Fi. Fa.; sometimes FF). Literally, "you are to make it to be done." A writ directing the sheriff to satisfy a judgment from the property of the debtor. Originally used for the seizure and sale of personal property, but eventually enlarged to include real property.

Folio. A leaf of a page or manuscript. It was the custom to number the leaves, and thus folio included front and back. Where each folio or sheet is separately numbered, it is usual to refer to the front as *recto* (right), or the folio number followed by R, and the other side as *verso* (turned), with V following the folio number.

Foreclosure. To shut out, to bar, to terminate. Often used when a debt is not repaid.

Freehold. This is an estate held for life or an estate in fee (which includes fee simple and fee tail.) Those appointed to juries, and county offices were required to be freeholders.

Gavelkind. Common in Kent, England, and used in some parts of the American colonies. The land descended to all the sons and could be disposed of by will. (This is sometimes referred to in documents as a conveyance in the manner of East Greenwich, County of Kent, England.) Usually, this particular type of tenure was established in the first royal deed or grant, and restated in succeeding ones: "to be held as of our [royal] Manor of East Greenwich in the county of Kent."

Gift Deed or Deed of Gift. A deed in which the grantor (seller) makes a gift of real or personal property.

Grant. In land, a grant refers to a particular type of transfer, that is, the conveying of a tract of land from a colonial or state government to an individual. Some colonies and states called these patents, as did the federal government.

Grant, bargain and sell. Terms used to convey real estate; the whole phrase was often used.

Grantee. One who receives property.

Grantor. One who transfers property.

Guardian. A person lawfully invested with the charge of another person. Appointed to handle either the person, the estate, (or both) of a minor, incompetent, or one otherwise incapacitated. A guardian ad litem is invested with that charge for a specific purpose (perhaps, as example, to transfer a specific piece of property).

Habeas corpus. An independent proceeding instituted to determine whether a defendant is being unlawfully deprived of his or her liberty.

Habendum clause. *Habendum et tenendum.* Portion of a deed starting with "to have and to hold ..." This determines what estate or interest is being granted by the deed.

Have and to hold. A common phrase in conveyances derived from *habendum et tenendum* (see above) of the old common law.

Heir at law. One who inherits property, whether real or personal, in cases of intestacy (no will).

Heir. See Heir at law.

Heirs and assigns. A standard clause normally indicating that there are no restrictions.

Heirs lawfully begotten of his body forever. A clause in a will or deed which established an entail.

Hereditament. Thing capable of being inherited, whether it is real, personal or mixed.

Holographic will. A will written entirely in the testator's handwriting.

Homestead Exemption. A law passed to allow a householder or head of family to protect his house and land from creditors.

Homestead. The dwelling house and adjoining land where the family dwells. Can also refer to the Homestead Act of 1862, in which land could be obtained from the federal government at no cost if certain requirements were met.

id est; i.e. That is, that is to say. As an example: I convey to my daughter my remaining personal property, *i.e.*, my kitchen chairs and table, and my cupboard.

Injunction. A court order prohibiting a specified act or commanding someone to undo a wrong or injury.

Imparlance. A continuance given to either of the parties to answer the pleadings of the other.

Imprimis. In the first place; first of all.

In room of; in the room of. Instead of. Usually replaces one person with another.

In witness whereof. The initial words of the concluding clause of deeds.

Indenture. In real property transactions, a deed in which two or more persons enter into obligations to each other.

Indictment. A formal written accusation originating with a prosecutor and issued by a grand jury against someone charged with a crime.

Infant. A person under the age of legal majority. (Remember, a 19-year-old male is an "infant" in the eyes of our legal system if the law says you need to be 21!) See also: Majority.

Inmate. In early usage, married or widowed; landless, living in the same house as another or in another building on the same property.

Instant (inst.). Indicates that the date referred to was in the same month as a previously mentioned date. In a newspaper notice of 25th April 1832, if the marriage took place on the 12 inst., it took place 12 April 1832.

Interlined. The addition of a word or words to a document, between lines or words already written, so that the document did not have to be rewritten. The clerk, in transcribing the document into the record books, usually noted at the end that certain words or sentences had been interlined.

Intestate. A person who died without a will. The resulting court proceeding may be called "intestate" proceeding or "administration" proceeding.

Inventory. A detailed list of articles of property, and their estimated or actual value.

Judgment. The official decision of a court in an action or suit.

Jurat. Usually means a clause or certificate indicating when, where and before whom an affidavit was sworn. However, in wills and deeds, the addition of the word "Jurat" after a witness's name indicates that the witness indicated went into court to acknowledge his or her witnessing.

Lease. An agreement between the landlord (lessor) and the tenant (the lessee).

Lease and Release. A companion set of documents, used in some states, in which the first (the deed of lease) established a lease for a nominal fund, and the second (the deed of release), dated at least a day later, gave the details of the actual price. This dual transaction was actually a sale.

Letters. When the court approved the appointment of an executor, administrator or guardian, "letters" were issued by the court making that appointment. Letters Testamentary, Letters of Administration, or Letters of Guardianship are commonly seen in estate matters.

Lien. A claim, encumbrance, or charge on property for payment of a debt.

Lineal. That which comes in a line, such as a direct line, parent to child.

Livery of seisin (also seizin). A common law ceremony transferring the land. It was a livery *in deed* when the parties went onto the land to perform the ceremony, or livery *at law* when the ceremony was not performed on the land but in sight of it.

Locus sigilli, (L.S.). In the place of the seal.

Majority. Full age; legal age at which a person is no longer a minor. The age at which, by law, a person is capable of being legally responsible for all of his or her acts. (This will vary for certain actions, depending upon the laws of the time, and the state. It can also differ for males and females.))

Male Tail. An entail which descends to males only, usually set up as the eldest. See also Entail.

Malfeasance. The commission of some act which is positively unlawful.

Manor house. A house, dwelling, or seat of residence.

Manucaptor. In early records a person who assumed the responsibility for the appearance of a person under arrest.

Manumission. The act of liberating a person from slavery or bondage.

Memorial. A document presented to a legislative body or its executive containing a petition or a statement of the facts.

Mesne conveyance. An intermediate conveyance between the first grantee and the present holder. A term for deeds, especially used in South Carolina.

Messuage. Dwelling house with the adjacent buildings. Formerly the term had a more extended meaning, *i.e.* dwelling house with the adjacent buildings and curtilage.

Metes and bounds. A way of describing land using compass points, natural points (a tree, river, etc.) and distances.

Mineral right. An interest in minerals in land, with or without ownership of the surface of the land.

Mortgage, and Chattel Mortgage. An interest in land (or personal property) created by a written instrument which provides security, usually for a debt. (A chattel mortgage was used as security specifically for personal property.)

Moiety. The half of anything, but sometimes used to reflect an equal part of three co-owners.

Next Friend. A person acting for the benefit either of an infant (i.e., under the age of majority) or of another person unable to look after his or her own interest.

Nuncupative will. An oral will. (Invalid in some states.)

Oil and Mineral Lease, or Oil and Gas Lease. A lease for the right to extract oil and the minerals only (or oil and the gas). It is not a lease to the land itself.

Orator. The plaintiff in a chancery action. (The term is generally no longer used and the orator is simply called the plaintiff.)

Ordinary. In some states, the judge of the probate court. Those states which used this term (such as Georgia) have generally now abandoned it.

Order to Show Cause. See Show Cause Order.

Orphan. A person who has lost both (or sometimes one) of his parents. Usually used with a minor.

Parcener. A joint heir; one who, with others, holds an estate before the inheritance has been divided.

Partition. The dividing of land (or personal property) by co-owners, usually resulting from an inherited parcel. This division may be voluntary, or compulsory through a court action.

Partition Deed. The deed evidences the partition, see above.

Patent. See grant.

Peppercorn. The reservation of a nominal rent was expressed by the payment of a peppercorn.

Personal Property deed. A deed of personal property, commonly household furniture, stock, etc.

Petition. A written request presented to a governing body.

Petition for Sale of Real Estate. Asks the court for permission to sell real estate, usually in a decedent's estate or a guardianship.

Plantation. In American law this refers to a farm, or a large cultivated estate. The term, used chiefly in the southern states, refers to a large farm on which crops were grown.

Plat. A map of a specific land area such as a town, section, subdivision or piece of land showing the location, boundaries and, usually, legal descriptions. See also *plot.*

Plot. A synonym for plat, but in common usage refers to a small piece of ground, generally used for a specific purpose, such as *a cemetery plot.*

Power of Attorney. An instrument in writing in which power is granted to another to perform certain specified acts.

Primogeniture. Firstborn or eldest son. In states that practiced primogeniture, any estate not disposed of previous to death or by will succeeded to the eldest son. (New England never practiced primogeniture, except for Rhode Island. Instead, the eldest son received a double portion of the estate.) In some areas, the eldest son could challenge his father's disposition of the land to others, claiming a denial of his "birthright."

Processioning. A survey and inspection of boundaries practiced in some of the colonies by the local authorities or those appointed by them.

Quiet Title. An action to remove any possible clouds on the title of the property.

Quitclaim deed. A type of release which passes any claim or interest that the grantor may have.

Quitrent. Rent paid annually by a tenant to the government.

Quod vide, *q.v.* Latin: which see. It is used to direct a reader to another location in the writing where further information will be found

Real property. Land, and generally whatever is erected or growing upon or affixed to land (such as trees).

Receipt. Written acknowledgment of receiving something.

Redemption. Usually means the right of a person to repurchase his property which has been sold at a forced sale because of a judgment.

Release. A written or oral statement discharging another from a duty or a payment.

Relict. A widow or widower. The survivor of a married couple, whether it is the husband or the wife.

Replevin. An action by which the person is entitled to repossess goods from someone who has wrongfully taken or detained those goods.

Respondent. One who responds to a complaint or bill (otherwise, the defendant). Usually used in court of equity causes.

Reversion. In deeds refers to any remnant left to the grantor.

Right of way deed. The right of a person to pass over the land of another. (Railroad rights of way include the land itself.)

Scilicet. In that place. See ss.

Scire facias. (Sci. fa.) Most commonly, a writ directing the debtor to appear and show cause why a judgment against him should not be revived. Alternately, a writ to have the judgment executed. (In most states this has been abolished.)

Sealed and delivered. These words are usually followed by the signatures of the witnesses.

Security. That which is offered to guarantee the performance of a contract (written or oral); also, one who undertakes to fulfill or guarantee the obligation of another.

Seisin, seizin. See Livery of Seisin.

Sine prole, s.p. Without issue.

Sister-in-law. The wife of a married brother; sometimes the wife of a married brother-in-law. In early records could be a stepsister, or occasionally an adopted sister

Show cause order. An order issued by the court requiring the appearance of a person to show why some action should not be confirmed or take effect. Also referred to as an Order to Show Cause.

Son-in-law or Daughter-in-law. The husband of a married daughter, or the wife of a married son. In early times often meant stepson or stepdaughter, or occasionally could refer to an adopted son or daughter.

ss. (Often written as an old styled double s which looks like an inverted f.) The clause for the acknowledgment or proving starts with the locality followed by ss. This indicates that the acknowledgment took place in that locality. *Black's Law Dictionary* states that it is "supposed" to be a contraction for *scilicet*. The location followed by "ss" is also used in other documents when a notary public or other officer of the court prepares a statement that someone appeared before him to sign.

Summons. Notifies a defendant that an action has begun against him and that he is required to answer at a certain date and place within a certain time.

Surety. One who has contracted to be responsible for another person, especially one who assumes the responsibilities or debts of another person in case of default.

Tenement. Commonly applied to houses and other buildings.

Testament. Under early English law, a written instrument that disposed of personal property after death. Today the words "will" and "testament" are equivalent, and the single writing may devise real property and bequeath personal property.

Testamentary. Pertaining to a will or testament.

Testate. A person who died leaving a will is said to have died "testate," and the subsequent proceeding is often referred to as the "testate proceeding."

To wit. That is to say; namely. As an example, in a gift deed: "I give to my three children, *to wit*, John, Joseph and Mary..."

Tort. A civil wrong or injury.

Township. 1) In federal government surveys a township is six miles square, a part of the rectangular survey method, and is also referred to as a congressional township. 2) In some states, townships are civil and political subdivisions of a county.

Travail. The labor of childbirth. Example: "I give to my wife Dorothy who is in travail ..."

Trespass. An unlawful interference with a person's property or rights.

Trust Deed, or Deed of Trust. In some states a type of mortgage in which the land was deeded in trust to a trustee to secure the property.

Turf and twig. A ceremony in which a piece of the turf and a bough or twig was delivered by the grantor to the grantee in making a livery of seisin (*q.v.*).

Ultimate; ultimo (ult.). In dates, refers to the previous month. A newspaper notice in May 1823 stating that a death took place on the 22nd ult. would indicate it took place 22 April.

Vacation of Judgment. The setting aside of a judgment entered in error.

Vagrant act. An act for the punishment of idle and disorderly persons.

Verbi Dei Minister (V.D.M.). Latin: Preacher of God's Word.

Versus. Against. In the title of a cause, the plaintiff's name is put first, then "vs." and then the defendant's name.

Videlicet, *Viz.* To wit, namely.

Warranty deed. The grantor (seller) warrants a good, clear title.

Waters of. Land that drains into a particular creek, river or other body of water. Does not have to adjoin the named body of water.

Widow's allowance. The amount which a widow may claim (usually set by law) from her husband's estate, free of claims, for her support and maintenance and that of minor children.

Widow's election. A widow may take what is allowed her in the will of her husband, or may choose to take what the law allows which is usually the amount that she would receive under intestacy laws.

Widow's third. A widow's one-third dower.

Will. An instrument which disposes of a person's real and personal property after death. Often titled "Last Will and Testament." See Testament.

Witness. A person who was present and personally saw an action or event. A person who declares under oath or affirmation as to actions or events personally seen.

Writ. A written court order directed to the sheriff or other judicial officer to do what is commanded by the writ or see that it is done.

INDEX

A

Abstracting documents, 10
Abatement, defined, 122
Abutter, defined, 40
Acknowledgement, defined, 40
Action at law, defined, 122
Administrations. *See also Estate Records.*
   relinquishment of, 95
Administrator(trix), cum testamento annexo, 72, 84
   de bonis non, 72, 84-85
   public, 96
   successor, 85
   with the will annexed, 84
Ads, defined, 122
Affirm, defined, 40
African-American search, 195-196
Agreement, defined, 40
Alienate, defined, 40
Allen County Public Library [Indiana], 9-10, 174
Anno domini, defined, 41
Appertaining, defined, 41
Appurtenance, defined, 41
Apprenticeships, 103
Assault and battery, defined, 122
Assign, and Assigns, defined, 41
Assumpsit, defined, 123

B

Bail bond, 142
Beneficiary, defined, 72
Bequeath, defined, 72
Bill, defined, 123
Births. *See Vital Records.*
Bockstruck, Lloyd, 59
Bond, defined, 72
Bondsman, defined, 72
Brother-in-law, defined, 72
Bureau of Immigration and Naturalization, 139
Bureau of Land Management, 166

C

Calendars and dates, 108, 164
Caveat, defined, 41
Certiorari, defined, 123
Chain carriers/chain bearers, defined, 41
Chain of title, 33
Chattel, defined, 123
Civil law, defined, 123
Clerk of Court, 128
Civil Court Records. (*See also Court Records.*)
   13, 127-141
   online, 169

COB (Court Order Book), 78
Codicils, to wills, 85
Colletta, John P., 138
Committee, defined, 72
Common law, defined, 123
Common law action, defined, 123
Complainant, defined, 123
Computer, using for notes, 23
   using in courthouse, 10
Congressional township, defined, 41
Consanguinity, defined, 123
Consideration, defined, 41
Contest (will), 72
Contract, defined, 123
Convey, defined, 41
Coram, defined, 123
Co-respondent, defined, 123
Coroner's records, 136
Cott Index, 20
Counties, existence of, 2
   parent, 2
Court of record, defined, 123
Court records. *See also Estate Records;*
see also Land Records
   abstracting and transcribing, 10
   affidavit, 118
   answer, 118
   bail bond, 142
   bastardy bond, 118
   bill, 118
   bond book, 114-115
   certified copy, 118
   chancery, 122
   changes of name, 131
   citation, 118
   civil, 127-128
   civil court process, listed, 130
   civil office, 128
   complaint, 118
   coroner, 136
   criminal matters, 141-142
   debt, 128-129
   decree, 119
   deposition, 119
   divorces, 140-141
   dockets, 116-117
   duty of criminal court clerk, listed, 142
   execution book, 117
   exemplified copy, 119
   fee book, 117
   file packets of, 121

Court records, con't.
  indexes of. *See Indexes*
  indictment record, 118
  injunction, 119
  jails, 142
  journals, 115
  judgment book, 117
  judgment, 119, 129-130
  juries, 143
  jury register, 118
  land books, 133-134
  law vs. equity, 113
  memorial, 119
  naturalizations, 137-139
  prothonotary, 128
  minute book, 115
  originals found other than in courthouse, 181-182
  order book, 115-116
  record books of, 114-115
  registrar of voters, 136-137
  road commissioners, 135-136
  roads, 135
  show cause order, 119
  summons, 119
  strategy in using civil, 130-131
  tax assessor, 134-135
  tax foreclosures, 135
  tax records, 131-133
  the system, 111, 113
  trial and appellate, 113
  types of, 111-113
  writ, 119
Courthouse, arriving at, 13-15
  fire, 24
  hints for success, 15-16
  open hours, 3
  what is expected, 14-15
  ladder hazards, 14
Coverture, defined, 72
Criminal court clerk, duties of, 142
Criminal records, 141-142
c.t.a. *See cum testamento annexo.*
cum testamento annexo, defined, 72
Curtesy, defined, 72
Curtilage, defined, 41

D

Dates and calendars, 164
Daughter-in-law, 74
Daughter of the American Revolution Library, 174
Death Records. *See Vital Records.*
de bonis non, defined, 72
Decedent Estates, 13
Deeds. *See Land Records.*
Demurrer, defined, 123
Detinue, defined, 123
Devise, defined, 72

Devisor/Devisee indexes. *See Indexes.*
Divorces, 113, 140-141
Documents. *See Court Documents.*
Double portion, to eldest son, 75-76
Dower, defined, 41

E

Eales, Anne Bruner, 59, 139
Ear mark brand, defined, 123
Eichholz, Alice, 1
Ejectment, defined, 123
Elder, in names, 56
Emancipation, defined, 123
Endorsement, defined, 123
Entails, 37, 43, 99-100
  defined, 41
  lands of minor, 97
  slaves, 39, 41, 99
Equity, defined, 124
Escheat, defined, 42
Estate records. *See also wills*
  account, 87, 91
  account of sale, 92
  administrations, 95
  adopted, 77
  bond, 89
  citation, 87
  court hearing, 87
  court order books, 78
  entails, 99-100
  Estate indexes. *See Indexes.*
  estate packets, 103-104
  estate packets, documents in, 104-105
  estate packets, following one case, 104
  file packets, 79-80
  final distribution, 93
  final settlement, 87, 93
  guardianship, 68
  heirs at law, 77
  kind of estate, 67
  inventory, 87, 90-91
  letters, 90
  office handling, 65
  per stirpes or per capita, 77
  petition for sale of real estate, 92
  primogeniture or double portion, 75-76
  probate minutes and orders, 78
  proceedings dockets, 69
  process, 86, 87
  process to sell real estate, 92
  proof of publication, 70
  public administrator, 96
  real estate sale, 87
  relinquishment of administrator, 95
  renunciation, 94
  sale bill, 87, 92
  sons-in-law, 77

Estate Records, con't.
   testate proceeding, 67
   understanding the law, 74
   widow's support, 87
   women and wills, 67
Estray, defined, 124
et al, defined, 42
et ux, defined, 42
et vir, defined, 42
Ex parte, defined, 124
Execution, defined, 124
Executor(trix), defined, 72. *See also Wills.*

F
Families, connecting through deeds, 58
Family History Library (FHL), 169-170
   catalog, 170, 171, 172
   ordering microfilm, 171
Federal-land states, 28
   named, 28
   patent process, 29
   rectangular surveys, 29-30
   surveying of, 29-30
Fees, high cost of ordering copies, 193
ff, transcribing as F, 8
Fee simple, defined, 42
Fee tail, defined, 42
Femme covert, defined, 124
Femme sole, defined, 124
Feoffment, defined, 42
Fiduciary, defined, 124
Fieri Facias, fi. fa., defined, 124
Files, what to take, 5
Folio, defined, 42
Foreclosure, defined, 42
Frederick County Maryland Genealogical Research Guide, 180
Freehold, defined, 42

G
Gavelkind, 42, 75
Genealogical Proof Standard, 58
Genealogist's Handbook for New England Research, 1
General Land Office, 166
German-English Genealogical Dictionary, 9
Grand jury, 143
Grant, defined, 42
Grant, bargain and sell, defined, 42
Grantee, defined, 42
Grantor, defined, 42
Grantor/Grantee indexes. *See Land records*
Grants, location of, 28
Grant/patent, process of obtaining, 29
Graves Index, 21
Guardian, defined, 73
Guardianships, 96
   accounts, 98

Guardianships, con't
   bonds, 96-97
   choosing a guardian, 97
   committees, 98
   entailed property in hands of, 97
   incompetents, 97-98
   minors, 96
   next friend, 97
Guide to Genealogical Research in the National Archives of the United States, 59, 139
Guidebooks (*See also Source References, p. 201*) , 1

H
Habeas corpus, defined, 124
Habendum clause, defined, 42
   example of, 62
Handwriting, books and tapes, 9
   reading, 7-8
Handwriting of American Records for a Period of 300 Years, 9
Handy Book for Genealogists, 1, 146
Hatcher, Patricia Law, 30
Have and to hold (clause), defined, 42
Hawkins, Kenneth, 28
Heir, defined, 73
Heirs and assigns, defined, 42
Heirs at law, 77
   defined, 73
Heirs lawfully begotten of his body forever (clause), 42
Hereditament, defined, 43
Homestead, defined, 43
Homestead exemption, defined, 43
Holographic will, 85
Hustings Court, 112, 115

I
id est, defined, 43
Illinois Regional Archives Depositary, 181
Imparlance, defined, 124
Imprimis, defined, 73
In laws. *See Estate Records*
In room of, defined, 124
In witness whereof, defined, 43
Indenture, defined, 124
Independent cities, 3
Indexes, abbreviations in, 34
   Campbell System, 19-20
   common law order books, 115-116
   consolidated, 16, 31
   Cott, 20
   court records, 120-121, 122
   deed indexes, 30-35
   devisor and devisee, 31-32, 69-70
   differences in, 16-17
   dockets as substitute, 116
   deed indexes inclusions, 34

Indexes, con't.
    entry book, 33
    estate files, 70-71
    finding a name, 21-22
    finding variations of name, 21
    first name system, 19-20
    general (consolidated), l, 16, 30-35, 68
    grantor/grantee, 30
    Graves, 21
    information included in, 34-35
    key letter system, 17-19
    lot and block, 32-33
    missing entries, 22
    mortgagor/mortgagee, 31
    order books, 115-116
    pecularities of, in land indexes, 33-34
    prepared by others, 35
    proceedings docket, 69
    published indexes, 71
    Russell indexes, 17-19
    tract index, 32
    using for maximum results, 22
    vital records index, 147-148
    Indictment, defined, 124
Infant, defined, 73
Inmate, defined, 43
Inquest jury, 143
Instant, defined, 124
Interlined, defined, 43
Internet, civil records, 169
    county forums, 165
    county sites, 165
    Cyndi's list, 163-164
    federal-land records, 166
    for calendars and dates, 164
    for dictionaries and glossaries, 164
    for handwriting and script, 164
    local land records, 167
    National Center for Health Statistics, 168
    online subscription services, 169
    state archives, 166
    tax assessors, 167
    unusual websites, 181
    USGenWeb, 164-165, 167-168
Intestate, defined, 73
Inventory, defined, 73

J
Jails (Goals), 142
Judgment, defined, 124
Junior, in names, 56
Jurat, defined, 43
Juries, grand, 143
    inquest, 143
    petit, 143
    special, 143
    trial, 143

K
Kirkham, E. Kay, 9
Kvasnicka, Robert M., 59, 139

L
Land record books. See Court records
Land ownership, importance of, 27
Land ownership, paperwork of, 27
Land records. acknowledgment/proof, 50-51
    Bureau of Land Management website, 166
    cemetery deeds, 35
    chains for survey, 49
    clues in deeds, 53-55
    colonial, 59
    consideration paid, 54
    dates in deeds, 53
    deed book, 47
    deed example with annotation, 61-63
    deeds, information from, listed, 50
    deed not located, 53
    deed not recorded, 56
    deed of heirs, 35-36
    deed of lease and release, 36
    devisor/devisee indexes, 31-32
    documents, bill of sale, 35
    discharge (military), 36
    dower in deeds, 53
    dower release, 36-37
    entails in deeds, 41, 97
    federal land case files, 59
    federal-land states, 28
    fractions for clues, 55
    General Land Office website, 166
    gift deed or deed of gift, 37
    history of property, 51
    indenture, 37
    indexes of land records. See Indexes
    land records aside from courthouse records, 58
    lease, 37-38
    local land records on Internet, 167
    maps on Internet, 167
    marriage contract or prenuptial agreement, 38
    military bounty land, 58-59
    mortgage and chattel mortgage, 38
    mortgage books, 49
    naming tracts, 27
    New York land tracts, 58
    occupation in deed, 53
    office of, 47
    oil and mineral lease or oil and gas lease, 38
    original deeds, noted, 52
    partition deed, 39
    personal property deed, 39
    petition for sale of real estate, 39
    photocopying, 55
    plats, plat books, plat maps, 48-49
    power of attorney, 39

Land Records, con't.
  power of attorney books, 49
  preparing chart for study, 58
  property description in deed, 54
  quitclaim deed, 39-40
  quitclaim of dower, 40
  record books, 47-49
  reconstructing chain of title, 33
  recording process, listed, 51-52
  right of way deed, 40
  signatures in deed, 55
  special clauses in deeds, 55
  state bounty land, 58-59
  state-land states, 28
  strategies for searching land, 57
  surveyors, private records of, 59
  surveys, 48
  surveys and field notes, 49
  tax assessors' websites, 167
  trust deed or deed of trust, 40
  warranty deed, 40
  when moving to another states, 53
  witnesses, noted, 52
Laws, finding, 177
Legal age, 24
Letter writing, 193-194
  stating the request clearly, 194-195
Letters, defined, 73
Libraries, *Allen County Public Library*, 174
  Daughters of the American Revolution Library, 174
  Family History Library, 173
  genealogical collections, 173
  Library of Congress, 175
  preparation for, 175-176
  St. Louis County Library, 175
  The Wisconsin Historical Society Library, 174
Lien, defined, 43
Lineal, defined, 73
Livery of seisin (seizin), defined, 43
Locating Your Roots: Discover Your Ancestors Using Land Records, 30
Locus sigilli, defined, 73
Location of search, 1
Lot and Block index, 32-33

M
Majority, defined, 73
Male tail, defined, 43
Malfeasance, defined, 124
Manor house, defined, 43
Manucaptor, defined, 124
Manumission, defined, 124
Maps, county highway, 6-7
  state/county outline, 6-7
  topographical 7.5 minute, 6-7
Marriages. *See Vital Records.*

Melnyk, Marcia D., 1
Membership cards, required, 5, 147
Mesne conveyance, defined, 43
Messuage, defined, 43
Metes and bounds, defined, 43
Microfilm, 169-173
  availability, 173
  problems, 173
Military bounty land, 58-59
Mills, Elizabeth Shown, 9
Mineral right, defined, 43
Minors. *See Guardianships*
Moiety, defined, 43
Mortgagor/mortgagee indexes. *See Land records*

N
Names, "1st" and "2nd," 56
  Elder and Younger, 56
  Sr. and Jr., 56
National Center for Health Statistics, 168
Naturalizations, 137-139
  formation of Bureau of Immigration and Naturalization, 139
  locating the papers, 138-139
  of women, 139
National Union Catalog of Manuscript Collections, 178-179
NETR online public records, 167
Newspapers, 178
Next friend, defined, 73
Nicknames, 57, 102
Nicknames Past and Present, 57
NUCMC. *See National Union Catalog of Manuscript Collections*
Numbering of record books, 16-17

O
OCLC (Online Computer Library Center), 177
Orator, defined, 124
Ordinary, defined, 124
Orphan, defined, 73

P
Packing for the trip, 4-5
Parcener, defined, 125
Partition, 39, 43, 73, 125
Patents, defined, 43
  process of obtaining, 29
  location of, 28
Peppercorn, defined, 44
Per capita, 77
Per stirpes, 77
Periodical Source Index, 179
PERSI. *See Periodical Source Index*
Petit jury, 143
Photocopying, 10-11
Plantation, defined, 44
Plat, defined, 44

Plot, defined, 44
Preparation, example of one-sheet summary, 6
Primogeniture, 75-76
    defined, 73
Probate records online, 167-168
Probates. *See Estate Records*
Processioning, defined, 44
Proceeding docket, 69
Professional Genealogy: A Manual for Researchers, 9
Property. *See Land Records.*
Prothonotary, 128

Q

Quiet title, defined, 44
Quitrent, defined, 44
Quod vide, defined, q.v., 44

R

Reading Early American Handwriting, 9
Real property, defined, 44
Receipt, defined, 73
Record books, numbering of, 16-17
    handling of, 4
Rectangular surveys. *See federal-land states*
Redbook, 1
Redemption, defined, 125
Regional archives, 181
Registrar of voters, 136
Release, defined, 125
Relict, defined, 73
Repeat Performance tapes, 9, 32
Replevin, defined, 125
Research in the Land Entry Files of the General Land Office, 28
Respondent, defined, 125
Reversion, defined, 44
Revolutionary soldier, a saga of, 199-200
Revolutionary War Bounty grants Awarded by State Governments, 59
Road commissioners, 135
Road records, 135
Rose, Christine, 57, 58, 102
Russell, Donna Valley, 180
Russell Indexes, 17-19

S

s, tailed, 8-9
Salmon, Marylynn, 67
Scilicet, defined, 44
Scire facias, sci. fa., defined, 125
Sealed and delivered, defined, 44
Seals, 84, 106
Security, defined, 125
Seisin, seizin, defined, 44
Senior, in names, 56
Session laws, 131
Signatures, seals, 106
Sine prole, s.p., defined, 73

Sister-in-law, defined, 73
Skills, practicing, 7-8
Son-in-law, 77
    defined, 74
Special jury, 143
Sperry, Kip, 9
ss., defined, 44
St. Louis County Library, 175
State-land states, 28
    patent/grant process, 29
    surveying of, 29-30
Statutes at Large, 177-178
    session laws, 177
Statutory law, defined, 125
Strategies. *See Chapter 12.*
    African-American records, 195-197
    allowing one record to lead to another, 183-185
    following the separations and divorces, 188-189
    for "knowing" our ancestors, 197-198
    letter writing, 193-194
    locating parents, 187-188
    locating the children, 185-187
    when the will is missing, 189-190
    widening the search, 190-193
Surety, defined, 125
Surrogate, 65, 74
Surveys, six-mile/rectangular. *See Federal-land states*

T

TAB. *See Trespass vi et armis*
Tapes from Repeat Performance, 9, 32
Tax records. *See Court records*
Tax Assessor, 134-135
    websites, 167
Tax foreclosures, 135
Tenement, defined, 44
Testament, defined, 74
Testamentary, defined, 74
Testate, defined, 74
Thorn, 8
Thode, Ernest, 9
Torrence, Clayton, 71
To wit, defined, 44
Tort, defined, 125
Township, defined, 44
Tract indexes, 32
Travail, defined, 74
Transcribing, 8-9
Trespass, defined, 125
Trespass vi et armis, 116-117
    defined, 125
Trial jury, 143
Turf and twig, defined, 44

U

Ultimate, ultimo, defined, 125
United States Military District, 29

United States Statutes at Large, 177-178
USGenWeb, 1, 164-165, 167

V

Vacation of judgment, 125
Vagrant act, 125-126
Verbi dei minister, V.D.M., defined, 126
Versus, defined, 126
Videlicet, viz, defined, 74
Virginia, grants, 28
   independent cities listed, 3
   military district, 29
Virginia Wills and Administrations, 1632-1800, 71
Vital Records, 13, 145-162
   births, 148-151
      delayed/corrected, 149
      local customs for recording of, 151
      cities, 146
      substitute records for, 149-151
   courthouse office handling, 145
   death, 157-161
      court record for, 160
      court record to prove, 161
      deeds to prove, 160
      guardianship records for, 160
      locate records, 160
      probate records for, 159-160
      register of, 158-159
      substitute records for, 159-160
      when register not found, 159
      from estates, 151
   marriages, 152-157
      applications and licenses, 153-154
      bonds, 154
      breach of promise, 156-157
      certificates, 154
      common-law, 157
      contract, 155
      by license or banns, 152
      registers, 154
      special notes on, 157
      substitutes records for, 156
      where solemnized, 155-156
   open to public, 146-147
   register book indexes and organization, 147-148
   registration of, 145
   town clerk, 145

Vital Records, con't.
   transcribing and abstracting, 148
Vital records websites. *See Chapter 11*

W

Waters of, defined, 44
Websites, unusual, 182
Widow's allowance, defined, 74
Widow's election, defined, 74
Widow's third, defined, 44
Wills, 84-85. *See also Estate Records*
   abstract of, 106-107
   apprenticeships, 103
   clues from, affirming, 101-102
      change of location, 101
      estimating date of death, 101
      former spouse, 102
      gravestones and religion, 102
      previous residence, 101
      wife's name and dower, 102
   codicil to, 85
      defined, 74
   executor of, 84, 103
   holographic, 84
   making it fair, 101
   more than one kind, 85
   naming children, 74-75
   naming of daughters, 76
   nuncupative, 85
   observations, 107-108
   of unmarried adults, 100
   original estate packets, 103-105
   original retained in courthouse, 52
   primogeniture, 73, 75-76
   transcribing of, 105-106
   signing of, 84
   two wills, 100
   witnesses, 103
Wisconsin State Historical Society, 174
Witness, defined, 74
Women and the Law of Property in Early America, 67
WorldCat OCLC, 177
Work Project Administration and *Works Progress Administration* (WPA), 180-181, 196

Y

Younger,. in names, 56